MIDDLE OF THE PACKER

Middle of the Packer

ANDREW BENNETT

SERENDIPITY

First published in 2003 by
Serendipity
Suite 530
37 Store Street
Bloomsbury
London

British Library Cataloguing-in-Publication data
A catalogue record for this book is available from the British Library

ISBN 1 84394 054 X

Printed and bound by Alden Group, Oxford

To all runners out there, irrespective of their ability; and to all race organisers, marshals and volunteers who work tirelessly to ensure our great sport goes from strength to strength

Contents

Acknowledgements

To all those featured in the book, and others who aren't.

Members and friends at Ackworth Road Runners.

My dearly loved Dad, the late Alf Bennett, for providing support and encouragement.

Dave and Ann Rhodes for publishing my early articles in 'Footnotes'.

The Wednesday evening splinter group who put me through my paces each week at Pontefract.

My Mum, Selina Bennett, Kevin Vickers, Paul Bedford, Cyril Jones, Trish Eaton, Christopher J. Greaves and Caroline Tempest for help and advice.

Derek Waterton, John Tucker, Trevor Posliff and Ken Barton for organising trips to overseas races.

Claire-Marie O'Grady at Eversheds.

Introduction

In my younger days, I was a pretty ordinary footballer, awful at cricket and my squash career never really took off.

Quite by chance, I was press-ganged, bullied and cajoled into running a local half marathon for charity in 1983. Inspired by the Coe, Ovett and Cram era along with the advent of the running boom, I never really looked back. Not that I was a brilliant runner, in fact quite the reverse; but in these types of races, there were many average runners out there just like me. Some of them have inevitably fallen by the wayside but others will have trodden a similar path to me in the subsequent years.

Running has enabled me to travel while taking part in events, socialising and staying reasonably fit and healthy. Being footloose and fancy free and with money burning a hole in my pocket, I have been fortunate to run in some of the great races both at home and abroad. I have been to places where only running would have taken me and have met many people and made friends along the way.

Twenty years on and over 600 races later, I am still going, not going strong but still going forward. *Middle of the Packer* charts my journey from those early days to the present, taking in many of the races and the places I have visited. I take a light-hearted look at many running related situations and incidents which the runner and non-runner alike will both relate to.

Introduction

IN MY YOUNGER DAYS, I was a pretty ordinary footballer, a useful cricket and my squash career never really took off.

Later in life, I was press-ganged, bullied and cajoled into running [illegible] half marathon for charity in 1983, followed by the [illegible] along with the [illegible] of the [illegible] I never really looked back. [illegible]

[illegible]

[illegible] with money burning a hole in my pocket, I have been fortunate [illegible] some of the great [illegible] and [illegible] would have taken me [illegible] along the way.

[illegible]

CHAPTER 1

The Start Line

As I looked around at the sea of faces, I couldn't help wondering what I was doing here. The date was Sunday May 18th 1983, the venue was Pontefract Park in West Yorkshire and the event was the first Five Towns Hospice Half Marathon.

Everyone looked lean and mean and well equipped to go the distance, while in contrast I was at best moderately chubby. They all appeared to have the proper gear; designer singlet, tight shorts with most wearing Hi-Tec Silver Shadow footwear. I was wearing cast-off football kit, a track suit top and trainers held together in one place by tape. Rarely have I felt so unprepared, inadequate and out of place.

Individuals were going through their own particular warm-up routines. Some were doing stretching exercises, others were limbering up and down while two men were undertaking a ritual I hadn't come across before. They were trying to push over a tree. The morning was pleasant and would become warmer, while the air was filled with the aroma of embrocation and rubbing compound.

A familiar face joined me in Frank, a friend and former squash partner who was partly responsible for putting me through this ordeal. Once the race was underway, we would run the early miles together. The man next to me asked what time I was looking for. This came as a shock as I hadn't realised that people looked for times. I presumed that just to complete the course was achievement in itself. Little did I realise that these thoughts would return to haunt me, time and time again in the years ahead.

The Five Towns Half Marathon was the first stage of my longer term plan to run the Leeds Marathon later in the year, or should I say the third stage? Stage one had taken place several weeks earlier in the shape of a long training run. I had run, jogged and plodded the four miles or so from my home town of Rothwell to neighbouring village Methley, returning home by the same route. It was a balmy evening, the likes of which we haven't seen in recent summers. A thunderstorm and subsequent downpour had soaked me to the skin but by the time I reached home I had dried out thoroughly. I treated myself to a hot bath but must have dozed, only to wake up in the freezing cold water. I had goose bumps on my goose bumps. The next day I could barely hobble but was feeling chuffed at my efforts the previous evening. Apart from a brief stop at the turnaround point for a breather, I had run continually for eight miles. Stage two took place a week later but this time I extended the run to somewhere around ten miles and believed that this would set me up nicely for race day.

I had seen one of the early London Marathons on television and can recollect reading about The Barnsley Six in a local paper. They had upset the hierarchy by awarding prizes to overall and category winners in the shape of household goods. Not only had they attracted a big entry of runners from Athletics clubs, but social, recreational runners and joggers alike. The Amateur Athletics Association were none too impressed as they believed this had contravened their policy of not running for prizes. How times have changed in recent years.

The first Leeds Marathon had received widespread media footage and had been dubbed 'The Tough One'. I stood at John O'Gaunts near Rothwell for well over an hour as the runners came through. The leaders were well spaced out, but as more and more runners emerged, the gaps closed making for an almost continuous stream. One thing, however, that stood out for me was that many of the middle and back of the packers were ordinary people and not the lantern-jawed, finely honed athletes I would have expected. I saw several people I would never have associated with sport, let alone run a marathon. Towards the back of the field, competitors were alternating between running and walking while others seemed to be able to maintain a steady plod throughout. At that point I turned to my Mum and Dad and made a bold statement that would change the direction of my life forever. 'I could do this,' I said. 'I'm going to enter next year.'

So Pontefract was just a stepping stone in my longer term plan but had created much local interest. Several local celebrities and sportsmen would run, along with a certain Sir Jimmy Saville. Proceeds would go to the Five Towns Hospice in Pontefract.

Little did I know that this would be the start of a magnificent journey that would take me the length and breadth of these islands and to places further afield. It would take me to over 600 races, to twenty countries and to capital cities throughout the world. I have been to many wonderful places both at home and abroad, some I would never have visited but for running. I have met many people, made friends and carved out a way of life in which my hobby enables me to travel, socialise and stay reasonably fit at the same time.

The mayor stood on the podium, last minute instructions were conveyed over a loud speaker and suddenly the race was underway. We didn't move for several seconds but then suddenly shuffled forward. The shuffle turned into a plod and then into a jog as we edged along the cinder track and out of the park. I could see a crocodile of runners on the road outside the park with the leaders at least 400 yards ahead. To this day I still wonder how they could open up a gap so quickly.

Running with Frank, we chatted away and soon passed the first mile marker. I started to regret not paying closer attention to how I dressed as the day was warm and I would suffer later on. Frank wished me luck and pressed ahead, while a stream of runners began to ease their way past, including work colleague Melvyn. A veteran of three marathons, he looked the part in impressive ensemble complete with headband.

In Glasshoughton, spectators began to line the route and friendly banter was exchanged with runners. This was probably the first time an event of this nature had passed through the Castleford suburb and everyone involved seemed to be contributing towards the atmosphere of the occasion. The first real hill was from Cutsyke to Whitwood, not a problem on the top deck of a South Yorkshire bus, but far more difficult to run up. The spectator noise level increased as a pocket of runners drifted by on the outside. I detected the distinctive leaning style of Sir Jimmy Saville who was flanked by his minders.

A welcome downhill followed, but with Sir Jimmy and his entourage disappearing into the distance and Frank long gone, I was left to tough it out on my own. Spectators were solid on the steep hill to Aketon and seemed to be sucking in the runners. As much as I fancied and probably needed a walk, I dug deep and made it beyond the brow. There were more regrets with my choice of kit as my football shorts, clearly unsuitable for this activity, caused me to chafe. A St Johns Ambulance volunteer came to the rescue with a generous helping of Vaseline which went some way towards soothing the irritation.

As more and more runners came by, I could picture myself towards the back of the field and the thought of finishing last crossed my mind. At eight miles we seemed almost within striking distance of Pontefract, but stewards in yellow bibs directed us along a country lane towards Ackworth. With the heat starting to take its toll, I fell in with another first-time runner who appeared to be in a similar state of disrepair. The drinks at ten miles were imperative and together we encouraged and cajoled each other up a long hill which I discovered in later years to be Castlesyke.

On the outskirts of Pontefract I finally submitted to a walk, quickly followed by another and then another. I conquered the tricky rise along the Bypass before dropping past the imposing Queens Hotel and into the park gates. An appreciative crowd encouraged me and fellow runners alike, up the gentle slope and across the finishing line. I was overcome with satisfaction and a wonderful sense of achievement particularly when a small medallion was thrust into the palm of my hand. I had finished just outside two hours and I hadn't come last. As I watched more and more people come through the finish, some the epitome of fitness and others in poor shape, I realised I was nowhere near last place.

On reaching home, I afforded myself another long soak in the bath. I told anybody who wanted to know how I had gone on, anyone who showed interest and those who weren't remotely interested. I wanted more of the same, where was the next race!!

While out for a drink in the market town of Otley, a poster on a wall told me the next race was in fact here. It was on July 3rd, it was a half marathon and would be sponsored by local car dealer, G. Eric Hunt. For this race I would be better prepared, I would have proper kit and I would have more training under my belt. And as the man at the Pontefract start had asked me, I would be looking for a time. I would be looking for under two hours.

I managed to fit in two fun runs before Otley, both in the Castleford area, recommended by Frank and his colleague Glen. The first was of an indeterminable distance, probably around nine miles, while the second was a hilly six miles which I completed in 51 minutes. Glen and Frank would become two of my early training partners along with Glen's brother Craig and the four of us would run many miles together.

Another warm day beckoned at Otley with the course very demanding, particularly to halfway. I struggled early on but settled in nicely, and encouraged by passing a few people down the steep Pool Bank, I was pleased to finish in 1 hour and 57 minutes.

Next on the list was an event in my home town of Rothwell organised by The Lions, which they advertised as approximate half marathon distance. The event was an organisational shambles from start to finish. Run in conjunction with the local gala, the afternoon start coincided with the hottest part of the day. The police failed to halt traffic at the busiest roundabout which resulted in runners and cars competing for the same section of road. There were inadequate marshals, insufficient drinks stations and infrequent mile markers. The later stages of the route were unclear, causing runners to take short cuts, either inadvertently or by cheating.

I got the impression The Lions had put this on at short notice believing it to be a quick and easy money-making event. They had neither put in the effort or done the research to make it a success. My lasting memory of the day was the sight of a runner and an official arguing over whether he could have a second drink. The runner said that he had just run thirteen miles to which the official replied, 'I don't care if you've run a hundred miles, it's one drink per person.' That just about summed up the day. I really struggled in the unbearable heat and not wearing a watch and with no official race clock, I never found out my official time. In my diary I wrote, 'More training, less beer, must do better.'

At the start of September, I was among 2,000 runners who took part in the Wakefield White Rose Half Marathon. The whole city appeared to get behind the race with the Wakefield Express providing both a start list and a pull-out results supplement. The course provided a welcome contrast of town and country, crossing Chantry Bridge, a well-known landmark in the area. Spectator support was good and friends gave me encouragement at pre-arranged places around the course. I felt I had made a significant improvement here, running my best time to date.

Work colleague Melvyn persuaded me to run the Robin Hood Half Marathon at Nottingham, enthusing that it was the best race around and I couldn't argue with his choice. The 5,000 strong field had a choice of either marathon or half marathon, taking in Nottingham Castle and several of the city's parks. The volume of competitors made for a slow start but I was well pleased with my efforts, dipping under 1 hour 50 minutes for the first time. The following Sunday I ran continually for three hours, filled in my application form and was ready for anything the Leeds Marathon could throw at me.

CHAPTER 2

My Sporting Life

'WAKE UP ANDREW,' was the call. We've had a letter. It was a Saturday morning in June and my mother was standing at the bedroom door. 'What is it?' I said, 'Have I passed my scholarship?' 'How did you know?' my mother replied. In all honesty, I had expected the letters to be dropping on the doormats if not today, then certainly next Saturday. I hadn't expected to be going to the Grammar School but then stranger things have happened.

Throughout the summer, I had attended meetings at my new school to become familiar with the set-up and expectations. My parents had me kitted out with school uniform and sportswear. My mother had carefully sewn a name tag inside each garment as these articles apparently had a habit of disappearing.

September soon came around and with it the first day of term, and I had become well aware of the initiation ceremony that greeted new starters; 'The Holly Bush'. Before class, at break and at lunchtime, a procession of hapless first formers were being marched away to be pushed through the 'Holly Bush', returning with leaves and brambles on their clothing and their hair dishevelled. For some inconceivable reason, I managed to get away with it. The next day in assembly, the headmaster announced that the ridiculous 'Holly Bush' ritual had once again reared its ugly head and must stop immediately. He then quoted three names, presumably the ring leaders, and asked the boys in question to report to his office after assembly.

I excelled neither academically or at sport for that matter. In the early years I turned out only once for the school cricket team, when I was roped in at short notice when two players were given detention. I was good enough to have played regularly but neither the sports master or the captain appeared to like me or to rate me. I only played once in the Rugby team, albeit for the younger year for which I qualified by birth date. I can't really say I relished being at the bottom of a loose ruck or maul in those days.

The sports master was Eric, a swarthy man perhaps forty years old. His party piece was taking a shower while smoking a cigarette. He hated football and everyone who stood for it. This was a Rugby school and all pupils were expected to play. Softies who didn't show an aptitude were given the ball and asked to run into an uncompromising wall of sturdy eleven and twelve year olds. Boys who chickened out of sport were made to run laps of the cross-country course and those who forgot their swimming trunks were made to borrow a pair, meaning some of those who liked a swim had to miss out.

One of the big events in the school sports calendar was the Ilkley Sevens Rugby tournament, for which coaches were provided and which pupils of all ages were expected to attend. This particular year had seen a disappointing attendance, the team hadn't figured well and Eric was looking for heads to roll. He lined up the class and asked if anyone had been to watch Leeds United. A telltale friend raised his hand and said, 'Please sir, Bennett did'. I was duly ordered to run four laps of the long cross-country course, ankle deep on muddy tracks, through a peat bog, and suffering the 'Holly Bush' where a prefect stood to make sure I didn't shirk out. Nowadays, parents and social workers appear to turn up at school over the slightest incident. When I look back upon those days, Eric and others would have regularly been hauled in front of the Head and the Board of Governors, and taken to task.

Eric's answer of punishing everybody who stepped out of line with laps of the muddy cross-country course had the opposite effect on me, and I loved it. Helped in no small way by cycling each evening on my paper round, I seemed to become stronger and was rewarded by being selected for the school cross-country team. Four schools took part in the competition with eight runners each. I finished something like twenty-third from the thirty-two competitors.

I was selected the following year after running well in the trial but a couple of days before the race, Eric lined everybody up and said that a boy who had been sick would run. The lad who he had replaced seemed chuffed when told he would be a travelling reserve. Eric then pointed to a boy who apparently hadn't tried in the trial and told him that he could do better and would run as a punishment, consequently replacing me. I would also travel as a reserve but wouldn't see any action unless somebody feigned illness or suffered an injury during transit to the race.

As a fifth year, I won a mile race in the games period and gained selection to run in the school sports. Running against older boys, I thought I might be in with a chance of coming last but I knew that a boy nicknamed 'Cancer Kid' was running. He had landed this nickname for having a sly swallow upstairs on the bus, behind the bike sheds, or wherever else he could get away with it, and surely I could beat him. Leading at halfway, I slumped to fifth out of eight with 'Cancer' bringing up the rear, half a lap adrift and earning the biggest applause of the day.

Like many boys I suffered at the hands of bullies, particularly one who lived several doors away who shall be called Ginger. When the school bus was full he would unceremoniously dump me from my seat to enable somebody else to sit down. One lunchtime when it was raining, pupils were sitting in the classroom, some on desks. Ginger walked in accompanied by the Head Boy. 'Get off your desk Bennett' he grunted. 'What about these other people?' I asked, to be told they were only interested in me.

I stood firm so they tried to cart me away, at which point I thumped the Head Boy. They bundled me away to the prefects' room and told me to stand outside in the corridor, but when they disappeared inside, I came away. They turned up as I anticipated they would the following day, and exacted their revenge by setting me on shovelling manure, along with two other poor sods. We didn't shovel it anywhere in particular, just from A to B, but it must have been seen fit to serve as a punishment.

Ginger and three mates bullied me one evening after school in the local park, splitting up a game of football to do so. Seizing my opportunity, I picked up his denim jacket from the floor and raced away down the park with Ginger in pursuit. After several hundred yards I stopped on a bridge over a stream and let Ginger close in on me, dangling his jacket over the side of the rail. 'Givus mi jacket,' yelled Ginger, 'Givus mi jacket!' his face pink as a salmon. I let Ginger come as close as I dare and at the very last minute, I let the jacket drop into the water before racing off again. Ginger was more concerned now about the jacket, rather than chasing me.

Continuing home, my Mum and Dad were surprised to see me so early and eventually forced the reason out of me. My Dad confronted Ginger who said that he was particularly annoyed as his cigs had been in the jacket pocket. The exercise was futile as Ginger only stepped up the bullying, regularly using my face as a punch bag.

I played football from my early teens into my thirties. I was a very good junior player, pretty average intermediate player and very average senior player. I figured mainly in second string elevens, reserve sides and a pub team. Starting as a tricky left winger, I ended up as left back as I lost speed and piled on the pounds.

I also completed stints as a club secretary and as team manager for Rothwell Athletic in the West Yorkshire League and wouldn't advise anyone to take on either of these responsibilities. As secretary, I had to fill in match cards, write newspaper reports and deal with registration forms along with a whole host of paperwork. In the bad winter months, I had to inspect the pitch on Saturday morning along with a local referee, hoping he would give the go ahead for the game to take place. I then had to make and take a host of telephone calls, to and from people who were wanting to know if the match was on or off. In case of a postponement, I had to inform the opposition, to prevent them travelling. We ran two teams, so I was reliant upon the away team's secretary going through exactly the same procedure, and informing me. I then had to go through the rigmarole with the telephone calls once again.

One particular season the weather had been inclement and there had been several postponements to games which had to be fitted in during lighter evenings. The Leeds and District Football Association had approached our club to stage one of their finals at our ground and it was my responsibility to liase with them regarding the state of the pitch. Throughout the week we had suffered heavy rain and the prospects of the game going ahead looked bleak. Each evening I inspected the field and then I would telephone the District Secretary with an update. Following a further downpour, the ground showed little sign of improvement, but on Friday and Saturday I was unable to contact local officials. Apparently they were all at Wembley for the FA Cup Final. When Sunday morning came around, two teams and officials arrived at the ground, to find it both unplayable and unprepared. I was duly hauled in front of the District officials to answer my case.

I was asked to sit on a chair in the middle of the floor akin to being on Mastermind. I faced half a dozen officials on a long table with delegates sitting in rows of seating behind me.

The District Secretary started to explain the sequence of events but was untruthful saying he hadn't taken any of my calls, so I found myself interrupting him. Immediately I was shouted down and shown up by the chairman, a man who I hadn't come into contact with before, but later found out was named Kilvington. Eventually I was allowed to put forward my case to the committee and then asked to leave the room.

From where I stood in the corridor, I could hear heated discussion and exchanges taking place with the secretary not appearing to come out of it too well. When I was called back in, I was informed that our club had been severely reprimanded, and this had to be minuted within our club records.

I thought the way I was treated had been diabolical, particularly as I was doing the job on a voluntary basis. The other aspect to annoy me was that some of the officials who down the years I had considered as friends either chose to ignore me or didn't want to be seen talking to me. The whole incident left a sour taste in my mouth and prompted me to hand the reins over to some other willing volunteer at the start of the following season.

If I thought being club secretary was bad, being team manager lifts the pressure up another gear, not least picking the team and dealing with players. I did very well in my first season but a shortage of goals at the start of the following year prompted me to leave out a player. I made a point of taking him to one side before the team sheet was displayed but he just wouldn't accept my decision.

He continued his argument in the pub trying to canvass support from anyone who would listen to him and even called at my house on Saturday morning to continue the argument.

He carried on in the changing room before the game and had to be evicted and it was no surprise when he packed in. My decision was vindicated with his replacement scoring in a 3-0 win. The same player also packed in from another local team after being substituted. When I eventually decided to step down, the player immediately made himself available again. Even more surprising was that the club decided to take him back on again, which I remember at the time seemed to be another kick in the teeth for me. The last I heard of the player in question, he was actually managing a team.

Even more demanding is running a junior team, as you have parents to deal with if their child is substituted or not selected. One Sunday I stopped to watch a game when I was out for a run, as I knew some of the people involved. One parent stood behind the goal trying to talk his son, the goalkeeper through the game, while another raced up and down the touchline flagging the opposing forward line offside whenever they attacked.

The local cricket team played on an adjacent field and an appeal for players prompted three of us to attend the nets. We were all selected for the Second XI and I kept my place on the strength of scoring eight runs while my colleagues both recorded ducks. I played for three seasons, at one stage opening the batting and keeping wicket. While not a prolific scorer I had the knack of hanging around for a while to frustrate the opposition.

I responded to the squash boom and played fairly regularly, never progressing higher than division thirteen in the local ladder. After I started running, I never considered returning to squash. With a keen eye for putting, I have often fancied myself as a golfer. I am sure I would have made the European tour but I will never know now.

CHAPTER 3

New Places and New Friends

Going into race week, I started to have butterflies which was ridiculous really as I had no need to be putting myself through this ordeal. I had sponsorship money for St Gemma's Hospice riding upon me getting around and when Tuesday's training session went well, I began to feel more upbeat. However on my short Thursday run I was hopeless and the doubts began to resurface, but a short one mile jog on Saturday went extremely well and brought my confidence flooding back again. I was ready to go.

Race day brought with it very strong winds which would make for poor conditions on the long stretch south of the river. I parked my car on the large Soldiers Field expanse, changed into my running gear, vaselined up and handed in my baggage. I still had the old trainers, one held by tape but very comfortable. If I did well today and decided to carry on, I would treat myself to a proper pair of running shoes.

The late appeal for runners appeared to have swelled the field to almost 3,000, among them Frank, whom I had started with at Pontefract, another friend Tom, and several more who I recognised from my handful of races. All had run in marathons previously and one runner who I later found to be Les Kitching, gave me a valuable piece of advice which I have tried to follow over the years. 'Keep running at all costs,' he said. 'Don't walk for drinks, don't walk for anything, keep running for as long as you possibly can.'

As the Lord Mayor made his way to the starting podium, some wag piped up, 'Does everyone get a medal like yours for finishing?' The runners snaked out of Roundhay Park and into Oakwood Lane. The atmosphere was friendly, the pace ideal and the light-hearted banter took my mind away from the task in hand. As the mile posts began to slip by effortlessly, I wondered why I had been making such a fuss and I actually started to enjoy the race.

A wooded country stretch near Temple Newsam Park brought respite from the stiff breeze and at Swillington Bridges I received a boost when friends of the family, Mary and Herbert, turned out to encourage me. A

Newcastle man down for the race, groaned as we we turned a corner to be confronted by the steep Pottery Hill stretch and it was on this section some years later that a Scotsman tragically collapsed and died. Spectators seemed to be drawn to the hill like a magnet to see most tough it out, while others resorted to a walk. Most gave words of encouragement but one or two shouted cryptic or sarcastic remarks.

As the route approached my neighbourhood, spectators began to recognise me and a fitting moment was provided by members of The White Swan Football Team, who lined the pavement to cheer me on. This was probably as much from curiosity as anything, since they didn't see me do a great deal of running in games. I was now on a high as more and more people recognised me and by the time I reached the prearranged place where my Mum and Dad would be, I was fair clipping along. I needed to ease back and did so on the country section before we hit the Leeds suburbs. Halfway in 1 hour and fifty minutes as Jimmy Saville and his minders slipped by quickly disappearing out of sight. Staff outside the Cameron Iron Works were vociferous in their applause and my mother and father, who was on an extended lunch break, once again popped up to lend their support.

Through the industrial heartland of Hunslet and across a footbridge over the motorway which vibrated scaring me to death. Street parties had been organised around the course to lend a carnival atmosphere to the event and in Holbeck, a brass band struck up to provide a timely boost.

I went through twenty miles with no ill effects but was about to enter uncharted territory. The numerous hills in the North Leeds area and along the Ring Road saw me resort to a plod, then to a shuffle and in the last couple of miles, I had to alternate between walking and jogging.

The downhill path into the Roundhay Park arena eventually beckoned, and I had reached my target in 4 hours and 5 minutes, with a finishing placing of 1,458, at least halfway up the field. Marathons were for the super-fit and slightly eccentric, but now at twelve and a half stones, I had succeeded against all the odds and couldn't wait for the next one. I was well and truly hooked, and the next day I posted my application for the 1984 London Marathon.

At the beginning of 1984, I was chomping at the bit to get started, enthusing at the new challenges ahead. Together with training partner Ken and a brand new pair of Brooks Chariot shoes, we pencilled in half a dozen spring races chosen from the *Running Magazine* events diary, and from application forms we had obtained.

Taking it in turns to drive and share the petrol cost, we completed half marathons at York, Doncaster and Lincoln and on each occasion, I improved my performance. At York, the course was predominantly flat, taking in parts of the historic city, the riverside and surrounding villages. Doncaster was a point-to-point course with runners being ferried to Rossington for the start, with the finishing post on the Racecourse. At Lincoln, the heavens opened, my car had to be pushed out of the mud on the car park and we had little opportunity to explore the city. My application for the London Marathon was rejected but that didn't seem to matter as there were plenty of races out there that would welcome me with open arms.

Travelling to various races, I would recognise the same faces at different venues, and make new acquaintances all with the same common interests and goals. Mini races would develop within the main race, one week somebody would beat me but in the next race, I would show them a clean pair of heels. A whole new life had opened up for me where middle of the packers like myself could rub shoulders with champions and Olympic Athletes.

I visited many of the races year after year, while new events came along and others disappeared from the calendar. In 1984, two aspects however came across very strongly. The first was that I had to put in the training miles to figure well in the races and the second one being that I had great difficulty running in the heat.

This was a very hot summer and I tended to plan my training runs in the evening when the temperature had dropped. Race starts tended to be mid-morning, when the sun was at its strongest and my performances and times fell away dramatically. When autumn came, the temperatures were ideal and I started to pick up my performances once again.

I ran in several marathons over the next few years including Bolton, Sheffield and Glasgow, as well as Leeds a further twice, and each race saw me better my performance and improve my time. Still unable to secure a London place, I ran the Bolton which at that time was televised and included the infamous Plodder Lane.

At the end of 1985, I completed the Barnsley Marathon on a bright crisp November morning and lowered my personal best to 3 hours and 35 minutes. The organisation here in keeping with the other Barnsley races was superb. Max McNally and his team claimed the running boom started here with the advent of 'The Barnsley Six' and who was I to argue?

New training partners came and went, as not everybody was able to sustain the same level of enthusiasm and commitment that I did. Ken was offered a career promotion and moved to Bristol while Craig, who I ran stride for stride with in the 1985 Leeds Marathon, sustained a series of injuries and never really took to the sport again.

Alan, Roger and Kevin preferred the shorter evening races throughout the summer which would provide the opportunity for some pub grub on the way home and a couple of pots. The four of us decided to diversify and tackled 'The Three Peaks Walk' in North Yorkshire comprising of Pennyghent, Ingleborough and Whernside. Alan and Roger packed enormous amounts of snap and would make inroads into this at each summit, and other strategic places along the way. We stopped at a tea wagon near Ribblehead Viaduct and at 'The Hill Inn' for a pint and ended up running in order to beat the twelve hour deadline. Not surprisingly the day ended with a bar meal.

I would set myself a weekly mileage of thirty to forty miles and make sure I got out at least three or four times a week. I knew the approximate distance of all my training runs, had a good idea of my pace and would be constantly trying to better my time. I became a recognised figure on the pavements, so much so that people would comment on the strange places they had seen me and the remarkable distances from home that I had been sighted. One guy who visited the firm where I worked, remarked that he would regularly see me pass his window, so I changed my route to teach him a lesson.

On a Sunday morning, I would go with my Dad to work and run home. Other days I would leave my car at work, run home and take the bus in the next day. The period when I shared cars served the purpose well as Bob would throw me out in all weathers part of the way home, and I would run the rest.

Leaving work in my running gear, I sometimes suffered banter and abuse but would get my own back with some of the car drivers. They would inevitably be held up at traffic lights and junctions in the teatime rush hour and I would just keep on running. Some evenings I would pass the same people over and over again. Running home also saved time particularly if I was going out. In winter I would stick to the main roads but in summer I could get off the beaten track, particularly along the canal banks.

One regular route took me past Elland Road, home to Leeds United Football Club. This particular summer, the new East Stand was under construction, the gates were regularly left open and I could see inside the stadium. One evening I was passing and the gates were open so I thought I would go for it. I turned into the ground and ran around the perimeter track alongside the pitch. Having never played there and never likely to, I did what I considered was the next best thing to playing on the hallowed turf. Construction workers were scattered throughout the stadium, but my lap of honour passed unchallenged.

My new-found fitness enabled me to do simple things such as run for a bus without losing my breath. Until I took up running, I never realised how out of condition I must have been. On a Thursday evening I tended to go out for a drink, and often as I came out of my house, the bus would be passing along the main road. I would think nothing of running half a mile and heading the bus off further down the route. I started hoping that I would miss the bus so I could have a run. Anywhere I needed to walk, I would appear to run.

I would sometimes play games with the buses and try to head them off or beat them to certain points. The little nipper shoppers' buses that trolled the estates and villages were easy prey as they twisted and turned, stopping so many times. Passengers would look out of the windows and probably think 'How did he get here so quickly?' or 'Not him again!' while adolescents on the back seat would either smirk or show two fingers.

While out on a long training run in preparation for the Glasgow Marathon with friends Tom and Graham, a work colleague and his wife drove past in their car and sounded the horn. We saw them again half an hour later when they once again acknowledged us. On Monday at work, he was curious to know where we had been and how long we had been out. While visiting his son, daughter and other relatives, he had seen us a total of five times. His wife kept nudging him and saying, 'Look Colin, it's those runners again'.

New running clubs began to spring up and unlike the traditional clubs, put out the welcome mat to runners and joggers alike of all ages and abilities. This was boom time for everyone connected with the sport. Manufacturers of running kit had never had it so good, despatching regular orders to the many new breed clubs.

Sports shoe retailers were having a bonanza and when I purchased my first pair of proper running shoes, I was directed to a specialist outlet in Leeds. The assistant knew me and offered generous club discount. She was a member of the local squash club and probably thought I was a member too. I continued to put my business her way and didn't let her believe any differently.

All kinds of running related businesses were falling on their feet, from print shops to trophy manufacturers and engravers. Some firms like the Running Imp in Lincoln, provided a full race service with numbers, tape, finish line clock and results. The running magazines were full of advertisements offering health products, energy supplements, sports clinics, training advice, charities and travel. The list was endless. In the early days, I experimented with some of the energy drinks but basically ate whatever I fancied. If nothing else, running would look after my weight.

I tried out the various forms of training such as fartlek, intervals and hill repetitions. I tried sprinting a lamp post and jogging the next, picking a point and focusing on it and timing myself on laps of a local athletics track. The truth was, however, that I much preferred the long steady plod.

After three or four years of improvement, my times began to level out. I needed to change something in order to take my running to a higher level. But this didn't happen and I would always seem destined to be a 'Middle of the Packer'.

CHAPTER 4

No Mean City

I GOT OUT OF THE CAR in Argyll Street on a miserable Friday September morning. We had crossed the Clyde several times and asked directions on a couple of occasions, before eventually finding the hotel. My Mum and Dad were going on holiday to the North of Scotland and a crack of dawn start had enabled me to hitch a ride. The lack of success in securing a London Marathon place had prompted me to turn to Glasgow, which seemed a suitable alternative.

After checking in at the hotel, I headed for Rutherglen where my firm had a depot. Horace and Tam were good enough to take me to lunch and show me around. I was introduced as 'The Marathon Runner' and took on something of a celebrity status.

Returning to Glasgow on the train, I walked from St Enoch's Station towards the hotel. On noticing people still inside the pubs, I decided to call for a drink myself. Scotland had opted for all-day opening with last orders at midnight, well before the licensing laws in England were relaxed.

The race registration was at The Anderston Centre along with an exhibition of running gear, equipment, travel and associated products, and these held my interest for over an hour. The Chicago Marathon stand caught my eye, with a sample of a finisher's medal the size of a gong. Steve Jones of Wales would set a world best at Chicago before too long.

When I came out of the registration, at Friday teatime, the heavens had opened so I decided to call for another drink. It was still raining when I left Glasgow on Monday morning. On Saturday morning, I tried to familiarise myself with the layout of the city, dodging in and out of arcades and doorways, trying to keep dry. Despite the appalling weather, I loved the place and returned year after year seeing it develop from mean to vibrant city.

The Central Station concourse was so clean you could have eaten your dinner from the floor. Around the perimeter were shops, cafés and bars, while kiosks for tea, coffee or fast food were strategically placed. The complex seemed light years ahead of some of the dingy stations I had become used to back home. Equally impressive was the glass-roofed St Enoch's Centre with its quality shops, eating mall and ice rink, and the upmarket Princess Square with designer outlets.

I had planned to watch Rangers on Saturday afternoon in the days when you could turn up and get a seat, well before the Graham Souness and Walter Smith glory years. The pitch was more suitable for water polo than football and the longer the game progressed without a goal, the more edgy the crowd became.

They were fairly liberal with their language and one supporter on my row seemed to have a downer on a lumbering defender by the name of McPherson, who didn't seem to be playing too badly to me. He called him a camel, a donkey, garbage and told him throughout to get a move on or get his finger out. McPherson was later to be transferred to Hearts only to be bought back again by Rangers, and eventually established himself as a Scotland regular.

You could have heard a pin drop as Dundee scored the winner minutes from time. This prompted many of the disgruntled crowd to make for the exits and out into the pouring rain.

The rain persisted into Saturday evening and one of the TV channels previewing the marathon expressed concern as to whether it would actually go ahead, as parts of the course were under water. There was little improvement on Sunday morning but at least the race would definitely go ahead. A tented village had been erected on Glasgow Green and this would serve as both the start and finish for many years to come.

Runners were already soaked through to the skin before a stride was taken. A pipe band led the way as runners were walked into Saltmarket where the race would start. The Tron, which had served as a weigh bridge and entry point to the city, dominated the skyline as we waited to come under starter's orders. After what seemed a lifetime, the gun fired, the runners edged forward and then began to walk as the adrenaline started to flow.

It took fully three minutes to pass below the start line banner, even though the estimated 20,000 competitors had been severely reduced by the weather. There were several twists and turns through the city and as quickly as gaps opened up, they would close again. The field would tighten up, the pace was slow and the name of the game was patience. I hadn't realised that Glasgow possessed so many hills, but once we hit the straight Sauchiehall Street stretch, the field began to spread out and the pace quickened.

Despite the miserable conditions, I was still able to appreciate the surroundings, particularly the West End, Kelvingrove and University area. The course took in many of the suburbs both to the North and South of the Clyde. To the North West we ran through the quaintly named

Anniesland Cross and Scotstoun where crowd support was strong and vociferous. A piper placed strategically at each mile-post played a fitting lament which provided a nice touch. Returning to the city over the George V Bridge, the course took in Paisley Road and the Bellahouston and Pollok Parks. We were regularly treading water as large sections of the course were flooded with the rain still refusing to relent.

Beyond twenty miles and I was still going strongly, onto the Clydeside Walkway where the cobblestones had been well documented, and on to the finish at Glasgow Green. I had just completed my fourth marathon and the first where I hadn't succumbed to a walk. I had lowered my personal best or PB, the term used in the running fraternity, to 3 hours and 42 minutes. My lasting memory as I came away from Glasgow Green were the dozens of empty beer casks floating down the Clyde apparently from a Brewery that had become flooded.

I returned to Glasgow in 1987, this time with Graham and Tom and we negotiated a good deal at The Post House, which served as race headquarters. We had arranged to meet work colleague Horace in the hotel foyer. As he arrived, who should come out of the lift but old stalwart Jimmy Saville, flanked by his minders. The party jogged towards us and as they approached, Jimmy sounded the familiar Oh Hoo Oh Hoo Oh Hoo cry. We saw him again later in the afternoon at Celtic Park pushing a young boy in a wheelchair around the ground.

Race conditions were far better this time, the three of us ran the best part of the way together and all recorded personal bests. In my twelfth marathon, I was probably in the best physical shape since my teenage years and lowered my time to 3 hours and 28 minutes.

Over the next few years, the local authorities decided that a marathon was too expensive to stage. This was first replaced by a half marathon, then extended to twenty-five kilometres before returning to the more familiar half marathon distance. The event continued throughtout the nineties, was usually blessed with fine weather and regularly attracted five-figure numbers. The added touches like the tea, coffee, biscuits and bananas at the finish as well as the usual souvenirs made the race stand out from the rest.

I returned year upon year and began to know the city well. I liked nothing better than to walk the streets, the parks and the river banks. I got to know the shops, the better pubs and the attractions, some of which I returned to many times.

The Museum of Transport in the Kelvin Hall complex captured my imagination and I have spent many a happy hour there. A fine collection of vintage cars, trams and buses are complemented by the hundreds of model ships which trace the history of shipbuilding on the Clyde. The Burrell

Collection in Pollok Park is a short train ride and walk from the city centre. It houses 8,000 acquisitions donated to the city by Sir William Burrell.

The spectacular People's Palace on Glasgow Green not only houses a botanical garden but also a Folk Museum depicting a history of the great city, through hundreds of photographs and exhibits. The tenement house near Charing Cross has remained unchanged since 1965, but can become claustrophobic if full of visitors. The Kelvingrove Art Gallery and Museum, and Mackintosh House are both worth visits.

Over the years I have visited Glasgow with different people but mostly on my own. In the late nineties, I arranged for a larger group of people to travel to the race. I was reliably informed that as much pleasure and enjoyment can be derived from the organising and planning of an outing, as the actual outing itself. Well, don't you believe it!

I agreed to make the arrangements for four of us. The word spread quickly, the four grew to eight, then to twelve and eventually to seventeen. In the end I had to turn people away. I plumped for a tried and trusted hotel, a mile from the city centre opposite Kelvin Park. After making the initial reservations, it seemed as if I contacted the hotel on an almost daily basis as our numbers increased and our requirements changed. I struck up a rapport with receptionist Donna, almost persuading her to take part in the race. We eventually filled every available room, and after they offered to put a fourth bed into a triple room, I decided to call a halt to the ever-increasing numbers.

Two couples opted to travel by car as did three lads who were staying for one night only. The next task was to arrange the transport for the remaining number and after much agreement and disagreement, we opted to go by mini coach. I received plenty of advice as there seemed to be plenty of experts in this field, but nobody offered to take on the task. I set about telephoning the companies I was aware of and those within the yellow pages. The difference in rates, terms and conditions between rival companies was surprising. One company would only hire to firms, another requested a further day's payment for an early morning return, while others had a mileage charge.

I was ready to sign up at two places until they began to explain the hidden extras. I was put off a third when the man at the desk was a former work colleague who had left rather quickly. I eventually decided upon a local company providing for easier collection and return and whose coaches looked to be in good shape.

Collecting the money was a shambles. I decided to collect the deposits on the evening of the summer handicap which proved to be another mistake. The clubhouse was full, raffle tickets were being sold, subscriptions being taken and lots of money generally changing hands. On returning home, I emptied my pockets, not really knowing who had paid. Having made a provisional list, I had lost my concentration and failed to keep it up to date.

Race weekend soon came around and on Saturday morning, I set out with our three volunteer drivers to collect the minibus. It was as we were signing documents that a surcharge for each mile over 200 per day, was brought to our attention. I felt we would be well within our limits but it was too late to do anything at this stage. 'Is that our bus over there?' I asked the proprietor. 'No, yours hasn't come in yet,' he replied. The half-hour wait made us late at the other pick-up points and put us behind schedule for the rest of the day.

A planned mid-morning stop turned into a late morning one. The greasy spoon came highly recommended by a transport driver in our midst and the tea and toast were a welcome diversion from the constant drizzle throughout the journey.

A change of driver brought a change in the weather and a fairly pleasant afternoon beckoned as we reached Glasgow. We found the hotel first time which was a minor miracle, taking into consideration the abundance of traffic lights and the many one-way streets within the city.

Expecting a party of highly-tuned athletes, the hotel staff were probably taken aback when a bunch of mishapes walked into the reception. The room allocation was an area in which I had envisaged difficulty, so I had made it clear well in advance who would be rooming together.

Meeting in the reception at two o'clock, it was to be decision time. Do we watch Hamilton and Clyde or Airdrie and Raith? One moron wanted to watch Rangers and wouldn't be told that all their home games were sold out for the season. He even had the receptionist phone Ibrox Stadium. We decided upon none of these options, instead taking a stroll towards the city and calling at Shenanigans on Sauchiehall Street. After a further drink to take in the final scores, we called at Burger King inside the magnificent Central Station concourse.

On arriving back at the hotel, I was made aware that the three lads travelling independently had brought a fourth person. Much to the disappointment of other members within the party, they had sneaked him into their room. No sooner had the dust settled on this than I received a complaint from one of the party, saying his room mate wouldn't take his turn to make coffee. He apparently said, 'I haven't made a cup in my life and I aren't about to start now.' I could have done nicely without all this aggravation.

Saturday evening started with a meal, before a long trudge to find The Horse Shoe Bar, another recommended establishment. The three lads, now four, ended their evening in a Karaoke Bar with one apparently taking centre stage towards the end of the evening.

Race day started with a light breakfast for the more serious runners and a traditional Scottish for those just hoping to complete the course. Another argument ensued when one of the volunteer drivers refused to take the coach saying it was overloaded. With that sorted out, we then made our way to a car park near Glasgow Green, and after changing headed for the start.

The thirteen mile course still crosses the Clyde taking in Bellahouston and Pollok Parks before finishing alongside the People's Palace on Glasgow Green. Everyone managed to complete the course in varying times and in various states of health. Those who had been too 'Heavy on the Heavy' the previous evening perhaps struggled. The guy who had wanted to watch Rangers moaned about having to wait for the slower runners before the coach could return to the hotel.

Meeting in the bar next door to the hotel, a search party was sent out for two of our number, who had left their room but had not arrived. They were found in a cellar bar further down the street, probably wondering why they were the only two in there.

With the suburbs left behind, we crossed the Erskine Bridge to Balloch on the south end of Loch Lomond. No arguments about this one but after a brief stroll it was decision time again. Fish and chips or a pub meal? I opted for the latter, tucking into steak and kidney pie with all the trimmings.

Some people wanted to head home first thing on Monday morning, others after lunch. Some wanted to stop at the services while others preferred a pub lunch. Decisions all the time. One guy persistently asked if he could be dropped off first, so he could get home in time to watch Leeds United.

I believe everybody had an enjoyable time and I received some satisfaction from the people who have since thanked me. Anyone looking for an enjoyable running weekend break could do worse than select the Great Scottish Run ahead of some of the better publicised overseas events. I'll continue to return each August. This is 'No Mean City'.

CHAPTER 5

The Big Apple

A CHANCE MEETING on a late night bus led to the trip of a lifetime. My rejection slip for the 1986 London Marathon had arrived on the door mat, and Tom who sat next to me on the journey had also been turned down. He said that his brother, Graham had been unsuccessful for three years on the trot and could see no way of being admitted until the numbers started to subside.

On the strength of this, Graham had sent away for literature on the New York City Marathon, and he and Tom were giving consideration to running there in November. I could recollect seeing the highlights of the previous year's race in which Italian Orlando Pizzolato had won a popular victory in blistering temperatures. Towards the end of the race, he stopped to look around and was reduced to walking and jogging to the Central Park finish. I remembered the spectacular bridge start and was keen to gain some first-hand experience.

I asked Tom to count me in too, so when the literature arrived, a meeting was hurriedly arranged in a local pub. Tom's friend Steve would make up the numbers and appeared keen to give a good account of himself. By applying to the race direct, we would have to take our chance in a lottery and wouldn't discover whether or not we had been accepted until August. By going with an approved tour operator, we would have the flight, the hotel, transportation and race entry all guaranteed. We decided upon the second option and chose a North West firm to deal with our arrangements.

We were keen to see something of the States after the marathon, and following a further meeting in the pub, decided upon Orlando, New Orleans and Niagara Falls, not necessarily in that order.

Graham and I visited a city centre travel agent and spent so long with the consultant that a queue had started to form behind us. They were unable to book flights exactly as we had planned, so we called another meeting, revisited the travel agent and finalised the arrangements. This time we were waiting for the consultant to arrive, and gave him little time to get his coat off or grab a tea.

Throughout the summer, I had something to look forward to which kept me focused. I completed the Selby and Nottingham Marathons in good shape, using the Bridlington Half on a cold and blowy day as my last long training run.

Steve's girlfriend Helen drove us to Manchester airport on a wet and miserable day and had cleverly pieced together a cassette with all the tracks featuring either New York or America. Simon and Garfunkels, 'Gone to look for America' and 'LA's fine, New York's home' by Neil Diamond were particularly poignant and stuck with me throughout the holiday.

The trip had come at an awkward time for me as I had recently made a breakthrough with Victoria, a girl I had been keen on for some time. I could ill afford eighteen days away from these shores. She had recently split up with a boyfriend but when I returned, the inevitable had happened and she had got back with him again. She did however thank me for my postcard and her mother and father had remarked what a neat writer I was.

The shuttle from Manchester would take us to Gatwick where we would meet the couriers and the rest of the party. With this in mind we were sent lapel badges from the tour company for easy identity. We met up with other members of the group, but no couriers showed up. As boarding time grew increasingly close, two guys, one with a briefcase, strode purposefully towards us. The first introduced himself as Tim Green and the second as Paddy Gunn. Graham said that he probably kept going off!!

Tim addressed the group and said 'Is Andrew Bennett here?' Immediately my heart sank into my boots. Apparently there was no record of me checking in, even though I had a boarding card and a seat number. The seat had apparently been double booked which resulted in me sitting well away from my friends. I sat in between Alison and a Dutchman who could have smoked for Holland. The Dutchman and his family who sat in the row in front, were all running in the marathon, as was Alison.

There seemed to be quite a bit of envy at work when I asked around for sponsorship as few people at that time had visited the States. My three colleagues had all previously been but it would be my first visit and I felt like a bit of a David Frost. This was the single longest flight I had undertaken, but it seemed to pass quickly. The time difference meant it was only mid-afternoon when we arrived in New York, but the horrendous traffic delayed the journey into Manhattan. The hotel on West 42nd Street was comfortable but basic.

In the evening, we ventured from the hotel onto the mean streets and within a hundred yards I was ready to turn back. We were offered drugs, approached by ladies of the night and at one stage, I could have sworn we were being followed. On top of all this, a peculiar steam seemed to drift up onto the pavements around street corners.

We survived the opening onslaught, and the four of us plus Alison went on to have an enjoyable evening, ending up in 'The Blarney Stone', a hostelry recommended by the couriers.

On the Friday morning we took a stroll, getting a completely different perspective of the city in day time. The traffic was unrelenting, the streets riddled with potholes and the tall buildings kept out the sunlight. Many runners by now would have sampled the full race package including expo, tour of the course and breakfast run and we took in the lot.

The tour of the course gave us a feel of the New York layout, but many stops for traffic lights and slow moving traffic really prolonged the journey. There was the opportunity for a photo call at the Verrazano Bridge and the chance to explore Central Park at journey's end.

The Expo was held at The Sheraton Hotel where race numbers were collected along with tee shirts and other freebies. Marathon week in New York has countless restaurants, shops and bars offering discounts to runners, and information about these was provided at the Expo. A hundred restaurants were taking part in the Pasta and Perrier scheme, providing food and drink for marathoners and their families at competitive prices in the run-up to the big day.

One souvenir handed out at the Expo was a huge rolled up poster which has stayed close to my heart ever since. The centre piece is a large bottle of Perrier Water surrounded by skyscrapers. The rest of the poster portrays a map of the course in cartoon style, with larger than life boats, buildings and bridges. The poster took pride of place on my office wall at work for some years but now stands rolled up along with similar posters at the back of my wardrobe. Some years ago I had a couple framed but the asking price for this one was £80. So in the wardrobe it will remain until the day I decide to treat myself.

Saturday morning saw us take part in the International Breakfast Run. This constitutes a gentle jog exclusively for overseas runners, from the United Nations Building on the East River to The Tavern on the Green in Central Park. Runners from each country are encouraged to jog the five kilometres or so, behind their own nominated flag carrier.

Once in Central Park, runners had to scramble for coffee, bagels and muffins in a free-for-all which I understand has been much better organised in recent years. Along with other members of our party, we sat on the temporary seating erected for the marathon finish and looked out across Central Park to the skyscrapers beyond.

One young member within our group had to purchase running shoes as his baggage failed to arrive at the airport, and had not been recovered in the days since. Fortunately it arrived safely, later on Saturday afternoon, but this taught me an important lesson. Always pack your running shoes in your hand luggage. Other kit can be replaced but broken-in running shoes can't.

This incident reminded me of the man who checked in at the airport. He asked to go to New York but asked for his luggage to go via Abu Dhabi and Dar es Salaam. 'We can't do that,' the attendant said. 'Why not?' he replied, 'You did last week'.

On Saturday afternoon, we took the Circle Line Cruise from the quay at the end of 42nd Street. The passengers who seemed to be mostly runners were crammed like sardines, but fortunately we managed to get seats near a window on the lower deck. At almost three hours, the trip was probably a shade too long but certainly the best way to see New York and gain an appreciation of the city. The journey completely circles Manhattan, going into the harbour close to the Statue of Liberty, and under twenty or so bridges. Continuing along East and Harlem Rivers, the boat swings left into the wide Hudson River passing below the George Washington Bridge. Once out of the city, the colours of the autumn foliage were spectacular in the late afternoon sun.

The pasta party was held at the nearby Lincoln Centre where people were continuously shunted in and out in order to seat as many as possible, in the shortest available time. The experience rather put me off pasta parties and since then, I have tended to give them a wide berth. The rest of the evening was spent writing postcards and with the big day fast approaching, I turned in early.

Arising at crack of dawn, we were transported on one of a convoy of buses to the race start at Fort Wadsworth on Staten Island. We missed breakfast as the couriers had forgotten to place the orders at a café, close to the hotel. One of them arrived just as we were about to board the coaches and looked as if he had been dragged through a hedge backwards, and he seemed very apologetic.

The facilities at Fort Wadsworth were plentiful and well organised. A tented village provided for changing, breakfast and shelter but with the rain steadily falling it was very damp underfoot. There was even a church service provided for those who needed a little divine intervention. We all changed in good time, vaselined, plastered up and did the little things individual to each marathon runner. I then wrote my name on the reverse side of my number as we had been instructed to do. There was still a long wait before we would see any action, the 10.50 start was probably arranged to suit television.

It was my intention to run around with a camera, and with this in mind I had attached a small bag to a belt around my waist. In the weeks leading up to the race, I had done practice runs with the camera and all seemed to go well. What I didn't know was how it would react and how many times I would have to adjust the strap over the twenty-six miles. It was my intention to stop at strategic places on the way round to take photographs of buildings, views, the crowds or anything else that caught my eye. With this in mind, I even took a spare film along with me.

The rain fell like stair rods before the start but I became friendly with a nice marshal who shared her brolly with me until it was time to go. The sun eventually broke through and would make for hot and humid conditions later in the day.

I read somewhere that all American events are preceded by a rendition of 'The Star Spangled Banner' and The New York Marathon was no exception. I found this to be very moving and only wished that we were more patriotic towards our own country back home. We were soon to be underway passing the toll booths at the run on to the Verrazano Narrows Bridge, the longest single span bridge in the world, at least according to the courier. This was keenly contested by a member of our group from Hull, who was adamant the Humber Bridge was the longer of the two.

Nevertheless, crossing the Verrazano was an unforgettable experience with helicopters hovering above, small planes with streamers and water cannons firing from boats in the straits below. The Verrazano links Staten Island and Brooklyn and would be the first of five bridges on the course. On reaching the far side, I stopped, moved onto the pavement and turned around to take my first photograph. I put the camera back into my pouch and continued jogging.

The New York Marathon takes runners through all five boroughs including many diverse neighbourhoods. I found the most fascinating to be the Hasidic Jewish Community in Williamsburg, where men wore wide brimmed hats and sported curled sidelocks and beards.

Fourth Avenue undulates for eight miles before a right turn at Williamsburg Bank transfers runners into Lafayette Avenue. There was sufficient room to manoeuvre but the course was still very congested. The crowd support was noisy, supportive and solid for most of the route as we ran through many contrasting communities. The four of us were split up very early in the race but each remained distinctive in our Union Flag singlets.

One aspect that took me aback was the many people from within the crowd who shouted, 'Brits out of Ireland'. What it had to do with me I couldn't imagine. They had no idea if I was Unionist or Republican or where my allegiances lay. Some of these people were perhaps only third or fourth-generation Irish and had probably never even visited the land of their ancestors. They probably put their hand into their pockets to support the cause and perhaps marched on St Patrick's day. These incidents made me all the more determined to wear my Union Flag vest with pride, if and when I ran again overseas.

The Pulaski Bridge from Brooklyn to Queens seemed to cross industrial wasteland and a tributary to the East River, with good views of the Manhattan skyline to the left. My only recollection of Queens is that it was home to fictional detective Mary Beth Lacey played by Tyne Daley. I wondered if she would be on the pavements lending her support.

The Queensborough or 59th Street Bridge takes runners across the East River into Manhattan. The walkway alongside the bridge was carpeted to prevent athletes treading on the metal grid, but I opted for the safer alternative of running on the road. The 59th Street Bridge became famous in the Simon and Garfunkel song, but more recently appeared in the opening footage on the American sitcom 'Taxi'.

On leaving the bridge, the run off loops onto First Avenue where a wall of noise hit me. I imagined this to be similar to running out in front of a full house at one of our top football grounds. First Avenue was straight as an arrow, for as far as the eye could see and flanked either side by tall buildings. Archways of brightly coloured balloons identified each mile post, and from time to time, entertainment was provided by way of jugglers, stiltmen and musicians. The crowds were superb and very supportive and from time to time would single out an individual runner to support.

By now I had taken many photos and even changed film on the run. It was now time to put the camera away, concentrate on my running and dig deep. The Willis Avenue Bridge marks the gateway to the South Bronx for a brief visit past the world famous Yankee Stadium, before returning across the Madison Avenue Bridge into Harlem.

The large Hispanic and Puerto Rican communities in Harlem provided a real street party atmosphere with musicians and dancers lining the route throughout the neighbourhood. We entered Central Park at the 100th Street entrance but there were still three miles to go. The stretch through Central Park was much longer than I imagined and surprisingly undulating as I found to my cost. The 850 acres comprise lakes, woods, parkland and a skating rink. A garden known as Strawberry Fields is dedicated to John Lennon while the Sheep Meadow provides a picnic and recreational area.

We eventually left Central Park but ran along Central Park South which flanks the narrow end of the park. A giant pair of Nike trainers were secured to the side of a tall building providing an unmistakable advertisement for this particular manufacturer.

On re-entering Central Park and with the finish gantry in sight, I whipped out my camera for one last photograph, before crossing the line in 3 hours 43 minutes. The marshals in the finishing chutes were the most enthusiastic imaginable and made every runner feel like a champion.

A huge rectangular medal was placed around my neck, a silver foil cape placed around my shoulders and I was presented with a goody bag containing fruit, sandwiches and bric-à-brac. The baggage buses seemed a mile away and after meeting Graham, we returned to the hotel using the subway. Graham and Tom were a little disappointed with their performances and times but both appeared to be slightly under the weather. Steve was upset at not breaking three hours while I would have liked to have done better, but couldn't really complain taking into account all the photo stops.

We celebrated on Sunday evening in 'The Blarney Stone' with food and several pitchers of beer and relived the day's events. Highlights of the race were continually being shown on television throughout the evening and once again it was an Italian success story. Gianni Poli won the race with Italians finishing in fourth, seventh and ninth places. This prompted the controversy on blood doping to once again rear its head. Norwegian Grete Waitz led home the ladies for the eighth time and little did I know that one day I would meet the great lady.

Later in the evening, we found ourselves in the company of a young, well-dressed black man and his older companion. They seemed particularly impressed that we had taken the trouble to visit New York and run in their marathon. On leaving, they gave us an address in Greenwich Village and asked us to call the following afternoon when they would give us a tour of the neighbourhood.

Monday was to be our main sightseeing day and despite the heavy legs, we managed Battery Park, Wall Street and The World Trade Centre Building. On the observation deck, there wasn't a breath of wind and the views were outstanding. The Verrazano Bridge from where we had run was on the skyline with New Jersey across the harbour. Queens was to the east and beyond were The Bronx and upstate New York. The three main bridges can be easily put in order by remembering the logo BMW Brooklyn, Manhattan and Williamsburg. Apart from the bridges, the various boroughs are linked by tunnels with the Brooklyn – Battery and Queens – Midtown under the East River and Lincoln and Holland Tunnels linking Manhattan and New Jersey.

The tunnel entrances are a hive of activity as motorists pull up at traffic lights. Youths rush out with buckets and sponges to wash car windscreens, vendors sell newspapers and scantily clad young ladies try to attract the attention of truckers.

I obviously penned this chapter before the atrocities of September 11th and my heart goes out to the people who both live and work in Lower Manhattan and the financial district and to those who lost a loved one in the carnage. My hope is that the perpetrators can be brought to justice with the minimum amount of bloodshed and that the people of this great city can return to some sort of normality.

We called at Maceys department store to claim our free bags for which a token had been provided among the race souvenirs. From there, we called at a bar to the rear of a delicatessen, which had been recommended by a friend of Steve. Apparently we would have a strange experience and soon found out why. As soon as the barman realised we were British, he talked incessantly about the Royal Family and Queen Mother in particular. Having lived in Manhattan for all of his life, the barman had never visited the Empire State Building, or any of the other attractions for that matter.

We were unable to find the address on West 10th Street in Greenwich Village. On retracing our steps several times, it seemed as if the missing number was in fact a church. Knocking on a suitable looking door, we found our new friends to be men of the cloth. True to their word, they made us welcome and gave us an informative walk around the village.

This is a community apart with sidewalk cafés and a bizarre mix of shops and homes. The many bars and restaurants are frequented by writers, musicians and students. Highlight of the tour was Washington Square, a small park with roller skaters and street entertainers, but dominated by The Triumphal Arch. This was built to commemorate the centenary of George Washington's inauguration as President. We thanked our hosts, wished each other luck and said our farewells.

Monday's sightseeing ended with a trip up the Empire State Building to see New York at night, another recommended experience. We said our goodbyes to other members of the party before going our separate ways on Tuesday.

New York was wet and windy when we left but Florida was hot, dry and still and I thought I was in paradise. Over several days we took in Kennedy Space Centre, Disney World and Epcot but I was more than impressed with Church Street Station, an authentic wild west street. I appeared to be so suited to the ambience and lifestyle that I firmly believed I would be living here in the not too distant future.

New Orleans was just as good with the mighty Mississippi River, the lively French Quarter and the Cajun cooking. I wondered if they held a race here as I would have liked to return one day.

A tedious flight took us north to Buffalo, the airport for Niagara Falls. The plane touched down at Cincinnati, Nashville and Cleveland with passengers leaving and joining the plane at each stop. We caught the service bus to Niagara Falls across the Canadian border and the driver fixed us up with comfortable accommodation. Well past the holiday season and with many of the attractions closed down, we enjoyed several days near the spectacular falls. I had expected the falls to be in the middle of nowhere, rather than in the middle of town, alongside a promenade.

We caught an early morning taxi to the airport, Graham and Tom caught a flight to Cleveland where they were to stay with relatives, while Steve and I flew to New York and then back to England.

While everyone had an excellent time, I considered this to be a trip of a lifetime. Little did I realise that this would be the first in a long line of wonderful overseas running experiences.

CHAPTER 6

Howay the Lads

I STROLLED ALONG THE SEAFRONT and down a slight incline. Ahead and to the right was a large expanse of grassland, further to the right were the sea and sandunes, while on a headland in the distance stood Tynemouth Priory. It was a bright, crisp, January day.

I wouldn't have even considered a holiday or a day out in South Shields, but seeing it from a different perspective, I was suitably impressed. Far removed from the chaotic scenes at the at the finish of the Great North Run, it appeared to be the ideal seaside resort. There was sea and sand, parks and amusements, not forgetting plenty of fish and chip shops and pubs.

Sitting by the window in one of the two old railway carriages that form part of 'The Marsden Rattler', I observed the occasional pedestrians and the gentle flow of traffic along the Sea Road, in contrast to the gridlocked traffic I was used to seeing on the big day.

With the exception of seventeen Great North Runs, all there and back in the day, my only visit to South Shields must have been over twenty years ago. I was staying overnight on business, on a miserable winter evening and was looking for 'The Sir William Fox Hotel'. My main objective was that my clapped-out Austin 1100 kept going in the torrential downpour.

I bought fish and chips, always tastier out of the paper and by the seaside, and I ate them as I strolled past the many bed and breakfasts and small hotels towards the town centre. Beyond the Town Hall, I followed the signs to the Ferry Terminal, caught the ferry to North Shields and hopped on a bus to Whitley Bay.

Some years previously, I had parked at North Shields before the Great North Run and rode the Metro into Newcastle. I had then completed the race, caught the bus to the Ferry Terminal and then the ferry to North Shields. This provided for a quick getaway through the Tyne Tunnel before the build-up of traffic. That day, the ferry was crowded but today it was quiet, making me wonder how it managed to prove viable with so few passengers.

I had a quick stroll along the front at Whitley Bay as dusk started to settle. They told me this place was on fire at night but there wasn't a soul around this afternoon. Another quiet pint, after which I located the Metro station for the train back to Newcastle where my day had started.

Apart from my Great North Runs, and boarding a coach to take me to Morpeth for the New Year's Day race, I had never set foot in Newcastle. My hectic morning had taken in Eldon Centre, St James's Park and Bigg Market and towards lunchtime I had walked the Quayside beneath the famous bridges. I called in at Northern Runner to see a certain Mr White but he was out at lunch. I bought a pair of Asics that set me back nearly fifty quid.

All the walking was making me thirsty and I called for another pot in a pub down the quaintly named 'Pudding Chair'. A colleague at work told me that in years gone by, all the pubs were interlinked and you could go from top to bottom without getting wet. He also said that if you managed to get all way down, without having a fight, then you had done well.

So I had now come full circle as I waited to catch the train home to Leeds. I was so impressed that I returned one day in April and did it all again.

My first GNR was in 1985. I brought my parents for a day out and parked on the sea front at South Shields. Not being too familiar with the arrangements, I had to rush around at the Newcastle end due to a work-to-rule on the Metro. The baggage buses which transport your clothes back to South Shields, park on the dual carriageway at the back of the field, ready to set off in the opposite direction. The bus marked B for Bennett was obviously near the front, so I had to jog the half mile there and half mile back in order to take my place at the start.

The thing that caught my imagination about this event was that it catered for all abilities. Everybody was there from world class athlete to fun runner, from elite athlete to fancy dresser and from club athlete to charity fund raiser. I lined up in the 6,000 block, not too far from the start, but all I could see in front was a mass of bodies with many more on the grass embankments poised to join in. No doubt these people would wait for some movement at the front of the field and then make their move, filtering into the spaces created.

It took three minutes to cross the start line but as each block moved forward, so did an official with what looked like a lollipop stick. The time that it took them to cross the start line was recorded, and everyone in that block had their official time adjusted accordingly. All well and good provided everybody lines up where they should. The first few hundred yards were stop and start with no real space to run comfortably. One or two impatient runners put a hand on my back as they moved through the field, trying to make up for lost time. Someone stumbled beneath hundreds of feet but two kind souls helped him to his feet, while others swerved or stopped in order to prevent a mass pile-up.

One carriageway went through an underpass while the other went over the top. The familiar chant of 'Oggy, Oggy, Oggy. Hoy, Hoy, Hoy' rang out from time to time and spectators gathered on every bridge, wall and conceivable vantage point. At last I had made it into the big time, with this far and away, my most prestigious and biggest event to date. The downhill to the Tyne Bridge should have provided the opportunity to make up for lost time, but with the many runners in close proximity, I had to concentrate on moving forward and not being tripped.

The sponsor's name, Thorne EMI, was emblazoned on a large banner over the approach to the Tyne Bridge which seemed to vibrate with the constant pounding of hundreds of pairs of feet. The event was televised with a camera positioned as we came off the bridge. People changed course, swerved in front of others and risked life and limb, to give themselves the best possible chance of getting their face on the box.

As we came off the bridge, I noticed another Thorne EMI banner, and then another and another. They straddled the road, were on posters, on mountings, or just on bill boards along the road side. It was impossible for anyone involved, not to know who the race sponsors were. They were certainly getting value for money.

With only two miles gone, I became annoyed at the number of walkers I was having to negotiate. They should have submitted slower finishing times and started further back. Youngsters were been allowed to join at Gateshead, and families walking three and four abreast began to cause problems. In future years, a separate children's race was organised for the Saturday before the main event over a more realistic distance.

The spectators were noisy, supportive and were tightly packed along most of the route. Children held out their hands, hoping to be slapped by anyone running close to the kerb. The course through Gateshead, Jarrow and Hebburn was testing and appeared to become harder with each year. The day was hot and with one hill too many, I tired in the final miles. The smell of the sea air, hot dogs and onions and the crowd three or four deep signalled the end was in sight.

With the exception of the Tyne Bridge and the final mile along the sea front, I didn't find the course to be too spectacular. Run mainly on dual carriageways, the course is surprisingly undulating, particularly in the middle section. Over the years, I got to know each blip and rise, when to speed up and when to hold back and on which side of the carriageway to run at any given time. I'm sure as the years progressed they kept adding an extra hill.

Despite the delays at the start, winning times have proved the course is potentially fast, particularly if you can get away quickly. The predominant westerly wind would tend to be a following wind and would blow you all the way to the coast.

The first year I took part, Steve Kenyon won the race in 62 minutes, with Rosa Mota of Portugal, who would later become Olympic Champion taking the ladies' title. I believe Steve was the last British winner here to my knowledge, which pays testimony to the quality fields assembled. Local hero Mike McLeod nicknamed 'The Elswick Express' won the first two races in the early eighties and has had a couple of good second places, while in 2002, largely unknown Andy Coleman was second. Despite wins in the ladies' race for both Liz McColgan and Paula Radcliffe in recent years, it would be a dream come true for Race Organiser, Brendan Foster to see a British winner in the men's race and particularly a North Easterner.

Brendan had the idea for an event after taking part in the Round the Bay race in New Zealand as part of his preparation for the 1980 Olympic Games. Along with the help of John Caine and Max Coleby among others, the dream became reality with the first running in 1981. Each year a high standard has been maintained at the sharp end of the race, while increasing the mass participation and fun element. Everyone worth their salt in distance running circles has competed here and hopefully will continue to support this unique event.

Past winners have included Olympians Carlos Lopes, Rob de Castella and John Treacy while Olympic champion Gelindo Bordin was beaten into third place in 1989.

Former ladies champions include the great Norwegian duo, Grete Waitz and Ingrid Kristiansen along with Lisa Martin and Rosa Mota, although in recent years, Africans have tended to dominate in both races.

Many celebrities have competed regularly including the likes of Sir Jimmy Saville, Frank Bruno and TV sports reporters John Motson and Steve Rider. Ex-footballers, now managers, Kevin Keegan and Peter Reid have been there and done it while Paul Gascoigne pushed a young boy around the course in a wheelchair. Usually a celebrity starter is invited to officiate and these have included former England boss, Bobby Robson and football legend Bobby Charlton. Former Commonwealth champion, now North East Sports Shop owner Jim Alder has started the race, while this year's man with the gun was Olympic triple jump champion, Jonathon Edwards.

Entertainment is usually provided at the start of the race on a purpose-built stage inbetween the carriageways. In 1994, Mr Motivator led the warm-up exercises which just went on and on and on. Those who took part would have had nothing left for the race. In recent years, Jimmy Nail and Status Quo have provided the pre-race entertainment.

Commonwealth Champion Rob de Castella was disqualified in 1987 for reducing the size of his number but was later reinstated on appeal. I can't imagine what advantage can be gained by trimming your number down. 1989 saw the introduction of The Great North Mile when John Walker was victorious ahead of Steve Ovett. The Great North Walk and Cycle Rides were added in 1991 as the North East became fitness conscious and a year later, the first World Championships were held for the half marathon in conjunction with the GNR.

From a 'Middle of the Packer's' point of view, the GNR became a must do event. Coach space quickly filled up, and in the unfortunate occurrence of injury, numbers quickly changed hands, as everybody got in on the act. What started out as a summer event gradually moved back in the calendar to October, presumably to secure the best TV deal and coverage. The main sponsors have changed over the years with prominent ones being Thorne EMI, Diet Coke and BUPA.

The GNR provided a day out for the whole family with plenty to keep them entertained at South Shields. It was a good day out too for the Geordies who packed every grass verge, footbridge and vantage point, to secure the best possible view and become an integral part of the proceedings. Everyone knew somebody who was running, with every street, village and community represented.

Athletic clubs, scouts and similar organisations ran the drink stations while groups, bands and majorettes strutted their stuff on roundabouts and other strategically selected places.

The fancy dressers made up a fair proportion of the field with every conceivable costume and dress being worn. Paul Ash, who organised a coach to the race, tended to dress up for charity and took on a different outfit each year, with Rupert Bear being one of his early costumes. The following year, I happened to glance out of the house window shortly before leaving to board the coach. A man with webbed feet walked past and sure enough it was Paul, getting in some last minute practice for his role as Donald Duck.

Due to the considerable expense incurred in hiring these costumes, it would be only practical to hire them for the required weekend. Paul would therefore practice for the big day, late in the evening wearing a heavy overcoat, so the neighbours wouldn't recognise him.

Another year he ran, straddling a very small horse in a similar pose to Bernie Clifton on his Ostrich. Paul said he had run badly but the horse had done a personal best. Sadly injuries have lead to Paul packing up at least for now. He will be a great loss to the sport as a brilliant organiser, fundraiser and a wonderful character.

The GNR provided me with fifteen seconds of fame, let alone fifteen minutes. In 1991, Frank Bruno sent me sprawling as he made his sprint for the line. I realised that Frank had been behind me for some time, listening to the applause and banter from the crowd, but instead of running around me he appeared to run through me. The TV cameras showed Frank for the last 100 yards or so and colleagues who saw the incident didn't let me live it down.

I have always tended to run well here irrespective of my form at the time. My ambition at one time was to be in the first thousand finishers and to dip below ninety minutes. To date I have managed neither and shouldn't imagine I will do now, although I came close to ninety minutes in 1994. Not feeling particularly competitive, but having jogged to the baggage buses and back before the race, I felt remarkably easy. Once the race was underway, I was fortunate in not getting blocked in and reached the first mile post very quickly. Feeling very comfortable, I pressed on nicely gaining momentum. I picked up pace and each time I asked for more, I seemed to be moving up through the gears. I slipped past a couple of club mates who were usually well in front and couldn't quite believe what was happening. All good things come to an end and by eleven miles I felt as if I was treading water. The relentless pace possibly cost me the ninety minutes and a place in the first thousand. As the years advance, it would seem as if those targets are lost forever now.

I really went for it in 1987, but set off far too quickly paying the price in the later stages. Falling way behind my anticipated time splits, I appeared to be going backwards as a tide of runners streamed past. That was the year I first started to realise how hilly the course was. My yardstick tended to be how well I ran up John Reid Road. If I managed the long drag in reasonable shape, the impetus would take me along Prince Edward Road and on to the sea.

1997 saw red numbers issued to runners who had completed all GNRs, and green numbers to those with ten or more under their belt. This entitled them to an ideal starting position up front behind the elite athletes. Completing our final preparations on the coach before making our way to the start, I asked the question why most of my colleagues had white numbers while only a few of us had green. Fortunately nobody rose to the bait.

The recent autumn date for the GNR has no doubt been dictated in no small part by the BBC, but the event has gradually moved from being a summer to an autumn event. The race has enjoyed good weather over the years and I can only recall rain once. Lady Luck won't last forever so a return to a summer date and the big family day out would generally be well received.

Consideration should also be given to be given to the introduction of a staggered start, as happens in some of the mass participation continental races. The Dam to Dam in Amsterdam has four starts at fifteen minute intervals, and seems to cope satisfactorily, taking in much narrower roads, parks and villages. The Gothenburg Half Marathon in Sweden has blocks of 5,000 runners starting at five-minute intervals, and this appeared to eliminate a good deal of congestion in the early stages. A championship chip could be used to give everybody an accurate time.

My third suggestion would be to hold the entry fee or look at the possibility of a reduction. The £22 fee is getting beyond the reach of some competitors and there has been quite a lot of discontentment from die-hard GNR runners, who now seem to be boycotting the event. The cost of staging such an event must be incredibly high and there are also all year round operating costs. The appearance and prize money at the sharp end of the race has to be found, but surely the TV money and top sponsorship will offset this to a great extent.

I invited my Mum and Dad to a couple of the early runs and they thoroughly enjoyed good days out. In 1999, my Dad accompanied me once again. We parked up early on the seafront and while I was travelling to Newcastle and waiting to start, he read a paper and took a stroll along the seafront. He watched the leaders come through the tape and waited until I finished. After changing, we had a beer and a sandwich before setting off home, missing most of the heavy traffic. I was pleased that I took my Dad as he sadly passed away the following July and this was one of the last races he attended with me. The memories of that day will last with me forever.

CHAPTER 7

In the Line of Fire

WHEN I STARTED the Wednesday evening training runs with Ackworth Road Runners, road safety didn't seem to figure too high on the agenda. Sometimes the group would be twelve or fifteen strong, and they would tear across the road in front of vehicles, pay little regard to traffic lights and generally keep motorists on their toes.

Safety in numbers appeared to be the theme particularly when they crossed the first half of the road and ended up running down the middle along the white line. It was reminiscent of the film, 'In the Line of Fire' where Clint Eastwood played a bodyguard to the US President.

One evening while out on a run in the Pontefract area, a shot was heard as the leaves in a nearby hedgerow rustled. We stopped, looked around and saw a couple of figures disappear behind some distant farm buildings. They had probably aimed to miss, but some years later, one of our group wouldn't be so fortunate.

We had started the run as a larger group, but Kevin, Mick and myself had peeled off. It was a warm summer evening and we were nearing the end of our run on Halfpenny Lane in between Featherstone and Pontefract. We left the fields behind and entered a built-up area when Kevin suddenly grunted, staggered forward and said that he had been shot by an air rifle.

As he lunged forward, he turned and was sure he had seen movement behind a curtain in an upstairs window. After examing the small red circle at the back of Kevin's leg and establishing that he would live, we briefly searched for the pellet. We then decided to go to the house in question with Kevin and I knocking at the back door and Mick keeping an eye on the front. The garden was one of those strewn with motor parts and general debris, with parts of the fence, gate and hedge all missing.

After knocking several times, and a wait of five minutes or so, an adolescent youth appeared at the door with a cigarette drooping from his mouth. We told him that Kevin had been shot and asked if anyone in the house had an air rifle. He said there was no one else in the house and no gun. Mick carried a mobile phone and, not happy with developments, decided to call the police.

By this time, several neighbours had emerged from adjacent houses, had closed ranks and were giving us a hard time. The woman next door had said the people were on holiday but when the youth emerged, she started arguing with me. A gang of youths started a game of football where we stood and were narrowly missing us with every kick.

At this point, a second youth came out of the house and we asked him the same questions but to no avail. A second call to the police met with the same response as the first, but they eventually arrived twenty minutes later. They were two WPCs, one in her early twenties, the other possibly thirty. They seemed hell-bent on getting us into the panda car, and away from the area as quickly as possible.

'Don't you want us to point out the people who were in the house?' I said. 'No we'll come back later,' replied the older officer. 'Anyway, we would need a search warrant and would have to go in mob handed.' I remarked that their approach would give the youths time to remove the gun from the house, but this didn't seem to break any ice.

We were driven to the police station, given tea and made statements. The officers were very nice but I don't believe they took the incident any further. Apparently the area had been a trouble hot spot and recently the police had built bridges. I believe they viewed this as a possible setback and didn't have the inclination or resources to rock the boat. This was all well and good but of little consolation to Kevin.

Our club chairman promised to write to the local police authority, but seemed to regard the incident as amusing and I don't believe a letter was ever penned. As for Kevin, he was left with an irritating sore above his knee.

I have twice reported abandoned or stolen cars to the police when I have returned home from runs. The first time, the officer knew the exact spot and was very appreciative. On the second occasion, I was put through to a central switchboard where the officer seemed unfamiliar with the area. The line of questioning indicated he was more interested in me, than what I had to tell him about the car.

A constant problem that runners encounter is constant lip and abuse from kids and some pretty old kids at that. Running has been a regular pastime for many years now with runners and joggers, commonplace on neighbourhood streets. I would have thought the shouting of abuse and obscenities would have subsided by now as the novelty wore off. From my point of view, the practice has become more prevalent and is probably at an all-time high. Gangs of youths congregate around late night shops and recreation grounds and you can rarely get by without being targeted.

Some of the comments from younger children are comical and tend to bring a smile to the face, but in among the 'Get them knees up,' are the occasional 'Look at that silly old fart,' and 'Fat Bastard'. Tremendous restraint is required but every so often, I would love to throttle one of these horrible little swines. My friend Mick would take no prisoners and go wading in among them, but they kept telling me if I so much as raised an arm, I would be in trouble.

Close to home is a huge bush within chapel grounds and youths tend to congregate there for a drink, a smoke, or anything else that boys and girls do. Everyone who passes, from pedestrian to jogger alike, suffers abuse with no holds barred. In the centre of the bush is a clearing resembling a rubbish tip with cans, crisp packets, fag ends and the likes. I have stood and watched as many as fifteen people walk out of the bush in one session, and people regularly drop in for a pee on the way home from the pub. From a distance on an evening or under the glow of streetlamps, it resembles the burning bush shrouded in smoke or mist. While I don't usually mind being abused and tend to shrug it off, there's only so much you can take and there comes a time when you have to hit back.

While recently running around a former colliery landfill that is now landscaped with trees, paths and ponds, four children pushing bikes approached from the opposite direction. One boy who could have been no older than eleven gave me a mouthful that wouldn't have been out of place in a tap room. I told him any more and I would give him a thick ear. I continued my run but as I climbed to higher ground on what had been one of the colliery stacks, I could see the same children down below with a man, presumably the boy's father. When they saw me, a lot of pointing took place and the father appeared to grab his son's bike and set off in pursuit of me.

Unperturbed, I carried on running my planned route neither trying to hide or escape from the man. I must have completed two laps of the landfill before he was able to get anywhere near me. Each time I reached one of the high paths, I could see him down below pedalling frantically but failing to narrow the gap. On the climbs I was leaving him and he was making little impact on the descents or the flat. The bike was a child's and he looked like a pea on a drum trying to ride it.

When he eventually came within striking distance, he shouted something along the lines of, 'Hey you, I want a word'. I ignored him, and when he pulled alongside he said, 'Hey, I'm talking to you'. Deciding that attack was the best form of defence, I said, 'So you're his father, that explains the foul language.' I'd never seen the man before in my life. 'Stop, I want a word with you,' he shouted again. 'Don't waste my time again,' I said and once again began to put distance between the two of us. That was the last I saw of him.

It generally doesn't bother me being cheeked by kids from time to time, but there is no reason why runners should put up with this and occasionally I will retaliate. I was running along the road one evening and a boy and a girl were pushing bikes along the pavement on the opposite side of the road. They waited until I had nicely passed and then let fly with the abuse. I turned around and crossed the road running towards them. The girl mounted her bike and was away but the boy abandoned his and started to run. I focused on the boy deliberately keeping a short distance behind, without intending to catch him. My aim was to make sure he had a long walk back to retrieve his bike.

Another evening, I stopped to cross the road and a boy and a girl were having what seemed to be a play fight. 'Help me,' said the girl. 'I can't, I'm too tired,' I replied. 'Well fuck off then,' was the response. I couldn't believe it and just stared in amazement.

One evening I ran home from work passing close to the fringes of a shopping centre. Four or five youths saw me approaching and there was much nudging and sniggering. They deliberately timed and angled their walk so as to make me run in the road. There was no need for this and I was having none of it, so I dipped my shoulder and caught the end youth as I passed. Not surprisingly, there was loud abuse ringing in my ears as I ran on my way.

Another scourge to the runners' lifestyle is the 'White Van Man'. Not only does he inflict his appalling driving upon other motorists by changing lanes, cutting in front of cars and driving up bumpers, he is a constant pain to the runner often slowing down to shout insults and abuse. I got the full brunt one day when a white van pulled out of a side street and I ended up whacking the side of the van with the palm of my hand.

On another occasion, a driver wound his window down and shouted something along the lines of 'Silly Cunt'. He obviously hadn't realised I was with a group of runners who still had to come around the corner and unbeknown to him, there were temporary traffic lights ahead, and a tailback of traffic. This enabled us to catch up with the van and with three either side we vigorously rocked it backwards and forwards. Neither the 'White Van Man' or his mate seemed in a hurry to wind the window down when I rattled it with the ball of my fist.

Apparently, an indication of our country's economy at any particular time, can be gauged by the sale of white vans. If this is true then God help us. Not only do they go about their daily business in a shocking manner, but they have the audacity to display a sign in the rear window saying, 'No tools kept in van overnight'.

Boy racers are another minority group who prey upon runners. In their highly tuned Escorts or Fiestas with baseball caps turned back to front, they tear around neighbourhoods and along main roads blasting their horns and fingering anyone who takes their fancy.

A car painted in the Starsky and Hutch logo whistled past me one evening with horn blasting. All four baseball caps turned like synchronised swimmers to take the mickey.

They seemed to dish out the same treatment to other pedestrians further along the road, but obviously seeing me as a sitting target, they returned for more of the same. They came by a further five or six times, each time driving close to the kerb, with the baseball cappers leaning out as far as they dare. They gave me what for, putting me well and truly in my place and having a terrific time.

Towards the end of my run, I saw the unmistakable car parked in a driveway and thought all my birthdays had come at once. Do I put a brick through the windscreen or do I let down the tyres? Better still, I could ring the door bell and knock seven bells out of whoever answered the door. Alternatively, I could get seven bells knocked out of me. I decided upon none of these options, instead choosing to complete my run and reflecting upon another entertaining evening.

While out running on the canal towpath, a motorcyclist and pillion passenger decided it would be good fun to build up speed and pass as close as they could without actually hitting me. I had visions of spinning round like the proverbial policeman on point duty. They did this twice but on the third occasion I decided to slightly change the line of my running at the last minute leaving them with little room to pass. In order to miss me, they were forced to go into the long grass, with both falling off, and the bike coming to rest ten yards further on. If I'd moved to the other side of the path, they could well have gone down the embankment and into the canal. I didn't wait to see rider and passenger remount, but probably the only thing hurting was their pride.

My favourite experience happened one Friday teatime when I managed to leave work early and fit in a run. It was autumn and starting to get dark, so making the most of the daylight, I chose to run along the canal bank towards Leeds. I would return along the busy Hunslet Road, one of the main arterial routes out of the city.

A white Fiesta pulled up at traffic lights and caught my eye when the passenger, another baseball capper, hurled a load of abuse my way. The footpath was separated from the pavements by flowerbeds but there were several gaps through which I could see the traffic. As the car pulled away from the traffic lights, the passenger abused me and the same thing happened at each subsequent set.

Suddenly in the half light, I stumbled across just the thing I needed, as if it had been sent as a gift from above. It was an abandoned hubcap and crying out to be picked up so I duly obliged. With the flowerbeds now gone, the footpath ran alongside the road, and I knew the Fiesta would be the third car to come through the lights. I ran as close as I dare to the pavement's edge clutching the hubcap in my sweaty palm, and listened as the cars moved away from the lights.

Sure enough, I heard acceleration and one car passed and then another and as the torrent of abuse started I threw the hubcap Frisbee style. It passed through the open window hitting the passenger, and probably dropped into the foot well. My jaw dropped as I saw the car indicate to turn into the petrol station a hundred yards or so on the left, but still undeterred, I seized the upper hand.

When I passed the garage forecourt, the driver of the car was standing at the fuel island, but I couldn't see the passenger. I pointed a finger as I ran by as if to warn the driver and hoping to put the fear of god into him. He remained motionless and failed to respond.

A hundred yards or so further on, the road forks with the low road heading towards Pontefract, and Wakefield Road going up the hill to the right. I took the Pontefract Road, and when nothing happened for several minutes, I presumed the idiots must have taken the other road.

But they weren't letting me get away so lightly and as I entered a tunnel under the railway, the car came screaming past with the passenger hanging out of the window shouting, 'You Bastard'. I had premonitions of them stopping the car, getting out, dragging me into a field and beating me to a pulp. That however was the last I was to see of them, although I did managed to spot the registration number and memorise it, by repeating it over and over again to myself in that last mile. When I arrived home, the first thing I did was to write down the registration number. It was my intention to scour the streets and estates and find the car, inflicting as much damage upon it as possible. I still have the number written down and often wonder what happened to that hubcap.

These are just a selection of numerous incidents I have encountered with motorists, vehicles and the public at large. I could have gone on ignoring them but just occasionally, I believe we should stand up for our hobby and give these morons a dose of their own medicine.

CHAPTER 8

Another Brick in the Wall

NEW YORK had reinforced my appetite for further overseas running and the Berlin Marathon seemed to fit the bill perfectly. It was the most publicised marathon on Mainland Europe and organised with German military precision, the course was flat and a field of 12,000 seemed quite manageable.

I had my name down to go with a group from a local running club, but a couple of steep price increases after the provisional booking had been made put it beyond reach of those who had planned to make it a family trip. Consequently the venture was cancelled with a tentative promise to rekindle the idea for the following year.

Undeterred by the setback, I decided to make my own travel arrangements, not fully realising how difficult Berlin would be to reach overland. Opting to go by train, I must have been fully half an hour in the British Rail ticket office, while the attendant explored the various options and possibilities. As a queue started to build behind me, I started to become slightly irritable and edgy.

The race was run exclusively in West Berlin, isolated in East Germany and completely surrounded by the Berlin Wall. This was before the unification of the two German States, when the borders of Eastern Europe were opened and the much publicised wall was torn down. Only certain routes could be undertaken and security in the East would be particularly tight.

I left home on Wednesday tea time and wouldn't reach Berlin until a day later. My journey took me from Leeds to King's Cross, across London by underground to Charing Cross and on to Dover. The ferry would arrive at Ostend in time for the 07.00 train to Cologne. I was able to grab a couple of hours' sleep on an almost deserted ferry. On awakening, land wasn't in sight and I began to worry whether or not I would make the train. The rough crossing had delayed the arrival time but on docking, I breezed through passport control and customs.

Fortunately the railway station was situated alongside the ferry terminal and I was immediately able to locate my platform and train. The ticket inspector dutifully informed me I needed to move along the train as the section I was in went only as far as Brussels. This section was very basic and quickly filled with workers. Once underway, it made out across the flatlands towards Bruges and Ghent. At Brussels I grabbed my bags and made a dash along the platform and settled into an upgraded more comfortable carriage.

The terrain became hillier towards Liege but flatter again as we approached Aachen and Germany. Customs officers boarded the train and I received an often elusive stamp on my passport. The train reached Cologne in late morning where I would have three hours to kill before moving on to Berlin.

I used the time to visit the magnificent gothic cathedral of St Ursula, started in the 13th century but not completed until the 19th. I strolled alongside the mighty Rhine enthusing at the sheer volume of river traffic, plying its trade from Switzerland and Southern Germany to Holland and the North Sea. Lunch came in the shape of a large frankfurter sausage sticking out either side of a crispy bread roll.

The scenery was more spectacular on the next leg of the journey, travelling through steep wooded valleys to Wuppertal. Here an overhead railway on a gantry follows the river valley providing rapid transit for the community. The industrial town of Dortmund is twinned with Leeds, Bielefeld is a large textile town while Gutersloh houses the world's largest publishing firm. The train reached Hannover in fading light, pressed on to Brunswick and arrived in darkness at the East German border town of Helmstedt.

The train stopped and there appeared to be a good deal of movement both on the platform and alongside the track. Torches flashed as guards, some handling dogs, walked backwards and forwards with some boarding the train. Passports were checked but there was no friendly smile or stamp here. We eventually nudged forward through huge gates as if we were entering a siding. The train never gained any momentum for the rest of the journey to Berlin with guards constantly patrolling the corridor. It was late by the time I arrived at the hotel, so after a short stroll I turned in, ready to explore Berlin the next day.

I set out on Friday morning, complete with Berlitz travel guide, to look for the highlights and lowlights of the city. I knew little of Berlin apart from the Wall, the Brandenburg Gate and Checkpoint Charlie. I can remember seeing the film 'Cabaret' with Liza Minnelli and Michael Yorke which portrayed the seedier side of the Berlin night life between the two World Wars. I can also recollect the Iron Bridge where rival spies were exchanged in espionage films.

My first port of call would be to register for the race at a large exhibition hall on the outskirts of the city. This entailed using the modern U-Bahn underground train and the older S-Bahn railway. I quickly became used to the various colours and codes that made up the network.

At race registration, I was given a card that entitled me to free travel on all transport within Berlin over the Marathon weekend. The race exhibition was similar to its counterpart in New York with stands exhibiting footwear, health foods and anything remotely connected to fitness and running. I hadn't realised that a Breakfast Run was staged the day before the race so under the proviso 'in for a penny, in for a pound', I duly signed up. The Breakfast Run would start at Charlottenburg Palace and finish in the Olympic Stadium where the 1936 Games were held.

The next job was to locate Charlottenburg Palace so it was back on the U-Bhan once again. The palace is the only major one of its kind within the city to survive the wars. Several sections house museums but I was particularly impressed with the manicured gardens.

Returning to the city centre, I visited the large Ka De We department store and Kaiser Wilhelm Memorial Church. The broken stump of the steeple is a result of bombing in the Second World War. The burned out tower sits side by side with a modern octagonal church, but will remain unrestored as a symbol of the bombing that was inflicted upon Berlin by the Allies.

I afforded myself a coffee and a cream cake at the upmarket Kranzler Café on the city's liveliest street, Kurfurstendamm. From my vantage point on the terrace, I browsed through the race literature and handouts, and watched the people go about their daily business. The Europa Centre is a series of pubs, shops, restaurants and a casino within the heart of the city, but I suspect it may be a little dated now. I spent the rest of the afternoon generally sightseeing, walking the streets and looking in shops, not the ideal marathon preparation. I returned to the hotel thoroughly exhausted.

I turned out on Saturday morning for more of the same. The Breakfast Run was only four kilometres and I figured it would do me no harm. A lead vehicle kept runners below a particular pace to prevent a race developing. The Olympic Stadium is a massive bowl built below ground level and appears to be a low building on the approach. But when you enter the tunnel and run onto the track, a huge all seater stadium emerges with a capacity of 96,000. The allocation of breakfast was well organised with every runner receiving their own box containing rolls, banana, yoghurt and fruit juice. I sat high above the track taking in the atmosphere and pinching myself at the fact that I had just run into an Olympic Stadium.

Back at the hotel and showered by ten o'clock, I set out in search of the Wall. The Tiergarten is a large expanse of recreational land consisting of forests, meadows and lakes. Many Turkish families gather here for their

Saturday afternoon picnics and barbecues. To the South West corner of the Tiergarten are the Zoological Gardens and aquarium, to the north is the River Spree and to the east are the Reichstag Building and Brandenburg Gate.

The Reichstag Building, now the seat of the unified German parliament, went up in flames in 1933 and has only recently been restored by way of a spectacular glass dome. The Berlin Wall ran behind the Reichstag, in front of the Brandenburg Gate and alongside the Tiergarten to Potsdamer Platz. There was a viewing platform here where I was able to look over the Wall and across no man's-land to a similar wall on the East German side. Beyond were drab tenement buildings with the needle-like television tower in the distance.

The Wall was thirteen feet high with watch towers at strategic places. There were apparently searchlights, tank traps and a ditch sixteen feet deep. I could see a guard on patrol in the distance together with his Alsatian. I followed the Wall to Checkpoint Charlie, the main crossing point between East and West. In places the Wall had been sprayed with graffiti and daubed with messages which I didn't understand. There were posters at regular intervals announcing that a German exile now living in Canada, would return on a particular date, and at a certain time he would sit on the Wall. This wasn't necessary as later that year, the borders were opened and the Wall bulldozed down. When I revisited in 1993, there were still small sections of the Wall remaining, perhaps left as a grim reminder of the past and a symbol for future generations.

The Checkpoint Charlie Museum is a converted café apparently well used by journalists in years gone by. The museum documents the history of the Wall with photographs, drawings and exhibits, in particular the attempted and successful escapes.

The Wall had been built to stem the flow of refugees from East to West. The East was being drained of skilled people such as scientists, doctors and engineers. On August 13th 1961, barbed wire barricades were erected under the protection of Russian tanks. People still attempted to escape by swimming across the river or jumping from moving trains, but eventually the barricades were replaced by a more permanent concrete wall.

The most fascinating escape happened when a West German hid his East German wife inside his car seat. A model portrayed how she was huddled in a squat position for several hours in order to build a new life for herself in the west. Another escape occurred when the crew of a vessel sailing down the River Spree got their captain drunk and made him steer the boat amid a salvo of gun fire, through the border post and to freedom in the West.

Having walked a marathon, or at least it felt that way, I glanced at my watch to see the time was only one o'clock. There was still time for plenty of sightseeing. I retraced the Wall calling at the National Gallery, alongside the canal and on the edge of the Tiergarten. I enjoyed an hour here looking at the French impressionist paintings including Renoir along with those by German artists.

I treated myself to meatballs for lunch, browsed around a huge flea market before a steady afternoon and early night in anticipation of the big day ahead.

Uncertain as to how I would perform after hours of walking over the last two days, I ended up rushing to deposit my clothes and had to hurry to take up my place at the start. I was well back from the front but there was no sneaking in here as marshals ensured you lined up strictly according to your number. The setting was superb on the Avenue June 17th with the Brandenburg Gate as a backdrop and the Victory Column straight ahead. Lines of balloons flanked each side of the road with the woods of the Tiergarten adding a distinctly closed in feeling.

The start was slow, taking almost three minutes to cross the line but a straight mile enabled the field to spread out and the pace to pick up. We crossed the River Spree twice before reaching the Kufurstendamm where the crowd support was plentiful and boisterous. I was easily recognisable in my Union Flag singlet, and two soldiers stationed in Berlin picked me out and I was to run and chat with them for several miles.

The course was mainly flat, taking in seven different boroughs, various historical sites and much parkland and greenery, with a couple of sections alongside the Wall. I found the thirty-one York railway bridges in the Schoneberg district to be fascinating and I tried to count them as we passed through the sidings. The way I felt however, I didn't feel much up to sightseeing.

The final stretch was along Kufurstendamm for as far as the eye could see. The finishing gantry was in the distance at the Kaiser Wilhelm church but the harsh reality was that there was still half a mile to go. As encouraging as the crowd was, I didn't seem to be getting any closer, but I carried on running even though at times a walk appeared to be a better option.

The organisation of the race was excellent with the exception of the baggage reclaim which was a bit of a shambles. I changed into warm clothing and bought an ice cream which always goes down a treat after a race. In the evening I had arranged to meet some Irish runners, at an Irish bar of all places, in the Europa Centre. With a long journey home the next day, I said my goodbyes and left them in full flow.

The journey in daytime shed a different light upon Eastern Germany and the contrast to their western neighbours. Small houses like huts seemed to be commonplace next to allotments and where the train slowed for level crossings, queues of Trabants could be seen waiting. The border post comprised barbed wire and watch towers which stretched across the fields and out of sight.

I had time to kill in Cologne and again in Ostend, when the midnight ferry didn't materialise leaving me waiting until 4.00a.m. Had it all been worth it? I asked myself. At Dover, I was stopped and searched by a customs official who seemed to lighten up when I told him the purpose of my journey had been to run the Berlin Marathon.

Some weeks later, a glossy brochure arrived in the post with race photographs and a complete set of results. This confirmed my finishing position to be 8,543rd, well past the halfway mark. Not only could the Germans organise a race, but they could obviously prepare well and run a good marathon. My finishing time would have seen me much higher up the field in a similar race at home.

In 1993, I returned to Berlin to compete in the 25 Kilometre race which both started and finished in the Olympic Stadium. Although not as grand an affair as the marathon, the race was still enduring and particularly enjoyable. Run on a sweltering hot day, cut-off times were implemented at certain places around the course. Runners who didn't meet these times were asked to retire from the race.

I travelled with a group of Ackworth runners on the ferry from Harwich to Hamburg and then on the train to Berlin. Like most trips of this nature, I didn't have the ideal preparation as most of the runners like to take a drink.

I ran in a threesome for most of the race with John and Terry. We ran on edges of roads making the most of the shade provided by buildings and trees. I dropped off the pace when an ambulance pulled out across the course impeding my progress. On the way back to the hotel we stopped off at The Hard Rock Café and stayed put for several hours.

With most of the Wall now demolished, Berlin had taken on a slightly different ambience. We were able to walk through Brandenburg Gate and see parts of the East that resembled a large building site. I noticed more beggars and vagrants this time and some members of the group remarked about feeling uncomfortable on the streets, at times. Nevertheless, I would love to return one day, but it would have to be for the half marathon in April. With all the walking and sightseeing I tend to cram in, I wouldn't do justice to the full distance.

Unable to secure a London spot in 1998, my childhood fascination for boats, bridges and waterways tempted me to Hamburg for the spring marathon.

I knew little about the race but made an excellent choice and wasn't to be disappointed. I flew with Lufthansa from Manchester with the only significant part of the flight being the fact there were only six passengers aboard.

Hamburg is Germany's second city and premier port, the twelfth largest in the world, and sits hundred kilometres inland on the banks of the Elbe. The inner city is a pleasant mixture of parks, canals and squares with old architecture blending comfortably alongside new. The two magnificent Alster Lakes provide a vast area for recreation within the heart of the city. You must 'Think Bike' as Hamburg is a keen cycling city with marked paths along sidewalks and through parks. Crossing the road can be frustrating here, as unlike home, waiting for the green light is strictly adhered to.

As a keen football follower, I like to take in a match on holiday and I found out St Pauli, Hamburg's second team were playing Wolfsburg on Friday evening. The crowd was close to the pitch in the compact stadium, providing something of an intimidating atmosphere. The only significant fact I gleaned from the game which St Pauli won 2-1, was that the Wolfsburg manager was none other than Wolfgang Wolfe.

The happy home supporters streamed out onto the Reeperbahn which cuts through the city's red light district. The main entertainment centre is here with restaurants, clubs and bars alongside sex shows and other establishments of ill-repute. Most bars were small and insignificant, but just as I was beginning to think there was nothing here to rival the Bavarian beer halls, I stumbled across it like an oasis in a desert. The Thomas Read Irish Pub was a spacious hostelry with a welcoming atmosphere, so much so that I visited again the following evening.

The ladies in the windows along Herbertstrasse lure prospective punters, while young girls in brightly coloured windjammers tout for trade around the street corners. I was chatted up more in two hours than in a lifetime around Wakefield. My love of boats and bridges was put on the backburner for a while.

Race day was warm with little breeze. Changing facilities and kit storage took place at a large exhibition centre while the 11,300 competitors were accommodated across three starts. Race timing was with the increasingly popular championship chip secured to the lace on one of the running shoes. This sends out a signal which is picked up as runners cross a carpet at the start, again at half way and at the finish. The field was made up of mainly Germans with a sprinkling of Danes and Swedes. I considered the course to be excellent with the spectator support the best I have come across.

The early stages took runners through the Reeperbahn, unrecognisable from night-time and through pleasant suburbs before swinging onto the waterfront at St Pauli fish market. Here the crowds lined the pavement two and three deep. Some were blowing whistles, some shaking football rattles, while others banged any sort of receptacle that made a noise. At intervals there were live bands while music blasted out through loud speakers regularly along the route.

Passing the 'Rickmer Rickmers' tall ship, now a maritime museum, the course followed the waterfront towards Warehouse City, before an underpass brought us towards the city centre for a complete circuit of the Inner Alster Lake. Crossing one of two bridges that divide the lakes, we then ran along the shore of the outer Alster passing large detached houses and luxury apartments.

The shrill sound of championship chips could be heard as hundreds of feet crossed the matting at halfway, but the way I felt after a hectic day previously and a couple of beers in the evening, a calendar would have been a better way of timing, rather than a stopwatch.

The final five kilometres brought us back along the other side of the Outer Alster, where spectators came off the pavements leaving only a narrow corridor for runners to squeeze through. They waved banners and flags, were generous in their applause and vociferous in their encouragement. I followed a young man in a Brazilian football shirt, with 'Romario' across the shoulders. He milked the applause of the crowd and disappeared into the distance as effortlessly as he had passed me. There is a frustrated footballer inside most runners waiting to escape.

The finish below the TV tower was unspectacular but welcome, although the organisation beyond the finishing funnels left much to be desired. The baggage, changing and exhibition areas had become a free-for-all and it was unclear where to hand in your championship chip or find a drink. Fortunately there was help on hand to remove the chip from my shoe lace. Bending down to unfasten laces is not recommended and not the easiest thing to do after running twenty-six miles. It took me a full hour to return to the hotel, which I had passed in the final kilometre of the race.

For the best part I found Germans to be friendly, accommodating and helpful with the exception of one man who addressed me in a café. I told him that I didn't understand German and that I spoke English. The man retorted in a loud voice to anyone who would listen, 'He says he speaks English' making a grunting sound before repeating himself again. From the corner of my eye, I could detect him staring at me for some time.

Hamburg seemed a reasonably safe place apart from the Central Station forecourt where punks and other hard-looking individuals gathered complete with mean looking dogs as accessories. I felt inadequate when a beggar asking me for money spoke in perfect English. While threatening each new term to attend language classes, I never seem to make the time or a concerted effort.

The Germans are keen drinkers as I discovered when I stumbled across a Monday afternoon session in full flow in a station buffet bar. Food comprises meat dishes, burgers and sausages and with a strong pound at that time against the mark, meals were excellent value. All around the city, stalls sold frankfurters in crisp bread and confectioners selling cakes and pastries did a roaring trade. I spent a pleasant half hour with a coffee and cake in the Rathausmarket watching the world go by.

Hamburg is ideal for walking with large areas of parkland and lakes probably best explored after the race. A harbour trip is recommended from one of the boats operating from Landungsbrucken. The port of Hamburg was rebuilt as large parts were destroyed in the bombings of 1943. The area covers 75 square kilometres, 12,000 seagoing ships leave annually and 72 million tons of cargo are handled. Even though the port is crucial to the Hamburg economy, the main revenues are derived from the service and manufacturing industries. This is the media centre of Germany with fifteen top selling magazines being published here.

I took an Alster boat trip from Junfernstieg which lasted two hours taking in lakes, canals and parts of the harbour. There are various landing stages around the lake where it is possible to leave or join the ferry. Another boat trip is available from Baumwall along the narrow canals of 'Warehouse City' the largest warehouse complex in the world.

The Monday after the race, I brought life back to aching limbs by walking the nine kilometres along the riverside path to Blankenese, a coveted residential quarter that clings to a hill above the Elbe. I also visited Hanseatic city Lubeck, famous for the Holsten Gate and only half an hour away by train.

The TV tower provides panoramic views across Hamburg but is best visited on a clear day. The Rathaus (Town Hall) built in Neo-Renaissance style is a must while there are several art museums close to Central Station. Other museums based on the seafaring tradition can be found along the waterfront. Shopping in Hamburg is good with many stores inside covered arcades and malls.

I returned to Germany later in 1998 to take part in the Ford Cologne Marathon. This was only the second running of the event and the debut race had attracted record entries for a first time event, in an already crowded German Autumn calendar.

Cologne is an excellent city to visit for a weekend break, be it business or pleasure. There is plenty to do from visiting churches and museums to cruising along the Rhine. I stumbled across the Chocolate Museum on the waterfront which plotted the manufacture of chocolate, from the humble growing of the cocoa bean to the finished article. There was a model of a tropical rain forest and small operated production lines.

I stayed in a hotel off Neumarket, an excellent area for bars, restaurants and night clubs. The other lively area I found was between the cathedral and the Rhine where taverns and beer halls nestled in narrow cobbled streets.

I crossed the pedestrian walkway alongside the Hohenzollem railway bridge to register for the race at the arena. The return crossing afforded great views across the Rhine of the cathedral's twin spires and surrounding skyline.

The race preparation wasn't as good as it might have been. I called in The Corkonian Irish pub on Saturday evening to try catch the football results. Three pints of Guinness later and watching a boring 0-0 draw between England and Bulgaria, I left and called for a pleasant meal behind the cathedral, before returning to the hotel.

Throughout the night I was disturbed by people talking loudly and arguing. When I opened the bedroom door I caught a glimpse of furniture being removed. What on earth was going on?

Race day was wet and horrible. I caught the underground train which later surfaced becoming a tram, crossing one of the Rhine bridges to the race start on the east bank. There was nowhere to change or shelter and runners huddled inside the concourse of a suburban railway station. I made my final preparations, vaselined up and secured my number while on the station platform and handed in my baggage to an official at the appropriately marked truck. The truck would transport my baggage to somewhere near the cathedral for collection after the race.

Joining my starting position, I waited in the drizzle as 2,000 or so roller skaters set off at the start of their race. Just as in the foot race, those at the front were lean, mean and raring to go while in contrast, those to the rear would have been pleased just to make it around the course.

The marathon route showed the city at its best despite the appalling conditions. Crossing the Rhine in the opening stages, the course then follows the great river passing churches along the banks, the Trade Fair grounds and some beautiful urban parks. The terrain was pretty flat, and while I didn't consider the spectator support to be as good as Hamburg, the crowds were nevertheless dense in places.

The run in to the finish was along one of the straight pedestrian streets leading to the Dom Platz in front of the Cathedral. Bill Bryson writes in *Neither Here Nor There* that it is a shame for such a magnificent building to be hemmed in alongside souvenir shops and next to the station. I tend to agree that a more spacious setting would befit this magnificent building.

Not running particularly well at the time, I tired in the later stages of the race, feeling wet and miserable. Although I started brightly enough, I can't be too dispirited with my 3 hours 48 minutes. I have run much faster than this but am sure to do a lot worse in future.

On Monday I made a sentimental journey to Koblenz from where I boarded the train along the Rhine Gorge to Bingen. This rugged section of the valley sees the river twist and turn through a gorge. Vines grow on the steep slopes and fairytale castles perch on bluffs and escarpments. The railway line runs like a thread alongside the river, passing the occasional village or running through a tunnel.

One feature of the gorge is the imposing Lorelei Rock where shipping has to negotiate a deep channel, only a third the width of the river. Here a mermaid is said to have lured sailors to their death with a seductive song. Further upstream is the 'Mouse Tower' where legend has it that Bishop Hatto was eaten alive by mice, for his misdemeanours to the people.

I caught the slow train from Bingen to Koblenz alighting at both Oberwesel and Boppard where I spent some time. I visited Boppard for a family holiday when I was in my early teens, but we returned home after only a couple of days when news reached us of my grandmother's death. I more or less located where we had stayed but thirty years on I couldn't be sure.

The day was a touch nostalgic as I have always wanted to return. The train journey through the Rhine Gorge must be among the most beautiful in the world, certainly one of the most enjoyable I have ever made.

CHAPTER 9

Double Dutch

THE FIRST TIME I visited Amsterdam, I was on a long weekend with a local football team back in the late seventies. We took the overnight ferry from Hull to Rotterdam and some of our party became extremely drunk, remaining that way for much of the duration. We stayed in a very basic bed and breakfast on the fringes of the red-light district, with six of us sharing a room high up in the gable of a building.

The rain was torrential throughout the stay, so most of our activity revolved around bars and brown cafés. We walked the canals and saw the ladies in the goldfish bowl windows, some of whom would rap upon the glass or give the come on if trade was slow. As the first evening progressed, we split into smaller groups. When we met up with the main party later on, a couple of lads said they had spent money, and it had been well worth it.

The next day, it appeared more people within our group had forked out money for pleasure, and as we sat drinking, one lad appeared not to be able to contain himself any longer. 'It's no good, I'm going to have to go,' he said, getting out of his chair and moving towards the door. Rather than approach any of the ladies in the windows, he probably walked around the block two or three times before returning to the bar to tell us how good it had been. Similar instances occurred throughout the weekend until eventually I became one of a small minority. We were tormented, ridiculed and labelled spineless when in actual fact, I don't believe anybody bought any favours from the women. It was all bravado.

The next time I visited was in 1989 for The Hague Ten Mile Race, with a party from Ackworth Road Runners. We were based in Scheveningen, a seaside resort several miles from The Hague, and pretty deserted on a cold November weekend. There was everything you would expect at a seaside resort with beach, sand dunes and pier. There was a casino, a shopping mall with bowling alley, restaurants and pubs.

We visited Amsterdam on the Saturday evening before the race for a guided moonlit boat tour along the canals. This was apparently the last weekend in the year they were operating which came as no surprise. After the cruise we headed off towards the much publicised red-light district.

A man who was probably a tout for one of the clubs, seconded some of our party to watch a show. Four of us hesitated undecided whether to follow him or not. ' If you aren't coming, then piss off' he said. After I picked him up by the lapels and dropped him like a sack of spuds to the ground (if only!!), he led his new conscripts into one of the narrow streets, with the four of us following at a distance. All of a sudden, the group, led by the tout, walked back towards us, and disappeared into a another side street. They returned again this time walking up an alleyway, and repeated the scenario further down the street. It was like an excerpt from the 'Keystone Cops'. The four of us who remained visited several brown cafés, had an enjoyable evening, and were reluctant to return to the coach.

Despite the horrible weather, the conditions booked up for race time on Sunday afternoon. The race started and finished on the promenade at Scheveningen, with an out and back course passing the picturesque harbour. For long sections we were treading water underfoot. I ran a satisfactory race recording 73 minutes, but most of the plaudits went to an elite group from Essex who were with Sports Travel. The evening ended with an enjoyable meal and a few drinks and we met the grand old lady of Marathon running, Madge Sharples.

The Hague Ten is now based around the city and I gather, finishes in an indoor arena. The other big race in the area is the City-Pier-City Race, from the city to Scheveningen and back. To date I haven't had the opportunity to run in this springtime event.

With New York and Berlin under my belt, Rotterdam came highly recommended as one of the top five marathons in the world with a superflat, superfast course. I enjoyed exploring the city of Rotterdam, particularly the waterfront and renovated dockland area.

The race start at the Coolsingel was slow, taking five minutes to cross the start and fifty minutes for the first ten kilometres. The course comprised a short out and back before crossing the Wilmsbrug over the River Maas. Most of the course was uninteresting through industrial areas and flatlands.

While the race organisation was good, I didn't take enough out of the race to make me want to return. I made a friend for life in Graham Hall of New Marske Harriers, the two of us running most of the way together. A railway strike put a dampener on the weekend, when a taxi from Rotterdam to Schipol Airport on the outskirts of Amsterdam proved costly.

In 1995, I returned to Amsterdam with Kevin and John to run the marathon. The long coach journey from Leeds started at midnight on Thursday and we wouldn't reach Amsterdam until Friday lunchtime. There were numerous pick-up points on the way to Dover with the trip becoming slightly long and tedious. The trip had been organised by local club Rothwell Harriers who had kindly invited us as guests.

On this trip I began to appreciate the cultural side of Amsterdam, the architecture, the picturesque canals and museums. The Rijksmuseum has splendid examples of the 17th century 'Golden Age' of Dutch paintings. Rembrandt is still regarded as the outstanding painter of that era and 'Night Watch', cordoned off from other works, takes pride of place. I could have stood and admired what I saw all day, but the museum had to close. The shades, the colours and the alignment of characters on such a huge work of art was truly remarkable.

We ate and drank wisely but well on the evening before the race, probably eating a little too well. I somehow got through a giant mixed grill at a Uruguayan Steak House.

The race started at an exhibition centre on the outskirts of the city, comprising two laps, taking in many of the city's interesting features. The course included the Damrak, Rokin, parts of the harbour and many of the canals. Kevin and I were going the full distance while John had entered the half marathon alternative.

I ran well for fifteen miles but never felt comfortable, believing that I needed to pay a call. I could feel last night's mixed grill laying heavily on my stomach, and when I saw a portaloo around the twenty-mile mark, the offer was far too good to turn down. I was never able to get going after this with the small inclines to the many bridges almost killing me. The rain started to fall like stair rods and we were running through standing water which caused several blisters to once again surface on the balls of my feet. I managed to scrape inside four hours but the experience hadn't been an enjoyable one.

It was on this trip that we were to meet the Luton foursome of Bob, Tom, Patrick and Flash who like us, enjoyed mixing running with pleasure. We have since met up with them at many long distance events around the country and have remained good friends. Patrick and Flash have set their stall out recently and turned in some excellent performances.

During the trip to Amsterdam, I heard of another race, which was apparently the best the city had to offer by some distance. Similar to our own Great North Run, the Dam to Dam catered for runners of all abilities. The course was point to point from Amsterdam to Zaandam, north of the city.

The race received no publicity back home so I had a fair bit of ringing around in order to find the date and the entry information. When the application form arrived, an accompanying letter stated that if I didn't understand anything in Dutch, I would be welcome to call a number. To me it seemed 'Double Dutch' but my Mum suggested we visit Mrs Roberts, a Dutch lady who married and settled in England after the war. Mrs Roberts started to translate the document but after breaking off for tea and cakes, we never got around to the small print.

I travelled from Leeds and Bradford airport one Friday morning in late September. I caught the express train from Schipol into the city, and stayed at the Victoria Hotel opposite Amsterdam's Central Station. This would be handy for the race start and ideal for being dropped off on the return from Zaandam.

After unpacking, I left the hotel for a walk along Damrak, the city's main thoroughfare. I was immediately approached by a young white man who asked if I was from England, whereabouts in England, how long was I staying and so on. He then offered to sell me drugs which I turned down. 'You must buy them' he said, to which I once again turned him down and started to walk purposefully away. Along with his two minders, one Black Caribbean and one European, they started to follow me. To test out if they were actually following me or just walking in my direction, I stopped. They stopped, I started, they started, I crossed the road, they followed, I crossed back and so did they.

I was beginning to enjoy this and started to take the mickey. I turned back the way I had come and they followed, turned again and they came with me. I started to get cocky zigzagging and doing serpentines, and eventually they called a halt to the game and disappeared. On reflection I realised how stupid I had been. I tend to have no fear if I go alone to these places, but I could have easily been bundled into an alleyway and given the full treatment.

On this trip I was able to spend more time familiarising myself with the city layout. The canals stretch out from the Central Station like a fan or a spider's web. I walked some of the canals observing the different types of architecture, particularly the gables, most of which were fitted with a hoist or pulley. I ventured into the narrow streets and canals of the distinctive Jordaan district to the west of Dam Square.

Here, students, media folk and hippies live side by side with studios, craft shops and the renowned Brown Cafés. It made a pleasant change, far removed from the hustle and bustle of Damrak, and not being followed.

On Saturday, I took myself to see the real Holland catching the bus from outside the central station to Volendam, a former fishing village on the

Ijsellmeer. The town has perhaps lost some of its charm with the amount of souvenir shops along the waterfront, but some ladies still wear clogs and traditional costume.

I travelled to Hoorn, another former seafaring town. Abel Tasman was born here, as was Willem Schouten who discovered Cape Horn and named it after his home town. Returning to Amsterdam by train, I didn't see the need for an early night with an afternoon race start. I had a bite to eat off Museumplein and called at a couple of brown cafés before calling it a night.

After breakfast on Sunday morning, I walked several of the canals off Damrak towards the red-light district, and what I saw was very much a case of the morning after the night before. I was approached once again by a dope pusher, but probably more out of hope than expectation. The narrow streets were strewn with litter and discarded bottles, while scantily clad women sat on doorsteps, some with head in hands, no doubt reflecting on last night's events. The area was a real eye-opener.

The race start was at midday with the elite runners going first and the rest of us staggered in blocks, going at fifteen minute intervals. The slower runners were in the earlier blocks and I started at 2.00p.m. The first mile was through The IJ tunnel under the harbour with a steep pull up to the far bank.

The rest of the course was flat with the exception of inclines leading to some of the traditional Dutch bridges. For a reputed field of 20,000, the route surprisingly came away from the main roads and took to the parks, canal banks, bridges and typical Dutch villages. Carnivals and street parties were organised in some villages with bands and dancers providing entertainment. Everyone appeared to come out and watch the race as banners, tickertape and archways of balloons straddled the narrow streets.

The first snag I encountered was that I soon caught up with lots of back markers from the previous start and walkers from even earlier starts. These people walked two and three abreast and proved difficult to pass on the narrow roads. By the time I reached Zaandam, the roads were solid. Checkout was hectic along with baggage recovery and the return of championship chips. The return transport to Amsterdam ran remarkably smoothly and the coach dropped me off within 200 yards of the hotel.

Despite the problems, I ran remarkably well recording seventy-one minutes, and thoroughly enjoyed the race. I wouldn't hesitate to do it again should the opportunity arise and would recommend it to any standard of runner. I received a race photograph within several weeks but was hardly visible amongst the masses of runners approaching the finish. I never received the advertised results booklet.

A Monday evening flight meant I had almost a full day to spend sightseeing. I visited the Historical Museum in Kalverstraat which depicts Amsterdam through the ages, with paintings, furniture and artefacts. The centre piece is Athoniszoon's Bird's Eye View painting which was the first known map of Amsterdam. I moved on to Rembrandt House Museum where many of the works were portraits of people such as beggars and organ grinders.

Following a beer, a coffee and another beer in Leidesplein, I returned once again to the Rijksmuseum and stared simply in bewilderment at 'The Night Watch'.

CHAPTER 10

Tears for Souvenirs

ON THAT MAY MORNING back in 1983, a small medallion bearing the Five Towns crest was thrust into my sweaty palm. I was proud as a peacock and over the next few weeks, I carried it around with me so I could show anyone who was remotely interested. Within a few months, I had accumulated more hardware than I had done in fifteen years of playing football. Each race awarded a medallion or certificate to every finisher as a memento and record of completing their particular race.

I pinned my early medallions to a board and displayed them with pride, but as the months and years rolled by, the board filled up, so I just pushed others into drawers and eventually into a shoe box. Even in the early days of the running boom, I could recollect runners choosing a race that awarded a medal rather than a certificate. The races that advertised the classy Birmingham Mint Medal were on to a winner.

At events such as the London Marathon, a large medal on an attractive ribbon would be up for grabs, and specialist firms displayed medal cases at the exhibition, holding anything up to thirty-two medals. Individual cases were also available to house medal, race photograph and certificate.

Down the years, more and more races started to award tee shirts rather than medals. I began to accumulate drawers full of them, and gave them away to charities, friends, relations and anybody who wanted one. The tee shirts would vary in standard with the likes of the Great North Run being of good quality and nice design, while many tended to be substandard. The Barnsley Races tended to lead the way, awarding a nice sweat shirt to all finishers in their races.

I would see youths walking around in single colour Nike, Adidas or Global Hyperbowl tee shirts at £15 a throw while I had drawers full with far better designs for every day of the week. Races that advertised a long sleeved tee shirt tended to attract a good entry as these would double for training shirts in the winter months.

A nice design tee shirt or one from an overseas race tended to be suitable for posing. One of our members is reputed to have packed a suit case full of tee shirts for his summer holidays. Each time he went out he would wear a different one, and on a particular evening he is said to have worn several layers. When he went to the toilet he peeled off the top one, displaying a fresh one underneath. He gave the top to his wife for safe keeping. By the end of the evening her handbag was bulging.

But runners became greedy with some people saying 'Giz another wun luv' and young girls who usually handed them out would duly oblige. Supplies quickly ran out culminating in back of the packers not receiving a tee shirt and the under fire race organisers hurriedly arranging a reprint. On top of all this, they would have to pack and post them all out.

Races needed to diversify to attract runners and did so. The East Yorkshire races awarded Fangfoss Pottery, the Heart of England races awarded horse brasses, while some of the Lakeland races awarded souvenirs made from local slate. Some races awarded plates, others mugs, while one of the best souvenirs I ever received was a Joe Scarborough print. This was awarded to all finishers in the Sheffield full and half marathons, and painted by a distinguished local artist. There was bags of detail, lots of colour and larger than life buildings, factories and vehicles. A friend had his framed and on display in the bathroom. He tells me he can spot something different each time he sits down.

One of the outstanding souvenirs over the years has been the traditional panel of Nottingham lace awarded to finishers in both full and half marathons. Each year is a different design usually based upon the Robin Hood theme. I must have ten of them all neatly packed away in a cupboard, but I keep threatening to put them on display.

Some runners display every piece of memorabilia in their homes which have been turned into shrines to running; mugs on the mantelpiece, plaques in the porch and plates on the pelmet. One of the best innovations I have seen is a wooden glass topped coffee table with a board underneath. Dozens of medallions had been stuck onto the board forming a mosaic pattern or similar.

The races I like provide hot food instead of, or sometimes as well as, a souvenir. Some events in the Yorkshire Dales tend to do this, while the excellent Marsh House Seven near Huddersfield provided excellent pie and peas on a winter's morning. A generous barbecue was on offer at the end of the Grantham Canal Run which was usually well earned after 33 miles. Some of the Christmas races provided festive fayre particularly in the prize list. The Percy Pud at Sheffield awards a Christmas pudding to each finisher of the popular race around the Dam Flask Reservoir.

The races that awarded nothing were likely to run into trouble. I can recall a runner taking exception with an official at a ten kilometre race on the moors near Huddersfield. 'You're telling me that all I get for running this is a cup of water?' he said. The organisers must have taken heed however as the following year they awarded tee shirts to the first hundred finishers. The other two hundred or so competitors would have been none too impressed.

In another race with the same concept, I finished 100th or was at least the last person to receive a tee shirt. With drawers and boxes at home full of the things and some not even out of their packets, I had enough tee shirts to last me a lifetime. The least I could do was offer it to the runner behind, but for some reason, I didn't.

Even though the Kilburn Seven Race in North Yorkshire offered generous prizes to the winners of each category, they didn't offer a souvenir to each runner, during the first staging of their event. I heard a runner ask an official if he got anything for finishing. One of the local wags replied, 'Send him over here and I'll give him something'. Since then the organisers have somewhat redressed the balance by awarding a horse brass.

Among the best mementos I have received are those awarded for the Leeds Country Way Relay, an event run in pairs over six stages. Different items of pottery have been awarded each year such as salt and pepper pots, sugar bowl and cream jug. If you miss the race one year, you are able to purchase the memento to maintain the full collection. One year the memento was very impressive, but nobody knew what it was supposed to be. It turned out to be a candle holder with holes in the side to create a flickering effect.

Races occasionally get screwed by runners. There is the old scenario of runners not entering the race but fastening four safety pins to their vest where the number would have been placed. They would tell officials at the finish that the wind had blown their number off even on the calmest of days. More often than not, the overworked officials wouldn't want any aggravation and the runners would get away with it. One runner I know genuinely turned up late for a race and didn't have time to sign on. He ran a good race but did the 'Four Safety Pin Trick' telling officials at the finish that his number had blown off. He must have made a mental note of my number and quoted a similar number to the official. On telling the story of what he had done while we were changing back at the cars, a man parked next to us started to take a particular interest. 'That's my number,' he said, holding it up for all to see. 'Nothing to do with me,' I replied. 'Sorry about that mate,' said my colleague before making a hasty departure.

Some races started to award goody bags with medal, tee shirt, certificate, chocolate bar and sports drink complete with a wad of leaflets and flyers. The high profile overseas races tended to award the best goody bags and those in the States were particularly generous in their supply of groceries. The Châteaux du Médoc Marathon in France was the best value for money race I have entered. I can recollect being awarded a tee shirt, medal, block of cheese, cheese board, couple of bottles of wine and a glossy results booklet. A plentiful supply of sandwiches and cakes were also available at the end of the race.

Apart from souvenirs given away, the merchandise sold is big business. Most big city races and some of the smaller ones send miniature photographs, from which you can order enlargements. Other firms rely upon trust and send the full size photographs on a sale and return basis. One of my colleagues reckons he has never returned any of these photos, but has had numerous reminders to do so. He has been warned that no further photos will be sent but they still keep arriving.

Race videos can often be ordered but I have only ever bought one which was the Humber Bridge Marathon back in 1992. I have seen others but with one or two notable exceptions have been mostly overrated. I saw a video of 'The Tough Guy' race at Wolverhampton which just ran and ran. If anything it stiffened my resolve never to enter this torturous race.

A friend of mine, Terry, ordered a London Marathon video where they had promised to capture him at the finish and at several places on route. When the video arrived, there was little to be seen of Terry, but plenty of Mick and myself who ran most of the race together. Terry said that one of us could keep the video.

The best race video I came across was one produced by Ray and members of the Goole Viking Striders club to commemorate their river bank race. The main picture followed the bulk of the field at particular points on the course, while the race leaders were superimposed into a small bubble. All of this was against the background music of Gladys Knight.

I recently sent off for a model limited edition trolley bus, complete with Robin Hood Marathon logo along with my name, finishing time and position. This was simply a one-off purchase with the proceeds going to charity. On my travels, I always tend to return with a model house, church, windmill or small figure as a reminder of where I have been, and this would sit alongside them in the cabinet.

The exhibitions at the large races sell a full range of souvenirs from tea towels to table mats and beakers to bobble hats, but unless I really require any of these, I tend to steer clear.

So what do I do with all the souvenirs and memorabilia I have accumulated over the years? Maybe at some point I should have an exhibition and donate the money to charity. If I'm lucky, maybe some of the rare medals may be worth a bob or two in years to come but I won't hold my breath. For now, I'll be content just to know my time and placing in events until my drawers of tee shirts start to subside.

The Cleveland Major race was held in the late eighties and early nineties on a course from Stockton to Middlesbrough. I only ran here once but the tee shirt presented has always held pride of place. Even after using it for training and throwing it away, I cut out the verse which was taken from a psalm, and reads as follows.

> 'They shall wait upon the Lord,
> shall mount up with wings like eagles,
> they shall run and not be weary.'
>
> Isaiah 40:31.

CHAPTER 11

Prince of Scandinavia

IN BERLIN, I was handed a form for a race that I couldn't stop thinking about and no matter how I tried, it wouldn't seem to go away. The form was printed in German so I didn't understand the small print, but the photographs captured my imagination. Each time I tidied the drawer, the form would stand out almost crying out to be filled in.

The race was the Stockholm Marathon, but with the high cost of living over there, I couldn't possibly afford to go to Sweden on my meagre salary. A representative from a large international organisation came to my rescue by putting me in touch with his Scandinavian counterpart who fixed me up with some sponsorship and accommodation. All I had to do was fix my flight and spending money. I eventually filled in the application form with the help of a German–English dictionary and I must have done alright as I soon received confirmation and race details.

June soon came around and my flight from Manchester touched down in Copenhagen, on route to the Swedish capital. The poor girl sitting next to me was terrified at both take-offs and landings and my assurances appeared to have little effect. She was to demonstrate computer systems at Mora, up country from Stockholm and would have to go through the take-off and landing procedure all over again.

The drive from the airport to the city filled me with anticipation of what lay ahead and I had to keep pinching myself that I was here. The airport shuttle bus passed blue lakes, green fields and pine forests, all enhanced by a beautiful summer day.

Acknowledged as one of the beautiful cities, Stockholm is known as the city that floats. Situated at the point where Lake Malaren meets the Baltic Sea, the city sits upon fourteen islands linked by forty bridges. Greater Stockholm houses 1.4 million people.

My hotel was situated on the large island of Södermalm, and from my bedroom, I looked out over the road and railway bridges across the water to the old town, Gamla Stan.

I registered on Thursday afternoon for the race, travelling by bus to the exhibition centre at Wasa Harbour. I collected race details, reduced tickets for travel in and around Stockholm, tee shirts and other freebies, and wrote postcards home over a cup of coffee. I visited the Wasa Museum, apparently Stockholm's number one attraction. The main exhibit is a seventeenth century ship which had capsized in the harbour and was only salvaged in 1956. An exhibition of pottery, coins and glassware are among 24,000 items recovered from the ship. I caught the ferry back to Slussen saving some time, but I lost it all again watching the various boats and craft of all shapes and sizes, passing through the giant lock gates.

In the evening I discovered the Old Town situated on the smallest of four main islands. I wandered the labyrinth of narrow cobbled streets and alleyways, fascinated by the fairytale shops and taverns. I walked the same area in the daytime, visiting the Royal Palace and Parliament Buildings to the north of the island. The Riddarhuset or House of Nobility, considered to be Stockholm's most beautiful building, lies on the west shore.

On Friday morning I was given an informative tour of Spendrup Brewery and my hosts provided a generous buffet. This reminded me of the time a couple of Swedish businessmen visited the factory where I work. We laid down the red carpet for them with no expense spared. A lavish buffet was set up and a tour of the factory arranged. All the machinery was in pristine condition and everyone was scrubbed up and told to be on their toes. After all the expectation, two scruffs got out of a taxi in denim, one sporting a beard like a down-at-heel version of Benny from Abba. They could only stay briefly, had to catch a flight, and that was that.

Talking of Abba, I caught the underground train to The Hard Rock Café where some of their memorabilia was exhibited. Then it was back on the train to the ivy-covered Olympic Stadium to familiarise myself with where I needed to go the next day for the race start.

More sightseeing entailed the Royal Chapel and Hall of State within the Royal Palace. The Royal Jewels are displayed in the treasury, while tapestries, paintings and furniture are displayed in the Royal Apartments. the Palace Museum, the Museum of Antiquities and the Armouries are all situated in the palace complex. I would imagine it would take several days for a serious museum buff to do these beautiful buildings justice.

The long light evening provided me with a great sense of well-being and I strolled the streets, the waterfront and the jetties before calling it a day. I gazed out of my window at the distant lights and the reflections across the water and all seemed well with the world.

The race start was Saturday at 3.00pm which meant I would have to endure the highest temperatures of the day. On the plus side I would be able to have a Scandinavian smörgåsbord breakfast which would be thoroughly digested by start time. I stayed with the tried and trusted cereal, rolls and fruit juice, promising to experiment the following day.

I had familiarised myself so well with the underground that I was even able to tell a Swede the correct train to catch for the Olympic Stadium. Changing was in an adjacent outdoor arena, with baggage stored outside in long rows. I remember hoping that it wouldn't rain. Runners were doing warm-ups, exercising or gently jogging but to kill the time, I sat below a tree with a book, trying to keep out of the sun.

Eventually we assembled in designated areas and were walked to the start. 11,000 runners lined up outside the stadium and would finish outside the stadium as renovation work was taking place within. If I had been looking for a spectacular finish on the track, I had chosen the wrong year and would be out of luck.

Leading into the race, I had been in the form of my life, setting several best times in local races. I was very nervous but usually tend to do well when in this frame of mind. The sun had now broken through the overcast sky producing temperatures probably into the eighties at start time.

For such a big field, I crossed the start in under a minute. The early stages were run on wide tree-lined avenues, with the shade they provided extremely welcome. The next stage was across an open expanse and runners making up for lost time kicked up sand from the verges which turned into dust clouds. We passed Kaknästornet, Scandinavia's tallest building, with television transmitter and observation platform.

The open expanse was soon replaced by the Djurgården or Royal Park, an area of outstanding natural beauty. Stockholmers retreat to the expanses of green and woodland for jogging, horse riding, sailing or less strenuous activities such as picnicking.

The course passed open-air museum Skansen before entering the city. I was feeling particularly comfortable as we crossed a couple of small bridges, ran alongside the harbour and under a tunnel into Slussen. Spectators and runners alike were all fair of face and athletic looking and I was indeed in the midst of beautiful company. At particular places along the course, an attractive girl on a white charger stood out above the crowd, probably criss-crossing the city to follow the race.

The next stretch was along the waterfront at Södermalm and this was quickly developing into the most scenic and enjoyable race I had done. Like New York, this race also had a long bridge in the Västerbron which had to be negotiated twice. The first time around, I really accelerated to the centre point and relaxed down to the far bank for a further section on the waterfront, this time at Mälarstrand. Turning inland and away from the water, the temperature became stifling and the going became tougher. There were several short inclines and one or two heartbreaking long stretches, but a welcome boost came in the sight of the Olympic Stadium. This would mark the start of the shorter second lap, which was pretty much the same as the first except for missing out parts of the Djurgården.

The heat was now scorching and the second crossing of the Västerbron was very much one foot in front of the other. I was becoming more lethargic with each stride, my energy draining away at an alarming rate. There would be no personal best today and just to complete the course would be satisfying enough. The feed stations were well stocked with energy drinks, oranges, bananas and chocolate. I made full use of these in the later stages sampling everything as much out of desperation as necessity.

I was hanging on for grim death, but was encouraged as the crowds became thicker and the ivy towers of the stadium came into view. Opening up into an obligatory sprint or what felt like one, I crossed the line in 3 hours 37 minutes exactly. While reasonably contented with this, at the back of my mind I knew I could have done much better.

By the time I had showered and changed, it was almost nine'o'clock. I wandered the steep cobbled streets of Södermalm hardly having the energy to drag my weary body around. I called for my now customary couple of beers which were quite expensive, but being in celebratory mood I was none too bothered. I came across several people proudly wearing their medals and who can blame them for a job well done. I turned in quite late and slept like a baby.

On Sunday morning I rested aching limbs and took a boat trip from Gamla Stan through the archipelago and along some of the city's waterways and canals. This provided a different appreciation of the city which seemed to float on the water.

This was one location that I intended revisiting, and I had the opportunity four years on, this time to run in the Stockholmsloppet, the city's half marathon. The race held in late August covered much of the same course as the marathon, but in reverse. This time I would be able to finish on the track inside the Olympic Stadium.

The weather was not as kind as in my previous visit, and the day after the race I was soaked during a boat trip to Vaxholm. On an almost deserted boat, I had the company of a down-and-out. Although I couldn't understand a word he said, I bought him a tea and kept nodding and smiling at the appropriate places.

A friend of mine swears by the Stockholm races, returning over and over again for the marathon, half marathon and Lidingøloppet, a mass participation cross-country event. I suspect he returns more for the easy on the eye scenery as for the athletic competition.

The Ultimate Guide to International Marathons written by Dennis Craythorn and Richard Hanna rated Stockholm as the number one International Marathon, ahead of London, New York and Berlin and I wouldn't argue with their choice.

I had a chance to visit Sweden again in 1992 when Trevor organised a trip for eight club members to Gothenburg on the west coast for the Göteborgs-varvet. We travelled by mini coach to Harwich and sailed on Wednesday afternoon on the *Prince of Scandinavia* reaching Sweden's second city twenty-four hours later. Four of us shared a cabin in which you could barely swing a cat around. The one thing that I can remember about the journey is that I went to sleep eating a Mars bar and awoke the following morning with chocolate on the back of my neck. No matter how hard I scrubbed, I couldn't seem to remove it all and was conscious of it all weekend.

The Swedish weather was very warm with a stiff breeze blowing off the sea. We docked, cleared customs and were taken by coach to the Panorama Hotel on a steep hill high above the city. Registration at the hotel was long-winded and we were kept waiting while rooms became available. The eight of us were spread across the hotel on different floors, no doubt as a precaution ahead of the European Football Tournament where English fans were expected to cause trouble. This was the tournament in which host nation Sweden defeated England and the newspaper headline the next day was Swedes 2 Turnips 1.

We took a tram ride to the race registration in a large sports hall on the outskirts of the city. Only a couple of months earlier, a tram had careered off the track down a steep hill. Surely they wouldn't be able to find a flat course here? The registration was similar to other big city races with many stalls selling sports goods and souvenirs. We received our race numbers and all bought matching tee shirts to pose in that evening, and let people know who we were. I was particularly taken by the stand advertising other Scandinavian races whetting my appetite for further travel.

On returning to the hotel, it was agreed a training run was in order, but the four miles or so only confirmed my belief that the race would indeed be hard and hilly.

Friday morning was spent sightseeing and this included a boat trip to the island of Nya Älrsborg, an ancient fortress at the harbour mouth where in years gone by, the Swedes and Danes had regularly done battle. Much to the delight of the other members in the party, John and I missed the boat back to the mainland after paying a call. We had seen a boat passing the island but it must have turned sharply at the last minute, setting down and picking up the passengers and apparently refusing to wait for us.

With a ninety-minute wait for the next ferry, John tried to commandeer a boat to get us back to the mainland, but I didn't relish rowing across the busy shipping lanes. He then tried to negotiate with the owner of a small vessel to make the journey but met with little success. To pass the time away, we each had photographs taken with the guide, a young blonde girl in national costume. When we eventually caught the ferry, a group of Swedish schoolchildren used us to practice their English language skills.

Friday evening started with a visit to Liseborg, a huge amusement park close to the city centre. The visit included a trip up the observation tower to see Gothenburg by night. The revolving carousel didn't meet with everyone's approval and some of the knuckles were a bit white when we came down.

We found a lively pub where the group were playing British sixties and seventies hits and the young revellers were going crazy over the likes of 'Yellow Submarine'.

Race time was 3.00 p.m. on Saturday afternoon and it looked like being a scorcher. After taking in a spot of shopping, it felt as though we had walked a half marathon before the race. When attempts to secure the hotel's courtesy bus to take us to the start had failed, we set out to catch a tram. Each stop we came to had long queues of runners and spectators heading to the start so we walked back several stops to improve our chances of boarding. Eventually we arrived at the small athletics stadium on the city outskirts, changed in an impressive ice hockey arena and handed in our baggage at another sports hall.

The Götesborgsvarvet is a half marathon and one of Sweden's largest mass participation events. The race started in seven waves with about 5,000 runners each. The waves started at seven minute intervals giving the runners in the earlier blocks time to get clear. Each runner was timed as their respective block moved forward and given a finishing position accordingly. Four of us had been allocated to the first block but we managed to sneak in another two. The remaining two, John and Trevor were happy to start in the fourth wave.

The early miles were through the Slottsskogen, a large park, and as expected the conditions were hot. Runners pushed, shoved and elbowed their way through, making up for lost time and gaining extra yardage. At three miles we were met with a considerable climb to the centre of the Älvsborgs bron, a long suspension bridge at the harbour mouth. Once past halfway, there was a welcome downhill and a more than welcome cooling breeze. The marker posts were in kilometres and came up very quickly. A pleasant residential section was followed by another park, and then back to the city over a second bridge, the Götaälvbron. The main factor here was trying to avoid the trams which were surprisingly still running.

By now the fatigue was setting in as the heat started to take effect. The final section meandered the city streets where spectators, many beautiful and blonde, came off the pavements to form the narrowest of funnels through which to pass. They handed out fruit, chocolate and ice pops as well as much needed applause and encouragement. An organisational masterpiece including a temporary bailey bridge within the stadium kept the thousands of runners moving through the checkouts.

While the heat and humidity affected the times, I was undeterred, running a good race. I tired in the final stages but was delighted to record ninety-six minutes. All eight of the group ran well with everyone quietly pleased with their performance.

On Saturday evening we had arranged to meet a Yorkshire lad who was going to show us a good time. We had met him in a restaurant the previous day when he told how he had replied to an advertisement in a national daily, and had landed a dream job as a draughtsman with Volvo. He had never been as happy and loved the country, the people and the job. He had a luxury apartment, luxury girl friend and money burning a hole in his pocket. Needless to say he turned up late, forgot his wallet, and most of us had to sub him for a drink.

In the two and a half days, we didn't do Gothenburg justice as there was lots more to do and see. A good excuse to revisit. The return ferry journey to Harwich was enjoyable but slightly tedious at the end of the break. The only incident of any note was when the purser kept threatening to throw some people off for singing, but doing no real harm. Whether he intended to cast them adrift in an open boat, like Fletcher Christian had done to Captain Bligh, is anybody's guess.

CHAPTER 12

Our Friends in the North

ALREADY HOOKED on Scandinavia, my next destination would be Tromsø for the Midnight Sun Marathon. Two hundred and fifty miles north of the Arctic Circle, Tromsø is the largest city in North Norway, has the world's most northerly cathedral, university, brewery and so on. Tromsø holds many accolades and has been known as 'Paris of the North' and 'Gateway to the Arctic'.

Tromsø has been the starting point for many Arctic expeditions down the years, notably those undertaken by Roald Amundsen and Fridjtof Nansen. Despite the long winters when daylight all but disappears for two whole months, Tromsø enjoys twenty four hour daylight in June and July, with many outdoor festivals and events organised throughout the region.

Situated on the island of Tromsoya, a bridge built in 1960 connected the city to the mainland. Prior to the opening, all goods and provisions were transported by ferry. A series of tunnels connect Langnes airport on the other side of the island to Tromsø, but a toll must be paid to travel through these. A myriad of pastel-coloured buildings line the steep streets of the city and the waterfront.

I arrived late on Thursday evening and as the plane descended through the dense cloud, I began to think I would never see daylight again. The weather on the ground was overcast with drizzle and there was no sign of the midnight sun. Trying to doze off in the half-light was a strange experience but I eventually nodded off only to awaken early.

Whilst completing my unpacking, I discovered various clothes had been stained by a liquid which had possibly seeped from an adjacent bag in the hold of the aircraft. One of the items damaged was my camera, so the first job would be to have it replaced. An electrical retailer offered me a discount on a new camera if I were to trade the old one in. More importantly, a race diary containing some of my times and positions had been badly stained, so I could look forward to a few evenings in the weeks ahead sustaining writer's cramp.

I needed a camera as there were lots of photograph opportunities; the harbour, the waterfront and Tromsø Bridge all against the backdrop of magnificent snow-capped mountains. The Domkirke is one of the largest wooden churches in the world while over the bridge is the modern Arctic Cathedral.

With a population of 50,000, I imagined Tromsø to be a similar size to Pontefract. The climate warmed by the Gulf Stream drift was pleasant and the air crystal clear. I wandered the same streets over and over again and along the waterfront where ferries and cruise ships were docked. Tromsø is a port of call on the Norwegian Coastal Voyage and was also a stop off point for Michael Palin on his 'Pole to Pole' journey.

The people play hard, drink hard and smoke hard and that's only the women. Some of the faces are weathered and hardened due to extreme winters and the outdoor culture with many occupations revolving around the fishing industry. Apart from the traditional 'fair of face' Nordics, some of the population are Sami or Lapps. With their oriental looks, some of the women can really turn the heads. The Sami make a living by selling their goods in the shape of richly coloured cardigans and skirts, moccasins, purses and jewellery from stalls on the waterfront. Passenger liners and cruise ships provide them with a lucrative trade.

At the race registration, I discovered there would be 2,000 competitors across the four races. There was a mini marathon for people of all ages, a ten kilometre race and a half marathon all at staggered times. The marathon started at 10.00 p.m. so I would start on Saturday and finish on Sunday, all being well running in the midnight sun. The marathon had 188 entrants including five from Great Britain and I saw one of these later on in a café, wearing a track suit covered from head to toe in badges.

The race pack contained a pass for unlimited travel, and on Saturday I studied the timetable, hopped aboard the Tromsbus, and explored the surrounding countryside and breathtaking scenery.

The races started and finished in the city centre on Stortorget and as I made my way to the changing area, I was able to see the tail end of the mini marathon. In fourth place was a Sami with husky dog at his heel, and despite the hundreds of competitors, I calculated I could have gone fast enough to earn a top ten placing. This would clearly be the race for me in future.

Leaving my belongings in a designated area of the race headquarters, I was ready for the start of this unusual event. Runners milled around and talked in groups but I sat on a wall until we were called forward. This was only the second staging of The Midnight Sun Races and the organisers were no doubt looking to build on their initial success. The unusual setting and time of day would no doubt be a decisive factor in attracting competitors from all over Scandinavia and overseas.

The first test in the race came within a few hundred yards in negotiating the steep incline on Tromsø Bridge. The downhill beyond the centre point provided views of the Arctic Cathedral and snow-capped mountains, visible even though the daylight was more like dusk. There would be no midnight sun today, but there was an irritating drizzle.

We ran an out and back section on two parallel roads before crossing the bridge back into Tromsø. The section ran through small hamlets where occasional pockets of spectators rang cowbells and enthusiastically supported the runners. The roads were narrow and from time to time we crossed a bridge, with the sound of clear mountain water gushing below.

Returning to the city, spectators were more frequent, and people singled out my Union Flag singlet for special applause. There was a further out and back section leading to a turnaround point at fifteen kilometres and by now wide gaps had opened with the runner in front a good way ahead. As the leaders came back down the other side of the road, I counted them until I reached the turnaround point in 105th place. Feeling pretty comfortable and running well within myself, I would see how many places I could pick up while trying not to be headed by anyone from behind.

I passed close to the finish before starting out on a full lap of the island staying pretty close to the coastline. Some of the well-used roads were badly potholed, no doubt worsened by the severe winters, but the quieter roads provided an excellent running surface. There were some testing little climbs and it was on one of these that I began to pick up places, and by my reckoning, I moved up to 92nd place. Near Langnes Airport, the half marathoners had their turnaround point, so once again there were runners on both sides of the road. With more runners present, I lost track of any further places I was to pick up. A nice gesture in the final stages was displayed by some of the half marathoners, who either clapped or touched a shoulder of those who seemed to be going the full distance.

There was a steady downhill into Tromsø and the half marathoners went hell for leather towards the finish in Stortorget. The marshals, no doubt spotting my number, directed me onto the left-hand side of the road, and I was left alone to take the plaudits running unchallenged to the finish. I recorded 3 hours 35 minutes, a very satisfactory evening, night and morning's work. My eventual finishing position was 87th from 187. One runner either didn't start, didn't finish, or must still be out there somewhere.

I changed, collected my belongings and enjoyed a cup of tea. On the way back to my hotel, I noticed the city starting to come to life. The streets were full of young people either leaving restaurants or in between bars. Some were watching the finishers of the respective races drift past as they queued to get into a night club. I even saw a scuffle which turned into a fight, showing that things change little wherever you are in the world. My hotel, The Grand Nordic, had both a night club and a cellar bar. After showering, I was very tempted, but I had my sensible head on and decided I had done enough for one day.

After ringing home on Sunday morning to let my Mum and Dad know I had made it in one piece, I set out for more exploring and tried to unwind a little. I took the cable car to the top of Storsteinen which at 1,380 feet provides panoramic views, over the mountains, the islands and surrounding inlets and fjords. An American couple pointed to the spot where the German battleship, *Tirpitz* was sunk by British bombers and thought it might be partly visible. The couple had arrived in Tromsø unaware of the race weekend, and unable to find accommodation had been fixed up with a local family.

My next stop would be the Northern Lights Planetarium where a special projection system takes you on a journey through the universe. The main function of the planetarium is to study the Northern Lights or Aurora Borealis. I called at the Arctic Cathedral to see the unusual organ and huge stained glass window.

There are numerous restaurants and pavement cafes in Tromsø providing a relaxed and laid back feel. On Sunday evening I set out to explore Tromsø at night by way of a few pubs. Mack beers brewed at the world's northernmost brewery were well represented wherever I went, and some of the pubs had British-sounding names such as 'Big Ben' and 'Football'. The people were very friendly with many people speaking fluent English. Locals were amazed that I had taken the trouble to travel so far to run in their marathon and wished me well. One man who said he was the captain of a merchant vessel insisted on buying me a drink. Around midnight, the sun eventually broke through the clouds making it all seem worthwhile.

Some months after returning home, I received race details for the following year's event and notification that I had become a member of 'The Midnight Sun Association'. Anyone who had run in the marathon since the inception of the race had this honour bestowed upon them. The award had to be collected in person but would still be available if I were to return in the years ahead. It seemed like a reasonable excuse to return sooner rather than later.

I did return but in 2001, ten years on, but this time I opted for the easier option of running the half marathon. I arrived on Thursday afternoon via Oslo to torrential rain and found myself dodging between shopping arcades and buildings with canopies. Trying to familiarise myself once again with the city, I noticed many more restaurants, cafés and bars than on my previous visit. 'Kelly's Corner' had even found its way here with lively Irish music blasting its way through the door.

In the cellar bar below the hotel on Friday evening, a group were setting up equipment for a spot later in the evening and trade was pretty quiet. A man appearing worse for drink made his way over to my table and immediately reminded me of Trevor, the wife-beating husband of 'Little Mo' in 'Eastenders'. On realising I was British, he stated that Englishmen, Irishmen, Scotsmen and Welsh were all the same. Running his finger along the table, he said he would cut them open, just like he would splice a fish. As he continued to glare at me, I decided it was perhaps a suitable time to drink up and leave.

Bidding my new friend goodnight, I quickly moved on and the next person who I came into contact with talked football. He was fanatical about English football, in particular Manchester United, and he irritatingly referred to them as 'United' just as our pundits do at home, as if there was only one United.

On Saturday I chose to take a trip on one of the ferries that ply their trade along the fjords, with a view to resting my legs before the half marathon in the evening. The first race to go was parents with push chairs and prams. The 4K race followed this, doubling as a fun run and a charity fund raiser. Many were in fancy dress including Vikings, Polar Bears and a couple of Eskimos although on reflection, these two could have been running in their civvies. The 10K race followed with the marathon going at 8.30.

The half marathon started at 10 o'clock, and I changed at the hotel leaving it as late as possible before jogging to the start. I felt remarkably comfortable, but was conscious of the fact I hadn't gone the distance for some time. On a small loop within the city, spectators packed the pavements to do the race justice. The course then followed the coast road towards the airport, returning the same way to form an out and back route. All the races remained on the island as they did ten years ago with the notable exception of the marathon, which negotiated the steep bridge to the mainland returning the same way.

Making a mockery of recent form, I cruised through 5K in 22 minutes and 10K in 44. Ten years ago, the conditions were similar to dusk, but tonight they were perfect and we would see 'The Midnight Sun'. The coast road was rolling without being too difficult and from time to time, there were excellent views across the fjord to the snow-capped mountains. Small pockets of spectators were most supportive, ringing bells, blowing horns and shaking old style football rattles. A lady no doubt with a programme, called out my name and provided me with a timely boost, while others patriotically waved the red and blue Norwegian flag. For once, I seemed to be overtaking runners but some of these may have been marathoners nearing the end of their own race.

All good things come to an end and I started to struggle, slowing noticeably in the final couple of miles. The run in to the finish was a narrow funnel from a few hundred yards out. Each runner was treated like a hero, and a unique atmosphere was generated which I shall remember for a long time. I recorded 1 hour 42 minutes, not spectacular but as good as I could have expected on the day. Italians came first and second, while I finished 93rd in a field of 300 or thereabouts.

Finishers received a distinctive medal along with beer, yoghurt, bananas and chocolate. Once again I meandered through spectators, clubbers and late night revellers and made my weary way back to the hotel.

On Sunday, I visited the Polar Museum which traces the journeys of Roald Amundsen, Fridtjof Nansen and other great explorers. I was surprised at the length of the expeditions, which in some cases lasted for three or four years. Not only did they travel by boat and on foot, but they explored the Polar Regions by airship and the 'Latham Flying Boat'. There was fascinating footage on Wanny Woldstad, a taxi driver from Tromsø, who became the only female hunter in the region. Apparently she harboured an unexplainable longing for the frozen wastes and returned year after year. Another exhibition is Polaria which examines the animals, flora and fauna of the polar regions and Spitzbergen.

Not content with the overcrowded football season at home, I opted to watch Tromsø on Sunday evening at their hill top ground. Several years ago they had given Chelsea a run for their money in a European tie played in a blizzard. They were soundly beaten this time by Stabaek, with the game petering out to a chorus of slow handclapping and booing.

At between £3 and £4 a pint and £7 to £8 for burger and fries, my wallet and credit cards were screaming for mercy by the end of the break. With a stopover in Oslo thrown in, I returned home looking forward to my next pay cheque and the one after that. The place and the race are well worth a visit but the travel and cost of living push the price well above the ordinary extended weekend break.

I never did get my 'Midnight Sun Marathon' membership so who knows? I may be back in ten years' time when I am sure to be running better. Roll on 2011.

CHAPTER 13

Norway in a Nutshell

ON THE RETURN JOURNEY from Tromsø in 1991, I had a stopover for one night in Norway's capital, Oslo and immediately fell in love with the city. The day was gloriously sunny, the place was spotlessly clean and everything about the city gave positive vibes.

Late the following summer and with holiday leave to come, I decided at short notice to run the Oslo Marathon. By now I was becoming familiar with the airlines and companies who specialised in Scandinavia and as a result, secured a good deal. Securing a good deal is one thing but spending money within Scandinavian countries would considerably stretch my budget.

The descent to Fornebu Airport is across the beautiful Oslo-fjord and when it seems as if the plane is destined to land in the water, the runway appears at the last minute as if by magic. Much work was underway at the airport and on a new rail terminal which would be completed in time for the Winter Olympics at Lillehammer.

Oslo sits in a magnificent setting at the head of the Oslo-fjord against a backdrop of pine forests and mountains. With only half a million people, Oslo is one of Europe's smaller capital cities. The centre, while quite compact, is easily manageable on foot and most of the main attractions can be captured over a long weekend.

Oslo houses a large merchant fleet and a spacious marina. In the heart of the city is Aker Brygge, a modern harbourside complex, with restaurants, bars and shopping malls. The main thoroughfare is Karl Johansgate which runs from the Royal Palace to Central Railway Station, passing attractive squares and gardens along the way.

The city centre is vibrant and throughout long summer days, people spill out from cafés onto the pavements. Oslo comes to life slowly in the evenings and by midnight is throbbing. Licensing hours were relaxed in the late 1980s and bars and clubs have sprung up across the city to suit all tastes. Until recently it was possible to drink around the clock but now a 3.00 a.m. curfew has been imposed.

Many cities offer a card entitling the holder to unlimited travel and entry to major attractions. Oslo is no exception and the Oslo Card enabled me to use buses, trams and trains along with some of the ferries. I could also obtain discount at some of the city's museums.

I took in some sightseeing the day before the race, boarding an underground train in the city centre. The train eventually came to the surface on its own dedicated track, before climbing steeply through woods to provide panoramic views across the city and Oslo-fjord.

The Holmenkollen is a ski centre with ski jump, an arena which doubles as a lake and concert venue, and a ski museum depicting the sport throughout the ages. Many of the early skis were on display along with equipment used in expeditions in the Arctic. From the museum I took a lift, then some stairs and then some very narrow stairs to the tower at the top of the ski jump. From here, I had an appreciation of how Eddie 'The Eagle' Edwards must have felt as he embarked down the ramp and over the edge into mid air. The Homenkollen stages an eleven day festival in March culminating in Homenkollen Sunday, to which Oslo people turn out in droves.

Back at sea level, I moved on to the Kon-Tiki museum which houses the craft in which Thor Heyerdhal travelled from Peru to Polynesia. There is also a fascinating collection of memorabilia collected from Easter Island.

I registered for the race at the well-to-do Radisson SAS Hotel, late on Friday afternoon where I had the privilege to talk to Norwegian distance running heroine and Olympic Silver medallist Grete Waitz. Although still running, Grete was non-competitive, concentrating her efforts on coaching promising young athletes.

Two other races at the exhibition caught my eye. The first was the Norske Fjell Marathon held up country in June. I didn't understand the commentary but the video showed happy runners being bussed to the race start, laughing, joking and singing. Despite the time of year, the roads were flanked by fields of snow. In places, the road had literally been cut through high banks of snow. There was a half marathon option which appeared to run predominantly downhill. Now that seemed like my kind of race.

The second race, the Viking Half Marathon was held in Balestrand on the mighty Sognefjord. The flat course appeared to cling to the water's edge like a thread of cotton. Apparently a competitive field was attracted to the race as Kenyans were among previous winners with times just over the hour.

The Oslo Marathon started at 1.30 p.m. with the half at the later time of 4.00 p.m. Both started outside the famous Bislett Stadium where many world records have tumbled over the years. I wasn't in the best form of my life leading into the race and with no recent long training runs as such, should have probably settled for the shorter option.

The conditions were humid with the course providing many twists, turns and inclines and in the early stages, we ran through Frogner Park past the sculptures. A football field was cordoned off with the route following the perimeter but someone must have taken a short cut across the goal mouth and everybody followed suit. Needless to say, some of the marshalling left a lot to be desired.

We climbed beyond the stadium towards the halfway mark which I completed in a modest 1 hour 43 minutes. I felt pretty comfortable suffering a slight cramp, but some favourable downhills brought us into the city and I started to pick up the pace once again.

The route circled Akershus Castle, by the Aker Brygge complex and along the beautiful fjord passing luxury yachts and craft. Needless to say, there were no cones, no tape and few marshals and it was a case of following the runner in front and trying to avoid bumping into pedestrians. This race was no Berlin or Stockholm!! The threatened thunderstorm materialised and the heavens opened. For a short while, my vest and shorts clung tightly to my body and legs, but despite the discomfort, I was running fluently. A good middle section of the race had put me in with a chance of a personal best, and I was determined to go for it.

The course continued to produce short inclines and testing little pulls, but I responded by working hard. There was an urgency about my running that hadn't been present at the end of my previous marathons and as we returned to the city I was zipping along. We completely traversed the Royal Palace on the way home to Bislett and I started to pass runners with ease. Moving easily through the gears, I was in dreamland, and when a car pulled across the road I indicated that I was coming through. I went under the clock inside the stadium in 3 hours 23 minutes, five minutes inside my previous best.

Not only had I run the second half of the race three minutes quicker than the first but it was the first time to my knowledge that I had achieved this. If only I could have bottled the way I had felt in that second half and reopened it for the next race. Rarely before, or for that matter since have I felt so comfortable and each time I asked for more effort, it was forthcoming. Ten years on, this is still my quickest marathon time.

I showered and changed in time to see the half marathon leaders enter the stadium. One of the Tanzanian brothers Simon Robert Naali easily outsprinted his nearest rival to take the title. I walked back down the course towards the city centre with a warm glow of satisfaction as I watched many of the half marathoners in the final stages of their own race.

Oslo really came to life on Saturday night providing a vibrant atmosphere. There were stilt walkers, fire eaters and jugglers drawing crowds to the main squares, along with the motionless bronzed and silver statuesque figures that suddenly move. The man who caught my attention was dressed as a clown and trying to push a balloon across a zebra crossing. He made the balloon out to be heavy and it wouldn't go where he intended. He held the traffic up for a fair while but nobody seemed to mind. For his next trick he fastened an imaginary tow rope to a car bumper, walking slowly forward and pretending to struggle.

North Sea oil had provided Norwegians with a standard of living unequalled in many larger European countries, and this was highlighted by the crowds on the streets and in the restaurants and bars.

On Sunday morning I made an early start and was among the first customers at the Defence Museum. I was fascinated by the models in glass cases showing how Norway had suffered at the hands of the Germans in the Second World War. I moved on to the compact Resistance Museum in the grounds of Akershus Castle. It was close to here that the Norwegian Chancellor, Quisling was shot at the end of World War Two.

The huge town hall dominates the waterfront and looks something of an eyesore, but the richly decorated interior and floor are particularly impressive. I walked the Aker Brygge, the city centre and the grounds of the Royal Palace, making the most of my last day and promising I would soon return.

I had to wait nine years for another visit to Oslo but I did return to Norway in 1997, this time to Bergen in Western Norway. The picture postcard city is built around a harbour and fish quay, sheltered by spectacular mountains rising vertically from the water. The gabled Hanseatic Warehouses that line the Bryggen are a UNESCO World Heritage Site. The predominently wooden buildings house a network of corridors, passageways and steps and regular guided tours take place. Many of the buildings now house art, craft and souvenir shops.

Bergen is known as ' Gateway to the Fjords' and this was where I intended heading, once the Bergen Half Marathon was out of the way. The two hour flight from Newcastle via Stavanger had left me with most of Friday afternoon and evening in which to familiarise myself with Bergen. The race took place on Saturday lunch time, but after that I had three days in which to explore the region.

Intending to take a short stroll and probably a couple of pints, I looked forward to an early night ahead of the race, but with daylight until almost midnight, it would have been folly to lock myself in the hotel bedroom.

Opposite the famous fish market Torget, was Scruffy Murphy's and I couldn't resist the temptation of a Guinness. Just as I had found some years earlier in Tromsø, the locals were extremely friendly with many speaking excellent English. I got into pleasant banter with a young Norwegian lady so I had to have two further Guinnesses before I could drag myself away. My lasting memory would have been the shafts of sunlight streaming through the windows at almost ten o'clock in the evening.

I called for a final drink in the pub adjoining my hotel, but what they failed to tell me was that this was the liveliest bar in town. I departed some time in the early hours with the hope of a promising run later that day rapidly changing into a happy to get around one.

The Bergen Marathon and Half Marathon are low-key races based at Fana Stadium on the outskirts of the city. A bus ride and a short walk gave me plenty of time to register, change and get to the start. The girl at the tourist information made a phone call confirming I could register on the day. She also sold me, among other bits and bobs, the Bergen Card, entitling me to unlimited travel, and discounts on ferries, cablecar, funicular railway and museums, over my four day stay.

There was no baggage storage area but an official kindly agreed to save my bag in his van. The marathon started at midday with perhaps sixty runners. The shorter option started half an hour later and would be an out and back course. The day was hot, I would sweat a lot and I would surely pay for last night's beer. The starter gave last minute instructions and then started to speak in English. He mentioned my name and went on to say I was the only overseas competitor and was very welcome at the event. I stood out like a sore thumb in my Union Flag vest, and several runners around me were all receptive with some turning around to shake my hand, and others wishing me luck.

The race started on a cycle way beside a main road but soon turned onto quiet and traffic free forest roads. With no more than a few hundred runners, there was no delay at the start with the field soon taking shape. The course ran through forests, past tiny chocolate box hamlets and crystal blue lakes. Many houses flew the national flag displaying fierce patriotism. Small pockets of spectators showed their appreciation, and one man in particular on spotting my vest, shouted some encouragement to which I replied 'Hi-ya!!' The man followed the race on a bicycle and appeared at strategic places along the course, each time shouting Hi-ya to me. He must have thought this was the thing we British shout.

Despite the scorching temperature, last night's beers were having no detrimental effect and I was going along nicely. It was hard to believe there were such spectacular surroundings so close to the city. At one point we passed a church where a wedding party had gathered outside, all in colourful national costume. A runner alongside me said that this would bring us luck. Towards halfway, the leaders returned on the opposite side of the road with several of them acknowledging me, further enhancing my growing celebrity status. Halfway constituted running around a marshal and returning from whence we came.

Still feeling quite good, I pressed on with the psychological factor being the kilometre marker posts appearing quicker than the mile markers would do back home. Moving into the final stages I felt particularly comfortable and thoroughly enjoying the experience in scenic surroundings. I finished in ninety-six minutes to generous applause. Not only did I receive a medal for completing my race, but they gave me a plaque otherwise reserved for marathon finishers.

I was invited to the club house for a drink, then another and another. They wouldn't let me leave and invited me for a training run on Tuesday or any Tuesday or Thursday if I were to return. They told me of beautiful Norwegian races particularly at Älesund and Sogndal, and the big race in Bergen, the Fanaløpet in autumn. It was no good, I would have to increase my lottery stake on a Saturday. They bid me farewell, wished me luck and encouraged me to return.

I arrived back in Bergen at tea time and dined at the Bryggen Tracteursted in the Hanseatic Warehouses, at three hundred years old, reputably the oldest tavern in Norway. On Sunday morning I took the eight minute funicular ride to Floyen, the city's mountain at 1000ft above sea level. From the top, there are magnificent views over Bergen, the seven mountains, the harbours, islands and skerries. The walk back down to the city took longer as I meandered the wooded hillside stopping periodically to enjoy the views.

Next stop was the Domkirke Cathedral and then onto the Hanseatic Museum. This depicted how traders of the Hanseatic League worked and lived in the 1700s with the rooms furnished as they would have been then. I called for a well-earned pint and a bite to eat and in the afternoon visited Bryggen Museum and the Aquarium.

The day of reckoning had finally arrived as I sat aboard the train pulling out of Bergen station. I was setting off on a journey that had captured my imagination over a number of years, a journey I had promised myself and I was determined not to be disappointed.

'Norway in a Nutshell' is a whistlestop tour by train, boat and coach taking in some of the more spectacular scenery of Western Norway. You purchase a ticket for around £40 at the Tourist Information Centre in Bergen, pick up a timetable and make your own connections.

The first stage of the journey is on the western section of the Oslo–Bergen line, a masterpiece in civil engineering. Passing through a series of tunnels, the line follows the Sorfjorden on the gradual climb to ski and tourist resort

Voss. Valleys are steep and barely wide enough to carry the railway and road, but occasionally the gorge broadens sufficiently to reveal a small hamlet or sparkling lake.

Out of Voss, the greenery is replaced by forests of fir and spruce, powerful rivers and waterfalls, with snow-capped peaks in the distance. The scenery becomes more rugged and barren as the line negotiates an abundance of tunnels and snow shelters.

Stepping from the train at Myrdal, I was glad to have packed a pair of trousers to replace my shorts and a warmer sweater as the mountain temperatures were somewhat chillier than in Bergen. The station buffet was a welcome sight with hot scones removed from the oven as if to coincide with the arrival of the train. Myrdal took me completely by surprise. It consisted of only a few wooden huts and a railway station with sidings and snow moving equipment.

The next stage aboard the Flåm railway must be one of the most exhilarating train journeys in the world. The line drops 2,800ft from the head of the valley to fjord level at Flåm, in only twelve miles. Passengers constantly move from one side of the train to the other in search of the perfect snapshot. There is a photo stop at the mighty Kjosfossenen Waterfall where passengers can step from the train, but run the risk of being soaked if they stand too close.

The track winds its way down the valley through tunnels and past cascading waterfalls, until in less than an hour, the train reaches Flåm, at the head of Aurlandsfjord. Leaving nothing to chance, there are five independent braking systems on the train, should anything go wrong.

Activity at Flåm centres on the arrival and departure of boats and trains within a few hundred yards. The two hour wait provided an opportunity for some exploring, a spot of lunch and a visit to one of several bars. I bought postcards and then strolled around Flåm, a collection of houses, hotels and souvenir shops, nestling below a steep cliff.

The passenger ferry would provide the next mode of transport along the Aurlandsfjord. a tributary of the longer Songefjord, before sweeping left along the Naerøyfjord to Gudvangen, a two hour journey. Finding a nice suntrap on the upper deck, I was soon engulfed by hoards of Japanese tourists on a whirlwind tour of Scandinavia. They provided good company and were reluctant to let a good photo opportunity pass them by.

Even though a commentary was provided, I found a map more than useful to pinpoint our progress. For me, this was the most intriguing leg of the journey, the mountain walls rising vertically from the fjord and the occasional waterfall plummeting down the rock face. A road followed one side of the fjord, occasionally disappearing into tunnels when it was no longer possible to stay close to the water's edge. The infrastructure of the area connects even the remotest village or farmhouse to the road network which perhaps justifies the huge demands placed upon the Norwegian tax-payer.

Passenger ferries and luxury liners travel the narrow fjord arms with some journeys necessitating a change of boat mid-fjord. Seagulls follow the ferries in search of tit bits and when the food is caught in full flight, this is usually greeted with a spontaneous cheer.

As magnificent as these fjords appear on a bright summer day, I could imagine how powerful, brooding and forbidding they would become during the long Scandinavian winters. The ferry made several stops before reaching Gudvangen where we disembarked for the coach journey to Voss.

Within a matter of minutes, the coach begins to negotiate the steep valley by way of a dozen or so hairpin bends. The road reaches a gradient of one in five and the driver has his work cut out either stopping or slowing to accommodate oncoming traffic. The view improves with each bend and when we safely reached the summit at the Stalheim Hotel, the driver received a well-earned round of applause.

The Stalheim Hotel is an imposing well appointed building with spacious gardens to the rear. The view looks out over the road we had travelled, which twists and turns into the valley bottom. Souvenirs and refreshments can be bought and if time allows, the Stalheimfossen waterfall and Stalheim Folk Museum are both nearby.

The coach journey continues after a short break, with the mountain roads passing lakes and forests. We followed a crystal clear river arriving at Voss with half an hour to spare before the train departure. I had time for a hot beef sandwich on the patio of the fine Fleischers Hotel next to the railway station. From my vantage point, I was able to take in the surrounding countryside reflecting on the day's events with some satisfaction.

The final leg of the journey was the morning leg in reverse, but tired as I felt, the Norwegian landscape in the early evening sunlight was well appreciated. An hour and a half later, the train emerged from the final long tunnel and into Bergen station, marking the end of a memorable day and one that I would like to do all over again.

I never tire of visiting Scandinavia and would love to return and run some of these races again with some new ones thrown in as well. The strong pound currently makes Norway an attractive proposition, so who knows, fingers crossed in the years ahead.

CHAPTER 14

Book of Excuses

LOOKING BACK at my early running days, I can remember all too well the excuses people provided for underachieving on race day. When I joined Ackworth Road Runners in 1991, the intensity of the excuses moved onto a different scale. Not only were there a bag full of excuses for not running well in the race, but a whole host of excuses for not having to bother running at all.

I found this particularly strange as I presumed the main function of a running club and its members was to run, but apparently not. On the annual sortie to the Great North Run, there would be as many runners who had cried off as there were taking part, and there would be any amount of numbers going for a song.

I can recollect one runner passing on his number to someone else, and amazingly claiming his souvenir tee shirt from the lad who had done the race for him. Likewise, another runner complete with number joined in for the last mile in his civvies just so he could claim his beloved tee shirt and gong. His dilemma was probably at what point to slip into the race. He may as well have gone the whole hog and slotted in just behind Benson Masya. With the advent of the championship chip, this guy would have been unceremoniously dragged off the course, and sent to the nearest Tyburn, never to be seen again.

Excuses can realistically be divided into three categories. The first category covers excuses to prevent you having to run while the second is for excuses in anticipation of a poor showing. The final category covers incidents that may occur during the race which contribute towards a bad run.

In the first category, apart from the usual excuses of aches, pains, pulled muscles, illness and so on, there are some gems of excuses for not having to bother running at all. 'I forgot my running shoes,' or 'I've brought the wrong pair of shoes,' are just about good enough, not to have to run, although it's not unknown for a half marathon to be run in a pair of Stead and Simpson hush puppies.

'I can't run, I've just come off nights,' is a good enough excuse even if you don't work shifts. 'I'm not running, I'm saving myself for London in three weeks,' is widely used. 'I'm not even bothering to run, the handicap I've been given is ridiculous,' has been known to enable faint hearts to pull out, or at worst, just go through the motions or plod around.

Many excuses only surface on the way to the race, courtesy the various modes of transport. One of the better excuses I heard was from a fellow who paid a call in one of those toilets situated in the stairwell of a coach. As the coach had gone around a corner, the guy had been thrown across the toilet and into the wall, then unceremoniously dumped onto the floor. Consequently he had wrenched his neck.

This reminded me of an incident on a local bus when a man stood up for the next stop. He was thrown down the stairs as the bus screeched around a corner. The passenger picked himself up, and as he was alighting said to the driver, 'Who do you think you are, Nigel Mansell?' The driver replied, 'Get lost, dickhead'. As the passenger walked along the pavement, the bus cruised alongside and the argument boiled over, each time the driver addressing the hapless passenger as 'dickhead'.

Another runner twisted his ankle stepping from a coach, and had to withdraw. 'My bus was late,' is another suitable excuse for not making start time, while a better one is 'My bus didn't turn up'. 'I caught the wrong bus' is perhaps scraping the barrel. 'My car broke down on the way to the race,' or 'I had a puncture and had to change the wheel,' are equally impressive.

One runner is reputed to have entered races where he knew that a souvenir tee shirt would be sent ahead with the other race literature. He not only wouldn't have to do the race but he had no need to bother with the training either. While his mates were pounding the highways and byways, he could be tucked up in bed and looking forward to a full English. He would record a 'Did Not Start' in his log book as apposed to a 'Did Not Finish'. He would meet up with his mates in the pub later on for a celebratory drink and an inquest about the race.

However the ultimate excuse for not running is turning up a week early or in the case of two friends, a week late for a short race at Whitby. They changed ready for action and perhaps wondered why there weren't any other runners milling around.

The excuses provided in anticipation of a poor run are equally impressive, and again the ones concerning running shoes rise to the surface. 'I brought the wrong shoes,' 'I forgot my running shoes and had to borrow a pair' or 'I'm breaking some shoes in for a friend' have often been heard.

Certain excuses that prevent some runners from starting can also be used to justify a poor performance such as coming off shift, a puncture or a breakdown. 'I left my number at home and had to go back for it' is usually good for five minutes adding to your finishing time. 'I lost my number and had to register on the day,' is pretty convincing, while apparently dogs tend to chew race numbers with alarming regularity.

'I don't run well on a morning,' 'I don't run well on an afternoon,' 'I don't run well on an evening,' 'All my runs are on an evening,' 'I never run well after my Sunday lunch,' are all quite plausible. 'I don't like flat courses,' 'I don't like hilly courses,' 'I don't like out and back courses,' all carry some credence. My excuse is that I can't run cross-country while others say they can't run on the road.

'I'm using this as a long training run,' is often heard along with, 'I'm just trying to get a friend around, it's his/her first half marathon'. 'I'm only doing it to meet my weekly mileage,' 'It's my fourth race in a week,' 'I'm only running here because I do it every year,' have all been offered as excuses.

I had seven pints, fish and chips and two bread cakes last night, seems like a reasonable excuse whether you actually have or haven't.

Once the race has started, a whole range of excuses present themselves in order to justify a poor run, and once again, the ones involving footwear start flooding back. 'The sole came off one of my shoes,' 'I tied my laces too tight and had to adjust them' are good excuses. On a similar note, 'I got some grit in my shoe that worked its way to the ball of my foot, and I had to stop,' and 'My shoe came off in the mud and I had trouble finding it,' are quite believable.

In big fields, it's possible to become boxed in, to be tripped or to start too far back. In the Great North Run, you sometimes regularly have to pass slow runners and walkers in the early stages. These incidents justify several minutes onto your anticipated finishing time.

'I can't run in the heat,' ' I can't run in the rain' and 'I can't run in the cold' are others. 'I didn't take enough liquids on board,' is another invented by David Coleman. 'I fell over the kerb,' 'I stubbed my toe,' 'The camber was too steep,' 'I tripped over a small metal ring that blew across the road' and 'A bin bag stuck to my face and I fell over'.

'A car pulled out in front of me,' 'I was clipped by a car,' 'A car ran over my toes,' 'I gave two Indians a hand to push their van,' are just about good enough to justify a modest time. Then there are the animal excuses such as being chased or bitten by a dog, becoming entangled in a dog's lead, or being trodden by a horse.

Others that spring to mind are, 'My number blew off into a field and I was chased by a bull,' 'I didn't do my warm up and stretching exercises' and 'I didn't have my usual pork pie before the start'. An excuse that prompted a friend to have treatment from the St Johns Ambulance at the London Marathon was the fact that he had been tripped by a small Chinese lady.

The poor marshals also take a lot of stick for the misfortune of runners. 'The first 100 were sent the wrong way adding 600 yards,' 'He sent me the wrong way and then called me back,' 'They said it was all downhill from here,' 'They said there was only a mile to go,' 'The sixth mile marker was out,' or ' The seventh mile marker was missing'. In an evening race in which I ran, two marshals left their positions, probably to have a kiss and cuddle, before all the runners had gone through. A search party had to be sent for the missing runners, who were recovered the best part of the way to Barnsley. They had probably run fifteen miles in a ten kilometre race.

One incident that happened to me was at the Ripon Midsummer Run when three of us were still getting changed at the car when we heard the starting pistol sound. We set off together, catching up with the rear vehicle after a mile. We eventually started to pass back markers, working our way through the field to respectability. At least in that race, nobody passed me.

Another genuine excuse I used for a poor performance was when a friend and I called for tea and toast on the way to the Bridlington Half Marathon. With the best part of three hours to start time, a full breakfast at £1-90 looked like a good bet. Five miles into the race, I could detect the fat from the fried bread working its way through my system. The coaching manuals always tell you to listen to your body and I certainly did on that day.

My favourite excuse concerns a colleague who had taken a new girlfriend out on several dates. Each time she had worn trousers and looked very smart, but on the most recent date she had worn a skirt revealing chubby legs. My friend was distraught and said he didn't know what to do. He said that he had been unable to concentrate on the race for thinking about his dilemma.

As I grow older and take longer to recover from aches and pains, I find it much more difficult to push myself through the front door. Some of these excuses have come in handy such as dodgy knees, didn't get away from work on time or under the weather all week. I am sure I will use some of the others in the years ahead along with one or two of my own.

Never mind the excuses, keep on running!!

CHAPTER 15

Cape Crusaders

THE FISH HORN sounded out across the early morning darkness signifying a minute to go to race start. The scene was Main Street, Claremont, on the outskirts of Cape Town, the day was Easter Saturday 1995 and John and I were among seventy-five overseas competitors in a seven thousand strong field at the start of the Two Oceans Marathon.

Friends Sharon and Michael had emigrated to South Africa some years previously and I had remained in touch by letter and the occasional phone call. Michael reckoned South African sportsmen were head and shoulders above their counterparts elsewhere and that their athletes were the best in the world. Average club runners and the everyday 'Joe Jogger' could run faster, further and for longer than we Brits.

Their flagship race, the Comrades Marathon is run in Natal over a ninety kilometre course and attracts a five figure entry, while the closest we can offer is the London to Brighton which may have a couple of hundred competitors. A close second to the Comrades is the Two Oceans Marathon in Cape Town, which at only fifty-six kilometres is used by many as a long training run for the Comrades. Colin, a runner with nearby Kippax Harriers lent me a video of the race in which his brother had competed several times. From that point, the race quickly moved to the top of my events wish list.

When the idea was discussed, there were several people chomping at the bit, but when it came to the crunch, only John and I were sufficiently interested to go ahead and book. The Two Oceans was termed as an ultra race, being longer than the standard marathon distance. I put in the hard miles in preparation for the big day priding myself on how long I could keep going. I sometimes felt as if I could plod around all day long. Apparently a strict six hour time limit would be adhered to, with those still out on the course treated as non-finishers.

Penthouse Travel based in Cape Town arranged accommodation, race entry and all the little extras that made the holiday run smoothly. The fare with South African Airways was slashed by almost half to £510, by courtesy of the fact we were running in the event. Since then however, fares have come down in leaps and bounds with more airlines participating.

We travelled to Heathrow on a National Coach and after numerous hold-ups on the motorway, talked ourselves into Harry Ramsden's fish and chip tea, and couldn't wait to tuck in. Unfortunately, the restaurant in the terminal couldn't match the original one at Guisley, with the portions nowhere near as generous.

We arrived in Cape Town before lunch on Thursday and were ferried by mini coach to Breakwater Lodge, our home for six nights. The Lodge was situated on the fringe of the Alfred and Victoria Waterfront, a renovated dockland area. Old and new buildings sat side by side with restaurants, shops and hotels. There were craft shops, wine merchants, a cinema, a museum and plenty of bars.

The view from our bedroom window at Breakwater Lodge looked out across a large building site and through a giant dust cloud. Beyond the city stood Table Mountain, its top shrouded in mist, flanked on either side by Devil's Peak and Lion's Head. I gazed longingly before I realised that Table Mountain reminded me of my own career path, climbing nicely before levelling to a plateau, and then plummeting back down sharply.

On our first walkabout, a woman appeared from a shed made from pallets and pieces of wood, stacked against a wall, and asked us for money. While obviously feeling sorry at her plight, her aggressive attitude didn't endear her towards me. She grabbed my arm and said I must go to a bank and draw out money for her. We eventually managed to get away remembering to return by a different route.

Asking directions to the Villager Rugby Club where we would register for the race, Danny, a parking lot attendant, went one better with the generous offer of a lift. He even went home for his wife, while we were registering and then ran us back into town, reluctantly taking the money we offered. The registration comprised a series of marquees against the beautiful mountain backdrop. As overseas runners, the officials made us extremely welcome presenting us with kitbag, peaked cap, headband and a sponge which remained ours for the duration of the race. There were also a couple of tee shirts included but they threw in an extra one which seemed like a nice gesture.

The day before the race, Good Friday, was a holiday in Cape Town and the city was extremely quiet. We had booked a city tour but when the coach arrived to pick us up, there was only one other passenger onboard. Imagine our surprise when we found him to be a Leeds University lecturer, in Cape Town for a seminar. When he found I would be running for Alzheimer's Disease, he promptly donated a couple of quid.

As we were the only people on board, the driver who doubled as guide, suggested he take us where we wanted to go. Our first choice, Table

Mountain was a non-starter as a blanket of cloud still covered the top. We did go to the lower cable station and to Signal Hill where we enjoyed magnificent views over the 'Mother City' and harbour. In the distance was Robben Island, home for several years to Nelson Mandela while he was in captivity.

The tour took in the Castle of Good Hope, the Parliament Buildings and the brightly painted houses and minarets of the Malay District. After a tour around the harbour by small boat, we ended up sitting outside a restaurant on Victoria and Alfred Waterfront eating deepwater hake and chips.

We were up at 3.30 a.m. on race morning, eating rolls and drinking coffee and fruit juice. The coach transported us through dark and empty suburbs to Claremont, where Penthouse Travel provided a splendid marquee adjacent to the finish. We were able to change and leave our clothing here to be collected, hopefully within the six hour time limit.

The start area was floodlit and announcements were being made both in English and in Afrikaans. I was really up for this race and couldn't wait to get going. Two weeks ago I had run the London Marathon, finishing pretty comfortably and reckoned I had a further nine miles left in the tank. Some of my long training runs had been completed on an evening, courtesy of a work colleague who would drop me off in the middle of nowhere, from where I had to run home. I was regularly used to being on my feet for over three hours and had plenty of miles in the bank.

At last we were called forward to assemble, a man on a podium blew the fish horn signalling a minute to go, apparently a race tradition and at last we were underway. Progress was slow in the early morning gloom, with my main concerns being to move forward and to remain on my feet. It was strange seeing the reflections as hundreds of runners passed in front of shop windows. The suburbs soon changed to residential flatlands and as daybreak came, the mountains of the Cape Peninsula rose in front of us like statues.

The programme notes had profiled the course and commented on the smell of fresh bread steaming from Lakeside Bakery. I looked forward to this and wasn't to be disappointed. Eleven kilometres gone and steady away, exactly my kind of running. I was comfortable and easy and felt as if I could run at this pace all day. However my mind kept wandering as to how John was feeling and faring.

False Bay was reached and with it the Indian Ocean. We ran through the picturesque fishing hamlets of St James and Clovelly with pockets of spectators emerging as the day became lighter. Bands and musicians gave the race a feel of a Great North Run or London Marathon but in far more spectacular surroundings. A passenger train on an adjacent track appeared to slow with passengers shouting words of encouragement through open windows.

At Fish Hoek, until recently a dry town, the road turned inland towards Louws corner. The commentator here gave everyone a tremendous boost by announcing the names of many runners as they passed below his rostrum. The drinks stations were well stocked with sachets of energy drink, water and coke along with chocolate bars and fruit. I grabbed an energy drink, but had to open it with my teeth and squeeze, just like the ice pops in my younger days.

A short off road section to Nordhoek brought us to the Atlantic side of the Cape Peninsular. Horses were being taken for an early morning gallop on the beach with the saltwater apparently doing their hooves the world of good.

It was here the serious climbing began, first up Little Chapman's and then the longer and steeper Chapman's Peak Drive. As I looked around, I could see a mass of unfamiliar running vests which seemed to be dominated by the green and white hoops of the organising club, Celtic Harriers. Some runners wore green numbers to indicate they had completed ten Two Oceans, while others had identifying marks to indicate a local runner or a master. The fact that I sported my name, club name and country along with a small union flag on both the front and back of my vest paid dividends as I began to receive support from runners and spectators alike.

Chapman's Peak Drive is a panoramic coastal road which hangs onto the cliff face like a thread. Constructed by Italian prisoners during the First World War, it was considered a significant breakthrough in civil engineering at the time. With the sea hundreds of feet below to the left and a sheer cliff face to the right, Chapman's would break your heart if you let it. Just as you believe the worst is over, you turn a corner only to be met with a further difficult incline. Part of the way up, a model Ostrich stands at the roadside while at the top, a sign says tongue in cheek 'New Legs for Sale'. At this stage I seriously considered investing in a pair.

A welcome downhill from Chapman's provided some relief but a difficult camber impeded my steady rhythm, and instead of relaxing, I found myself working harder by concentrating and watching my footing. Hoult Bay provides a rousing welcome from the locals and in particular, the mermaid sunning herself on the sea wall, apparently another race tradition.

The weather alternated between brilliant sunshine and showers, but with 34K completed in three hours, I began to project my finishing time, reassuring myself I would comfortably get around before the six hour cut-off point.

Hoult Bay is a working port manufacturing fish meal and fish oil and is a major source of the South African delicacy, smoked snoek. It is also a haven for seals and many birds such as gulls and cormorants. The route leaves the Ocean for the last time passing the 'Twelve Apostles', a continuation of Table Mountain.

The marathon check point was reached in 3 hours and 48 minutes, and I was directed into a funnel where a tag was removed from my number. I made use of the many drinks stations on the course and wiped my forehead with the sponge that I had fastened to my shorts by way of safety pins and elastic.

The second difficult climb is Constantia Nek and begins before you realise depending upon what shape you are in. It was now that I really began to appreciate those long runs home as I was able to effectively apply myself. The road to Constantia Nek twists and turns up the hillside with many runners resorting to a walk. With runners spread out across the narrow road, it seemed inevitable that I would become boxed in and need to walk at some stage. Having seen the race video and realising this hill could break me, I had run the steepest hill near home, Fanny Pit Lane, over and over again, usually towards the end of long training runs. This put me in good contention on the day, and even though I slowed to a plod at times, I made it over the summit.

We were greeted by TV cameras, another announcer and hundreds of yelling spectators. The popular cry seemed to be all downhill from here, but there was still a fair amount of work to do before being afforded that luxury. The road through Constantia undulated through magnificent forests and sloping vineyards. Every drinks station was now an oasis as the mid-morning temperatures soared. Many of the volunteers wore fancy dress and each drinks station had a theme which was published in the race programme, with an award for best dressed table. One young girl who handed out a drink must have taken a shine to me, running alongside for a few hundred yards. We exchanged life stories, before she wished me luck and sent me on my way. The residents of Constantia sat out on the verges and lawns of their magnificent white gabled Cape Dutch Homes.

At last the course began its final descent past the world renowned Kirstenbosch Gardens and to the finish at Villager Rugby Ground. The last few hundred yards were on grass and I had finished arguably the most beautiful race in the world in 5 hours and 14 minutes, well inside the allotted six hour limit.

The Penthouse Travel marquee at the finishing line provided a place in which to change back into warm clothes. Refreshments, in particular the 'Hot Dogs' made from the delicious Boerewars Sausage were on offer along with tins of beer provided by race sponsor, Ohlssons.

I returned to the finish hoping to see John, but a combination of injuries and cramp prevented him from making the cut-off time. The way in which the cut-off time is implemented seems a little cruel and insensitive. As the clock slowly edges around to the six hour mark, a gun is fired and a rope pulled across the finishing line. Runners in the finishing straight are directed by the stewards, down either side of the chutes and runners still out on the course are advised not to continue.

One runner made a desperate bid to beat the clock, but on stumbling he just missed out. Dozens more made the home straight but suffered heartbreak as the clock eased past the six hour mark. To all intents and purposes, the race was over after six hours, marshalling and support for runners still out on the course was withdrawn, and spectators began to drift away. There was talk of the cut-off time being increased to seven hours to encourage runners into having a go. I understand this was put into place for the Millennium edition of the event, and a half marathon option was also added. My placing inside the first 3,000 of a 7,500 strong field represented an excellent morning's work.

We put the days after the race to good use, eating and drinking wisely but well, with a fair amount of sightseeing thrown in for good measure. The meals were excellent, cheap and of exaggerated portions so consequently our money stretched a long way. The bill for half a dozen telephone calls home amounted to more than the money we had spent on food.

When the blanket of mist finally cleared Table Mountain, we took the cable car to the summit. There was no glass in the windows presumably so the strong winds could whistle through. Being of a slightly nervous disposition, I stood bang in the middle of the gondola and let others scramble for the places looking over the sides.

A train ride to Newlands Cricket Ground where Sir Cliff Richard would be appearing was followed by an arduous walk back to the city calling in a couple of neighbourhood bars. The Wine Route tour was largely disappointing with the driver picking up late and calling at only two wine estates rather than the advertised three. Our free time in Stellenbosch was also reduced, the wine samples were pretty feeble, and anyone contemplating returning legless was sadly out of luck.

The tour of Cape Peninsular was far more enjoyable. Travelling across the Cape Flats, the route followed parts of the course we had pounded only days earlier, but today far more comfortably. After a brief stop in Simonstown, home to the British Naval Fleet, we followed dramatic coastal scenery to Cape Point. A combination of steep steps and the Flying Dutchman shuttle bus brought us to a viewing point where the cold waters of the Atlantic meet with the warmer current of the Indian Ocean.

At The Cape of Good Hope, the most South Westerly point on the African continent, I was about to have my photograph taken next to the sign marking the spot. All of a sudden, a coach pulled up and I was engulfed by hoards of Japanese tourists. The photo shows a dozen or so Japs with me perched on the end. The tour returned via an Ostrich farm and the notorious but spectacular Chapman's Peak Drive, much easier this time around in the coach.

All in all, a thoroughly enjoyable holiday was had. All my years of running seemed to peak for the big day and I produced the run of my life. I had the opportunity to meet old friend Michael and his young family and would love to return for a longer spell. The scenic Garden Route to the east of Cape Town has captured my imagination and I would quite like to travel along the coast towards Durban.

Somewhere in my heart of hearts, the Comrades Marathon beckons, and with that under my belt, I could retire to the winding roads in the sky as a happy man. However with dodgy knees and advancing years, it seems a long way away at the moment.

CHAPTER 16

Men Behaving Badly

'YOU GET YOURSELF OFF and have a good time,' was the response from his wife when he asked about getting his card stamped for a long weekend away, running. If he'd asked for a weekend away with the lads, there would have been no chance, and she would have found him jobs to divert his mind away from such thoughts. A weekend away with the lads may see him get too drunk, show himself up, fall over or at worst, end up in jail. No chance of any of these things happening on a running trip, or is there?

Travelling to Italy for the Florence Marathon, we ran into trouble before we even left the country. John, Kevin, non-running friend Steve and myself were heading to Gatwick by car for an early morning flight to Pisa, before going on by train to Florence. When I go on holiday, part of the enjoyment for me is eating out and generally eating more than I normally would do back home. On the journey down, we talked endlessly about a Garfunkels breakfast, and after parking the car and checking in, we were ready for a full English.

The service was a little on the slow side and we would be cutting it fine. We were delayed at passport control but heard no final call for our flight. We reached the departure gate with only a couple of minutes to spare.

A British Airways official asked where we had been, and we told him that we had been held up in traffic. Unfortunately for us, he had all the answers saying that we checked in over an hour ago. We were unaware that a bus would take us out to the plane, believing that we would just walk on board at the stand. We were rushed onto a coach and whisked across the tarmac with the words of the official ringing in our ears.

He told us that we were inconsiderate and had caused 170 fellow passengers to be delayed, due to the plane losing its take-off slot. He demanded to know where we had been, what we had been doing and why we were late. 'Who do you think you are?' he blasted. It was like being back at school again and I was made to feel like the lowest of the low. A fifth man who boarded the plane with us must have also been late but he kept quiet. While we received a rocket, he got away totally unscathed. I anticipated boarding the plane to a chorus of jeers and some aggravation so I kept my head down. Remarkably, everyone seemed upbeat and the cabin crew and fellow passengers were pleasant. Fortunately we got away with no undue delay, and there were no recriminations.

In Florence we soon ran into further trouble. The accommodation was pretty basic, and we had to ring to be let in late at night by the proprietor. The night life in Florence was pretty low-key and on this particular night, we returned around midnight. Someone tripped and we all laughed. A door opened and I sensed a pair of eyes glaring at me through the darkness. The following morning, an American lady came into the breakfast room, and strode purposefully towards our table.

'Don't you ever, ever, ever, ever, get back to the hotel at that time again,' she said. We told her that it was only midnight and that we hadn't made much noise. She then replied, 'Who do you think you are?' the second person to ask us this within a matter of days. She was none too impressed and with a shake of the head grunted, 'Typical of the British'.

On my previous trip to Italy with a local football team, we ran into deep trouble and in my opinion, some of the people involved were lucky to come away unscathed. The troubles started when the coach arrived at The White Swan at Rawdon, rather than The White Swan at Rothwell. The landlord had opened up early so we could have a drink, but the delay meant that by the time the coach arrived, some of the early arrivals were tanked up.

Some of these people took cans onto the coach and topped themselves up at Birmingham Airport. The coach transported us from Venice to the hotel in Lido de Jesolo, where two idiots stripped off down to their underpants, leaving their clothes strewn across the lobby. They dived into the pool returning to the lobby dripping wet. The hotel management were none too impressed, and that immediately got us off on the wrong footing.

Following a meal and more drinks, we split into smaller groups towards the end of the night. On returning to the hotel, two of our party were involved in an argument outside. I tried to break it up, but in doing so, a resident several floors up opened a window and shouted, 'What the hell at this time of night? Hey! you in the red shirt.' That was me.

In the early hours of the morning, I awoke to someone ferociously shaking me. It was roommate Howard who was trying to tell me the police wanted to see us in the lobby. I told him not to be so stupid and to get back to bed. I had hardly drowsed, when the next thing I knew, I was being jabbed in the side by what I realised later had been the butt of a rifle. Two police officers were in the room and were directing me to get dressed. I made them wait until I washed and then I went to the wardrobe for a shirt. 'No, you put on red shirt,' said one of the officers, noticing it draped over the back of a chair. Immediately my mind raced back to the man shouting from the window. I had done nothing wrong but he had obviously reported me.

When I arrived in the lobby, all our party were standing in a long line opposite police officers and members of staff. I was immediately made to stand alongside the police with no questions asked. The scene was typical of picking a football team from a line of boys, recapping my school days. I had no idea what was going on but found it rather entertaining.

Eventually, they pulled out another lad, Martin, who seemed to be put under pressure to name names. Two others were pulled out and along with our group organiser and an interpreter, we were all bundled into a couple of police cars. At last I was able to ask somebody what was going on. 'Three people pinched a truck for a ride back to the hotel,' was the reply.

The police station was a high classical building unlike the typical British cop shop. There was much discussion and poor Martin was being persuaded into pointing out faces from a pile of passports assembled on the counter. I never did like leaving my passport at the hotel reception desk and have flatly refused to do so ever since this incident. Eventually it was sorted out with one of the culprits being, of all people, the party organiser, Mick. No charges were pressed so we were kicked out onto the dark streets and left to find our own way back to the hotel. At no time did I get involved in the discussion and no questions were asked of me. The interpreter who doubled as a local bar owner apologised for my trouble.

Apparently while on their way back to the hotel, the gang of three had gone alongside the truck to pay a call of nature. One of them held the door handle, the door came open, and the keys were in the ignition. 'Let's have a ride back to the hotel,' was the cry. The truck in question was pointed out to me later in the week and was one of those council types with a corrugated hut and tools on the back. Two had jumped into the cab and the other one climbed onto the back. To anyone observing from the many pavement cafés or walking along the street, it must have looked like The Lord Mayor's Show. Martin had seen them, waved, and apparently become involved.

The following day, we were all required to sign a charter promising to behave for the duration of the holiday. A police officer was assigned to us each day and accompanied most of the lads onto the beach, into the bars or wherever they cared to venture. By the end of the week, he had been nicknamed 'The Keystone' and had become best of chums with some of the group, who had photographs taken with him on their shoulders.

Several of us looking for a quiet life, hired a car for a couple of days and travelled into Austria. I believe the perpetrators had a very lucky escape. Undeterred by all of this, two people still saw fit to remove a menu board from outside a restaurant and place it in our hotel garden.

Dublin 1994 was memorable but for all the wrong reasons. Our flight had been delayed, the rain bucketed down relentlessly so spirits were low. On Sunday morning, we set out for the start of the Breakfast Run but ended up having to ask directions. Only later did we realise there was a map of the course printed on the tee shirts we had been wearing.

Throughout the weekend, one non-runner who was along just to sample the local Guinness tried to set a record for the amount of people he could upset. The way he brusquely boasted about his no-holds-barred approach to life, reminded me of the Harry Enfield character, 'Alf Whitebread'. 'I say what I mean and I mean what I bloody well say.' By the end of the weekend, people were giving him a very wide berth indeed.

After the race, one girl with a ghetto blaster the size of a rabbit hutch organised a party in her room after the bars had closed. This lasted all of two minutes before being broken up by the hotel management.

As always however, we saved the best until last. At about seven o'clock on Tuesday morning, I had a telephone call from a friend a few rooms along the corridor. He said that his room was flooded and wanted me to take a look. I started to tread water immediately I entered the room with the carpet resembling a sponge. Towels had been laid all over in a frantic attempt to soak up as much water as possible. My friend was talking to a plumber-cum-handyman who said there were no problems with the plumbing. My friend assured him that no taps had been left on and that the water hadn't come from the bath, the sink or the radiator. Throughout all of this, his roommate lay on the bed, oblivious to anything that had been going on.

Later in the day before we checked out, the two of them were summoned along to the office to account for their plight and asked me to go along to lend moral support. The Assistant Manager said all the pipe work was functional and that the water must be down to my two friends. Not only was the carpet in their room spongy, but water had found its way into the rooms on either side. They threatened to bill us with one night's lost revenue for three rooms which amounted to £144. I was of the opinion that somebody had discharged a fire extinguisher under the door, so I sprang to the defence of my friends. I suspected one person in particular who had liberally thrown water about on a previous trip but the Assistant Manager assured us no extinguishers had been tampered with.

They failed to press home the charges but I suggested we tell our group that we had been obliged to pay. I anticipated this would prompt a whip-round to cover the costs at which point I would throw a wobbly and refuse to pay. I then expected the culprit would own up, but for some reason we never put this brilliant plan into action.

As we sat in the hotel lounge awaiting the taxis to take us to the airport, we watched in amazement as dowser after dowser of water was wheeled past us, no doubt from the offending three rooms.

This would be organiser Trevor's swansong, or at least as far as we were concerned. First we were threatened with being cast adrift in an open boat, following a sing song on the ferry home from Gothenburg. Then he had to account for a broken bedroom door in Berlin and now this. He justifiably must have had a bellyful.

Imagine my amazement when one of these two guys recalled the incident in the bar following a recent training night. His account was exactly how I remember it with the exception of one notable addition. 'When I went into the bathroom, the tap was running,' he said.

These incidents apart, we suffered someone throwing water into a lift as the doors opened to let out the passengers. The same guy carried a small statue of a kilted Scotsman from the hotel reception and placed it alongside me in bed.

Another member of our group slowly poured lager over a Scotsman's boot after accidentally having drink spilled over him. In Berlin, another person worse for wear tried to force everyone to systematically eat the leaves from a plant. A woman onlooker accused him of being a bully.

On the running front, the 'Men Behaving Badly' are a group of runners known as 'The Peelers' simply because they peel off just before the end of the race. They don't do this by accident and the incidents are by no means exceptions. They don't enter the race, don't pay a fee, don't have a number and don't finish. But what they do do is run on a accurately measured course, using the race conditions as a glorified time trial. They are happy to let others pay a fee while they use the marked course, the time of the marshals and more than likely, use the drink stations.

If every runner decided to take this attitude, no revenues would be forthcoming and the races would fold. What would happen if marshals who give their time free of charge didn't turn up or if they left their designated positions? What would happen if there were no marker posts?

This practice is becoming more abused but rest assured, the culprits are well-known, they will not be tolerated and they are slowly but surely being weeded out of our great sport. They are not wanted or needed. If spotted, they should be pulled from the race, their running shoes confiscated, and then taken through the highest criminal courts in the land.

When challenged, these tightwads come up with the excuses, 'Well, I didn't want a souvenir or a time, I've drawers full of tee shirts at home.' Well the simple answer is don't give them a souvenir although I've even known some of these people to scrounge one. Kick them out of the races and ban them throughout the region. These people won't be missed.

Another variety of 'The Peelers', not quite as bad but almost as irritating are those who have legitimately entered the race but are suffering or having a bad time. They find themselves struggling and being overtaken by runners they would normally expect to beat. Rather than suffer the indignity of seeing those people's names ahead of theirs in the official results, they decide to peel off in the last couple of hundred yards and don't pass through the checkout. To their way of thinking, a DNF (Did not finish) is far better than being beaten by a few slowcoaches. What on earth are they thinking about, if they can get to within two hundred yards of the finish, then ninety-nine times out of a hundred, they will finish. If found out, these people should be placed last in the results list, with their names in bold print.

They may have to swallow their pride but surely a modest time and placing are better than a DNF any day. I won't apologise for my strong views on the subject. Former Marathon World Record holder, Steve Jones finished last in the European Championship in Stuttgart after holding a big lead for much of the race. He didn't throw in the towel despite not feeling well and with the odds being stacked against him. He battled on to finish receiving probably the biggest cheer of the day. What was good for Steve on that day, should be a shining example to runners of all abilities. There is no shame in finishing in a modest time or a lowly position.

Another issue on which I hold strong views is the liberal tendering and exchange of numbers, particularly for the London Marathon. Despite being extremely difficult, nigh on impossible, for the 'Middle of the Packer' to secure a place for the premier event in the country, I disagree with running in someone else's name. I ran in a borrowed number at a low-key event some years ago but felt guilty doing so and certainly won't do it in future. Likewise I have let my number go to somebody else when I couldn't attend a race, but again, only once. I recently appeared in a set of results where I hadn't even run. Whether this was a mistake on the part of the organisers, I wouldn't like to say. A more likely explanation would be that somebody knew I wouldn't be running, didn't have a number themselves and used my name to get a start. What did actually happen, I will probably never know.

The incident that changed my way of thinking on the issue occurred in the early eighties at the Leeds Marathon. Two runners came down from Scotland for the event and inadvertently used each other's numbers. They had probably received both entries in the same envelope. One of the runners tragically collapsed and died on Pottery Hill at Woodlesford. Consequently, the police notified the family of the wrong man. Imagine that happening and putting a family through the trauma, then having to contact the correct man's family with the same devastating news. Ever since then I have been reluctant to pass on my number and would advise others not to do so.

The other practice I do not condone is the sending off of multiple entries for the London Marathon, in order to guarantee a place. People tend to apply still using their own name but use addresses of workmates or relatives.

However the London Marathon must share some of the responsibility for forcing people's hands, and to some extent have brought it upon themselves. I for instance applied for five years before being accepted and this was only by accumulating my rejection slips and appealing. I then was accepted again in 1990, the very next year. I know people who get in year after year, while there are people who have run in every race. So what is the secret formula for successful applications? Nobody seems to know. I have no issue with a southern weighting of places as I would expect a northern weighting, were the Leeds Marathon to be oversubscribed.

I am also uneasy with the provision of places being held over to the following year for those of us who are unable to run, illness and injury excepted. When the letters of acceptance drop onto the doormats in December, it takes a great deal of time, effort, sacrifice and self-discipline to arrive at Blackheath Common or Greenwich in April.

I've even known people send in double entries, be accepted under one application and rejected under the other, but enter the rejection slip into the draw for an allotted club place. This is why I believe a series of qualifying races should be completed to gain entry into the London Marathon, and reward the runners who regularly subscribe to races up and down the country. This should also have the additional impact of bolstering the fields at some of the regional races.

The race has gone charity-mad in recent years with large numbers of places being allocated to the mainstream charities. I have run for charities on numerous occasions but have tended to support local hospices, church appeals or hospital units rather than the national charities. Unless you have the necessary contacts, it is extremely difficult to raise the £1,000 which is usually the minimum amount these charities demand, in return for a guaranteed place.

A friend accepted one of these places and ended up running raffles and holding a barbecue to try make up the shortfall. Trying to raise £1,000 through friends and workmates is virtually impossible unless you can secure a couple of larger donations. I have raised this amount only once, when my firm pledged a further pound for every pound I had raised.

A further problem with running under another person's name at London is trying to imagine the catch-you-out questions you will be asked at the registration. One runner was sent packing when he couldn't remember his own telephone number. I once played with fire when as a joke, I deliberately gave the official the wrong answer to a question. On seeing the look on his poker face, I quickly changed my answer.

Another person I came across ran in his previous year's number, but used a John Bull printing outfit to reproduce the removable tag. My message to all applicants is be patient and await your opportunity. After a flurry of rejections, I have now run London six times from something like eighteen applications. I have probably enjoyed the races all the better for the wait and have had the satisfaction of seeing my name both in the programme and the official results.

Why not run in one of the excellent regional marathons or run a big city race abroad? They will welcome you with open arms.

CHAPTER 17

European Union

'THE BENIDORM BASH' in 1991 as it had been dubbed, was much talked about with everyone eagerly looking forward in anticipation. The stark reality was that I felt I needed a week's holiday when I returned home. Previous trips had tended to be over long weekends but this time we would be going for a full week's holiday in November to sunny Spain. There was a good mixture within the group; older couples, younger couples, single people, and a lot of people who liked a drink.

We arrived on Saturday, resplendent in our multi-coloured sweatshirts, courtesy Anne and Dave, which would see sterling service over the coming week. The races would be held on Sunday and we would return home the following Saturday. When we sent off the race application forms, I corresponded directly with the race headquarters in Benidorm and paid £5. Others gained entry through a sports travel company who had imposed a further handling fee of £15, and this didn't go down particularly well. Even then, people still felt aggrieved some months later and after collecting race numbers they went in search of the proprietor of the sports travel company. Apparently they knew where he was staying and gave me the impression they were about to tar and feather him.

Benidorm came to prominence in the early sixties as one of Spain's most popular resorts. Since then, hotels and apartment blocks had sprung up to flank the magnificent beaches, and Benidorm became the entertainment capital of the whole coast. The town is cosmopolitan, with restaurants to suit a wide range of nationalities and tastes. The night life is varied with many bars, nightclubs and discotheques. The Old Town is situated on a spur of land between the two beaches and the greatest concentration of shops are to be found here.

The race list comprised many Brits, and my club, Ackworth, had five going in the marathon and many more in the half. The marathon would start at nine o'clock with the half at midday when the heat would be intolerable.

We had a quiet Saturday night consisting of an evening meal, a couple of San Miguels and a spot of karaoke. The night ended with a coffee back at the hotel where we had to keep lifting one of the non-runners back onto a bar stool. The humanitarian thing would have been to take him to his room and put him to bed, but he was providing great entertainment value where he was.

After an early breakfast, we were transported to an Athletics stadium close to the railway station, where we would change and leave our kit. The morning was cold, with a chill blowing from the snow-capped mountains. The race started with three laps of the track before we ran out onto the road and a favourable downhill brought us into the old town. The course consisted two out and back laps taking in both the Levante and Pontiente beaches, the Old Town and orange groves on the outskirts of town. There was a testing pull at the end of each lap followed by a steep descent back down to the beach.

The promenade was deserted on the first circuit with the only people about, being holiday makers out for a stroll and half marathoners cheering on their club mates before the start of their own race. I ran most of the first loop with John until he had to pay a call in an orange grove. As I ran along the promenade, my left hand side which faced the mountains was freezing while my right hand side facing out to sea was warmed by the sun. This happened in reverse on the way back, a peculiar feeling.

As we entered the old town, a labyrinth of narrow streets, a man rang a bell to warn pedestrians that runners were approaching. Stallholders came out and shoppers turned around to applaud us, a nice touch, and one I looked forward to on the second circuit. A couple of elderly British holidaymakers gave me encouragement, no doubt noticing the club name on my vest. I responded with the tried and trusted line, 'I only came out for a paper'.

The temperatures soared particularly towards the end of the second lap when I began to suffer. There were far more people about on the streets and promenade, but some got in the way of runners. They were obviously oblivious to what was going on around them or not particularly bothered. Encouraged by our trusty band of supporters, and runners heading in the opposite direction, I made it to the finish. I was even able to pick up the pace when I saw the finish gantry and I recorded a very satisfactory 3 hours 31 minutes.

The five of us who had gone the full distance were able to watch the half marathoners pass both at five miles and at the finish. My heart went out to them running at midday in such stifling temperatures. There were many strugglers including some from Ackworth, who perhaps had too many San Miguels the previous evening. The representative from the sports travel company finished to a crescendo of booing and jeering which I thought was perhaps taking things a little too far.

The prize money on offer was particularly attractive. I finished just ahead of the fifth placed lady who received the equivalent of £200 in pesetas, which covered most of her holiday.

Paul, a born leader of men, had said on the Sunday night after the races, he would make sure we each drank a case of San Miguel. 'How many in a case?' I asked. 'I don't know, twelve, maybe eighteen,' he replied. This pretty much set the tone for the rest of the week apart from the occasional cultural interlude.

At night we toured pretty much the same bars and clubs, The Talk of the Town, Lennons, Steptoe's and The Hippodrome. The same acts were on each night, sometimes at several venues. There was Johnny Hackett of 'Comedians' fame, magician Howard Burnett and Roy 'Slither' Jay dressed in a convict's uniform complete with arrows. Then there was the redoubtable Sticky Vicky Leighton whose party piece was to pass a bottle around the audience. When nobody could open it, she would do so in a rather unconventional manner. One of our gang was infatuated with her, and followed her around the different venues.

Another comedian, Mike Curtis, got his laughs exclusively at the expense of an unsuspecting audience. If anybody had the impudence to answer him back, he made mincemeat of them. Anyone who passed in front of the stage to visit the bar or toilet were food and drink for Curtis who immediately cut them down to size. People sat there with legs crossed, prolonging the toilet until there was a lull in the proceedings or until the next act came on. When Curtis finally took his bow, there was a mad stampede to the back.

During the daytime while not in bars we explored the surrounding area, and particularly impressive was the impenetrable fortress of Guadalest, perched high on a solid rock. Guadalest was never conquered and even survived an earthquake in 1644.

Another day, we caught the train to neighbouring town Altea, taking in the waterfront market and climbing the 257 steps to the old village. Here people congregated in and around the church square and outside the bars and restaurants. The old village boasts an artists' quarter and a number of art galleries, and also provides excellent views of the surrounding countryside and coastline.

A handicap race was organised for Wednesday afternoon but no one seemed particularly up for it. We would run on a track to the rear of the hotel, with the strong wind really blowing the dust and litter around. Injured club runner Terry would stand a mile and a quarter or so along the track signifying the turnaround point. We were each given an anticipated finishing time which we had to try and beat. For many of the group, it was just a matter of going through the motions and I treated it that way going out. Turning in about seventh place, I couldn't recollect running as fast or fluently before, and I certainly haven't since. I finished third, beating my handicap by a good two minutes. I even had the confidence to draw level with one runner for a while and keep surging to make him hurt. If I could have run like that week in, week out, I'd have never run a bad race again.

It was all so easy but I came down to earth with a bump on the Sunday after we returned home. I figured if I could run twenty-six miles, then a four to five mile cross-country race would be small potatoes by comparison for a man of my calibre. How wrong I could be. I caught a real dose of 'The Benidorm Blues' as a procession of runners came by me. It was as if a bus had pulled up behind, and everyone getting off was passing me. To this day, I still look back upon the experience as putting me off cross-country for good. My legs felt like jelly and my lungs like asbestos.

The first club trip overseas took place in October 1988 to the Paris 20 Kilometre race. We travelled overnight down to Dover, and once onboard the ferry, there was a stampede to the restaurant for breakfast. The crossing took slightly over an hour so there was little time to spare, but some of these people could have eaten for England. We travelled across France arriving in Paris late on Friday afternoon. At that time I wasn't a club member and was only along as an invited guest to make up the numbers. My first impressions were that they were a serious bunch as most of them embarked upon a training run in the local park as soon as we arrived.

We stayed in student accommodation in La Defense business area, close to La Grande Arche, a huge rectangular office block. The accommodation was on the outskirts of the city and in the evening the area was dead.

On Saturday we had an informative tour taking in the main attractions such as Notre Dame and The Eiffel Tower. We took stops at strategic places, but large queues prevented us from going up the tower. The steep cobbled streets of Montmartre were intriguing. The area was formerly home to writers and artists and was said to be the birthplace of modern art. Students had erected easels with a view to painting tourists if they cared to sit still for any length of time.

The Basilica of Sacré Coeur is prominent on the Paris skyline and can be reached by the funicular railway or by climbing 250 steps. Close to Sacré Coeur are the neon-lit windmill sails of the Moulin Rouge Theatre. The dimly lit streets around this red-light area are where Edith Piaf is said to have risen to fame.

Sunday seemed to be totally tied up with the race. We left the accommodation for an early afternoon start, but a huge field demanded we line up below the Eiffel Tower in plenty of time. Eventually the barriers were withdrawn and the runners spilled across the Pont D'Iena from where the race would start.

I lined up with Roy and Mick, both veterans but pretty nippy, but with thousands of runners in front, they would have to be patient today. Some of our faster runners had tried to muscle their way further forward but when the gun sounded, it took four minutes before we even moved.

The race was a shambles with no clearly defined route. There were no barriers as I would have expected for such a big race and cars were parked on the course. Runners tried to steal a march by cutting across gardens and roundabouts, while some weaved their way through the tables and chairs of sidewalk cafes. One runner ahead of me helped himself to a croissant from the plate of an unsuspecting punter.

The course passed close to the Arc de Triomphe and used some of the wide boulevards before heading towards the parkland and forest of the Bois de Boulogne. Here the trees seemed to come alive as dozens of runners appeared to join the already bulging race. There was a circuit around the complex of famous racecourse Longchamps before heading back towards the city.

Despite being delayed at the start and at places around the course, I had done well to finish in 97 minutes, particularly as I had stopped from time to time to take photographs. Although I have no doubt the race organisation will have improved, I wouldn't particularly recommend this event. We had to arrive unreasonably early, the start was slow and the course wasn't clearly defined. Marshals were non-existent, cheats were allowed to join in and the checkout funnels were hopelessly slow. Despite all of these setbacks, I enjoyed the experience once the field spread. The gods blessed us with glorious sunshine, and I had the opportunity to notch up another overseas race.

An early morning departure was required enabling us to catch the ferry at Calais, and we arrived in Pontefract shortly before midnight on Monday.

Many of the same faces returned in 1992 on a long weekend, this time taking in the Paris to Versailles race. Even though the travel arrangements were similar and we didn't arrive in Paris until early Friday evening, we appeared to be much better organised this time around fitting far more into the weekend.

On Saturday morning, room mate John had itchy feet and wanted a training run. Even though we were located pretty centrally, we had no real idea where we were heading until suddenly we rounded a corner and the Arc de Triomphe towered above us. From here we had a superb run down the Champs des Elysées with only the water carts and street cleaners for company. Telling John the River Seine was straight ahead when it was actually to the right, we pressed on regardless. After eventually stumbling across the river and running over a couple of bridges, we had to eat humble pie and ask directions back to the hotel. We were late for the itinary and had to catch up with the main party later on. This will teach us in future to go on the official training run. We were probably out longer than we were the next day in the race. I certainly enjoyed it better.

Having to ask directions back to the hotel reminded me of when I attended a meeting at Cardiff. As always, I took my kit and decided to go for a run from the hotel which was prominently situated on a roundabout. I figured four left turns would bring me back to where I had started. About ten turns later and with no hotel to be seen, the hailstones started to pepper my cheeks. It was time to call in a newsagents and ask directions. I never lose my way in the car but seem to do so quite easily while out running.

I gained a far greater appreciation of Paris on this trip. The magnificent buildings appeared to be well planned in spacious parks and attractive gardens, enhanced by a warm autumn day. We visited the Trocadero where crowds gathered around pavement artists, jugglers and escapologists, and we strolled the parks and the river banks.

There were no crackerjack runners within our midst and with the race over an undeterminable distance, the main goal would be simply to complete the course. Therefore we let our hair down a little on Saturday evening with a meal, a few drinks and some more sightseeing. Fire eaters had now joined the other artists at the Trocadero.

As with the previous Paris race, the organisation left a great deal to be desired. We assembled inside a large pen with high sided barriers. As this filled with more and more runners behind, we were unable to leave our places to pay a call. Some runners who couldn't wait any longer used bottles or any receptacle they could find. Others shamelessly had a pee on the spot which I found a little disconcerting.

Every runner had a bar code attached to their number and when at last the race started, runners were directed into funnels and the bar codes scanned. At first this seemed to be a perfect system but proved to be painfully slow. Some of our back markers were waiting for two hours before they could even start. It would have probably been better to turn up late after the masses had already started, and breeze straight through the checkout. This would have probably caused a delay at Versailles with the coaches waiting to return.

With runners leaving the checkouts in dribs and drabs, there was adequate running space with no pushing, shoving or impeding. The route followed the banks of the Seine for several miles and every few hundred yards, we would run through an underpass providing claustrophobic conditions. A combination of the hot day and the beers consumed the night before caused the sweat to pour from me like a tap. On leaving the Seine, we climbed steeply through typical French villages. We ran through undulating forests until eventually, a welcome downhill brought us to the finish with the Palace of Versailles as the impressive backdrop.

There was little time to explore Versailles, the palace or the manicured gardens for as soon as our last runner finished, it was back on the coach and a quick change at the hotel before the river cruise. This was particularly pleasant, the pleasure boat cruising along the River Seine through the early evening dusk, with a commentary picking out landmarks of interest. We embarked at Ile de la Cite close to Notre Dame Cathedral relaxing for the rest of the evening.

Another enjoyable day was rounded off with a quick burst of 'Ruby, don't take your love to town', on the metro back to the hotel. We set off home once again early on Monday morning arriving late evening in Pontefract. The coach driver had taken a shine to Pat, one of our young ladies. His party piece was to leave the coach and re-enter through the emergency exit, sneaking up on her from behind. Every announcement he made over the microphone had some reference to Pat and while quite amusing at first, became pretty predictable by the end of the weekend.

As much as I enjoyed Paris and was so impressed with the parks and the magnificent buildings, I didn't get the spark or the must return feeling I have had with some of the Scandinavian and Eastern European cities. I never saw the results to either of these two races, but with such big fields, it would have been interesting to see if I had come in the top third of the field, top half or wherever.

One race in France where I did get the must return feeling was the Médoc Marathon or to give it the complete title, le Marathon des Châteaux du Médoc et Graves. The race is held each September at the riverside town of Pauillac, north west of Bordeaux. This is France's most popular marathon with the places filling up well before the closing deadline.

The race came highly recommended by Alberta, a running club member and prolific charity fund raiser, who had taken part several times. Four of us decided to go in 1995. Ken made the race and travel arrangements, Alan provided the car courtesy of his boss and William provided the map. I just turned up, nearly burning out the clutch when it was my first turn to drive.

We set off late on Wednesday afternoon arriving at Portsmouth far too early, so had time to kill in a dockside pub. The overnight sailing to Le

Havre was relaxing and prepared us for the long drive through the heart of France to Bordeaux on the South West coast.

Over the spectacular Pont du Normandie, along parts of the le Mans twenty-four hour circuit and down the A10. We crossed the Seine, Loire and Dordogne rivers passing close to Tours and Poitiers, but we mainly bypassed the towns. Our hotel, the Campanile, was situated on the outskirts of the city, and we arrived in time for a training run through industrial estates and past hypermarkets.

Bordeaux is the eighth largest city in France and stands on the Garonne, a tributary of the Gironde. The attractive old town features wide tree-lined boulevards, pedestrian precincts and bustling terrace cafés. Determined to try out my limited French, I decided to really go for it. 'Quatre biers sil vous plait', I asked as we ventured into our first bar. That was about as good as it would get.

On Friday morning, we headed for the rolling hills of the Médoc region with a view to having a reconnoitre for the following day. The Médoc Marathon is part of a three day festival to celebrate the harvest and revolves around wine drinking. The quiet roads to Pauillac are flanked with vines for as far as the eye can see. The gentle slopes facing the Gironde estuary and the fertile soil of the region are well suited for the growing of vines.

We were too early to register, but with the weather once again kind, we explored the Pauillac waterfront where the wine estates had set up stands inviting the sampling of their produce. William couldn't make his mind up, so revisited several of them on the way back to the car.

On overhearing us talking, a lady introduced herself, explaining she and her husband had made the voyage from Newcastle in a small craft. They encountered a rough crossing, were tossed about in the estuary and had decided to put down anchor. She urged us to go speak with her husband saying he would be delighted to hear some friendly voices. Locating the vessel, she told us to shout 'Dave'. We must have caught Dave off-guard as he appeared from the galley, his face covered in foam and a shaving brush in his hand. Their intention was to travel the Midi Canal, eventually reaching the Mediterranean. How wonderful if you could spare the time to do it all.

We spent time at the seaside resort of Montalivet, searched for the pitch and putt course to no avail, but did locate the nudist colony. We returned to Pauillac to register and to drink more wine.

Our insistence to have a hotel breakfast meant we were running late for the race start. We abandoned the car on a track in between vineyards, jogging to the start but being split up in our quest to secure a reasonable starting position.

In the early stages, I was caught at the back of floats, viking long boats, Chinese dragons and jogging Eiffel Towers, as we bottle-necked through the town's narrow streets. The country lanes and tracks of the Médoc Hills were soon reached, with little room to manoeuvre as the masses of runners kicked up dust and sand.

Half of the competitors seemed happy to plod around chatting away, this clearly not being the race for a personal best. We ran through stunning wine estates where the neatly knotted vines were close to harvest. The famous vineyards include Lafite-Rothschild, Mouton-Rothschild, Margaux and Latour, and at several drinks stations, wine was on offer to support the mandatory water and orange.

Most of the course is on quiet country roads, part on dusty tracks but all terrain is firm. The varied route takes many twists and turns but stays close to Pauillac, St Estèphe and St Julien. There are small villages, usually with trademark belfry tower where locals tend to line the pavements lending their support to the occasion. At no time did we stray far away from the vineyards.

The long drives leading to some of the châteaux provided special moments, and the manicured gardens and groomed hedges provided a welcome distraction from thinking too much about how I was suffering in the rising heat. We ran around spectacular patios, in between outbuildings and out across vineyards. In all we would run on parts of thirty different estates. From time to time, we would pass a pint-size chapel on the road side, providing workers with a refuge for prayer during the hectic harvest. When the grapes are ready for picking, estate workers are bolstered with the recruitment of students and itinerant workers. Armed with secateurs, they work solidly for almost two weeks under the watchful eye of the estate manager.

I afforded myself a cup of wine at twenty-two miles, safe in the knowledge I would finish but I gave the much celebrated oyster bar a miss. The final three miles tested the resolve along the straight waterfront road back to Pauillac, but crowd support was heartening and somehow I kept going.

The finish is on the waterfront and a series of marquees provide the competitors with refreshments and yes, you've guessed it, more wine!! A celebration dinner is held later in the evening with the race winners being presented with their equivalent weight in wine. The festivities ended with a firework display close to midnight. The activities don't end here as the following day, a recovery run of five miles is staged with more wine stops and wine at the finish.

For completing the marathon, we each received a couple of bottles of red wine, a boxed cheese, a cheese board, tee shirt, medal and bits and pieces.

We didn't hang around for the festivities, having found a supermarket with the best cream cake department in the world. As a treat for finishing, we had promised ourselves a top of the range gâteau.

Only now did I realise why we had opted to bring such a large estate car. We needed one to take home the vast amount of wine purchased. While William and I purchased a modest amount, Alan and Ken really pushed the boat out. Each time I had cause to go into their room, they had the bottles of wine lined up like soldiers across the floor and were meticulously checking these off against the supermarket tally roll. On the journey home, I cringed each time we braked or turned a corner sharply as the bottles of wine clattered into each other.

The Médoc Marathon came highly recommended to me, and likewise I would recommend it as one of the best races I have done. The aim should be to go there, take your time and enjoy the scenery and surroundings. It is ideal for slower runners and recreational joggers who would perhaps like to run a big marathon but are put off by the big city atmosphere. Some weeks after returning, I received a glossy results brochure through the post, but even though the text was in French, the outstanding photographs made a nice souvenir. I really will have to start the language classes. I certainly intend to return one day and do it all over again.

The Lisbon Half Marathon provided another welcome break in March 1994. With Barnsley, Burnley, Walsall and York City supporters in our midst, the topic of conversation for the next few days was more or less set in tablets of stone.

The plane began its descent over the Portuguese capital to a far warmer climate than we had left behind. Our organiser Trevor went to collect the race literature while the rest of us were ferried to the Hotel Capitol in a convoy of taxis.

On leaving the hotel for the Saturday evening meal, several of the party chose to stay close to the hotel, while others ventured up the steep lanes of the Bairro Alto in search of the night life.

Sunday was race day and after an early breakfast, a taxi ride brought us to the waterfront, where we would catch the ferry to the start on the far bank of the River Tagus. Unfortunately we arrived at the wrong terminal so it was back into the taxis to try our luck further down the foreshore.

The problems with arriving on Saturday evening were that we didn't have chance to familiarise ourselves with the city layout and were now struggling to find our bearings. The long 'April 25th Suspension Bridge' where we would run, dominated the waterfront but how did we reach the other side?

When we eventually found the ferry, It was basic to say the least. The early morning weather was bracing with the crossing taking twenty minutes. The start was still a bus ride and a brisk jog away with the clock rapidly moving around to start time.

Several of us were fortunate to secure places close to the front, moving into the space provided as the elite runners moved forward. Others, including club skipper Terry, weren't so lucky and had to join close to the rear.

The race started below the imposing 'Christ the King' statue, which dominates the hillside. The first mile spanned the spectacular 'April 25th Suspension Bridge' apparently the longest in Europe before the opening of the Humber Bridge, and we were running into a stiff breeze. The views of Lisbon were to be enjoyed as we slowly edged across the suspension bridge, and a superb downhill section on leaving the bridge caused the pace to somewhat quicken.

The course from here was out and back from Belem to Baixa. The main turnaround point was Commerce Square in the heart of city and the finish in Empire Square next to Jeronimos Monastery at Belem. The conditions started cool but by the end of the race were unbearably hot. The out and back course enabled us to see club mates, including skipper Terry who had to work hard to move through the field only passing me at five kilometres.

The organisation at the finish was disappointing with no water or fruit left for most of us. Goody boxes were being handed out from the back of a trailer and these had all gone too with some runners looking to have taken four or five boxes each. I approached a runner who was sat on the grass for one of several boxes in his possession but he became very nasty. I don't know what was in those boxes but he acted as if I was trying to steal his girlfriend.

I tabled these complaints to the organiser of the Gothenburg Half Marathon who was staying in our hotel and acting as an observer for the Association of International Marathons. He listened to my grievances but seemed more intent in trying to smoke a pack of Marlboro in record time.

All of the party opted for a celebratory Chinese meal on the Sunday evening but we rang the culinary changes over the next few days. Determined to try some of the local dishes I ordered a grilled cod which turned out to be the toughest and greasiest in the Bay of Biscay. All the meals appeared to be supplemented by a never-ending supply of crispy bread rolls.

Monday gave us our first real chance to see Lisbon in the daytime and first impressions were a city rich in monuments, attractions and curiosities. We explored the steep streets of the Alfama and Bairro Alto districts served by rickety tram cars, funicular and lifts, in which people were crammed like sardines.

We struck lucky again with the weather and caught the train to Estoril where the Tagus meets the Atlantic Ocean. More famous for its motor racing circuit and casino, some of our party will remember it more for the eccentric lady with a dog, who went under the name of Farty Fraser. She provided an entertaining half-hour and had some of the party in stitches. The next village along the coast was Cascais which appeared to be a well-preserved fishing village with enchanting beaches and coves. We did spot the telltale Union Flag logo outside the British pub.

The same evening, the bars were packed as people watched local favourites Benfica on the telly playing in the European Cup. Celtic had won in this football crazy city in 1967 and had been dubbed 'The Lions of Lisbon'. A group of us mingled with locals to watch the game with Nigel shaking more hands than Prince Charles. Needless to say, nobody in any of the bars had heard of York City. Benfica won the game with the celebrations continuing into the early hours. Cavalcades of cars seemed to cruise around the city flying flags and sounding their horns. We secured a stay back in a Tequila bar, until obliged to leave when a vase was accidentally broken.

The next day we visited St George's Castle with its well-preserved fortifications, strutting peacocks and magnificent views. Others headed for the Palace of Sintra, a short train ride away. We caught the lift to the top of the Discoverers Monument and on another fine day had panoramic views of the waterside, and Belem Tower which was under renovation.

An excellent time was marred by one of our group being threatened at knifepoint, but he managed to push away the assailant. Another member had his wallet stolen on the underground and there was a sting in the tail when some of the luggage failed to arrive at Heathrow. We had left behind scorching temperatures in Lisbon to be greeted by snow and sleet, when we left the train at Wakefield Westgate.

I had arranged to meet friends John and Kevin the day before the 1997 London Marathon. I was down for a long weekend taking in the race but they were staying Saturday night only. I was among the first customers in the British Museum at crack of dawn with my prime aim being to see the Magna Carta. We had arranged to meet early on Saturday afternoon to take in a football match which turned out to be Queens Park Rangers and Grimsby Town at Loftus Road. We sat among the Grimsby faithful, some of whom carried inflatable haddocks, but needless to say their team were thumped.

The other item on the agenda was to choose on overseas marathon in autumn from the literature picked up at the exhibition, but when they turned up, it seemed already cut and dried with Florence in November as the destination.

Despite being chastised for almost missing the plane and upsetting a guest in the hotel, we had a pretty good weekend. The weather was diabolical for most of the time but this didn't deter us from a fair bit of sightseeing. Florence is a testament to Renaissance architecture and no other Italian city has produced the likes of Leonardo da Vinci, Bruneleschi and Michelangelo among others.

Split by the River Arno, the red-roofed buildings are separated from tight streets by awkwardly narrow pavements, and everything appears to be tightly packed. Frontages of buildings are in desperate need of a clean and apparently in summer, the city swelters in the stink of traffic with no outlet to disperse the aroma.

The famous Duomo Cathedral with Bruneleschi's dome is the city's outstanding landmark, while on the Ponte Vecchio, the historic bridge across the Arno, silver jewellery is made and sold from kiosks. There is also a tradition of leather goods in and around the city.

The Piazza di Michelangelo situated on the left bank is worth the walk up the many steps for views over Florence and the Arno Valley. A copy of Michelangelo's David dominates the square where both landscape and portrait artists sit patiently to try make a living. There are many fine galleries within the city but some were closed when we planned a visit on Monday.

In the week leading up to the marathon, I had not been well and was on antibiotics for an abscess in my mouth. My cheeks were more puffed than Marlon Brando's in 'The Godfather'. At race registration, I enquired about switching to the half marathon and was told the two races followed the same course and if I felt like dropping out at half way, then that would be fine.

Race day was wet and the three of us set off for the race start at the Municipal Stadium, leaving Steve at the hotel with the promise we would look out for him somewhere on the course. John pressed ahead but I settled in with Kevin, momentarily forgetting my illness. I thought the course was superb, passing many of the city's attractions, the Duomo, Piazza della Signnoria and the Uffizi Gallery. There were many twists and turns along narrow streets and around compact squares, and generous sections along the river bank, through parks and past a huge fairground. There was a small section on the left bank with certain sections completed twice.

I felt fine beyond the half marathon cut-off point, running and chatting away to Kevin for thirty or so kilometres. When he pulled slightly ahead, I neither had the ability or inclination to try bridge the gap and I suffered badly in the final quarter, being relieved to finish in 3 hours 48 minutes.

The rain stopped part of the way through the race, but on large sections of the course we were treading water. I can't ever recollect my feet being so cold, and once back at the hotel I had to point the hair dryer on them to bring back the circulation.

We had a light meal and headed for a bar where Arsenal and Liverpool were on television. From a distance we could see people spilling out onto the pavement, but they were all trying to catch a glimpse of the tail-end of the game featuring local favourites Fiorentina at Napoli. When the match finished, the bar emptied leaving the four of us and only half a dozen others. The landlord was even able to transfer the commentary onto English for our benefit.

Rome was only two hours away by Express train but when we arrived the weather was no better than in Florence. We each bought an umbrella from a stall in the station concourse and set out to explore the sights. We saw the Vatican City, the Colosseum, the Trevi Fountain, the Spanish Steps and many more. We never took the umbrellas down while outside and ended up thoroughly miserable and dejected.

I enjoyed Florence and the marathon but on hindsight I should have probably settled for the shorter option. Any runner looking for a late autumn marathon could do worse, but there are many other good Italian races with the Venice Marathon attracting me like a magnet.

CHAPTER 18

Marathon Men

THE RUNNING CLUB Annual General Meetings were usually dominated by one topic, the Grand Prix. This consisted of several races, usually ten in all, run over different distances and spread throughout the year. Points were awarded with the first past the post gaining the maximum, and scaled down so every runner would gain some points. Usually the best eight scores counted with the overall winners being declared champions. Trophies were awarded to the winners of the various categories and to the most improved runner.

The Grand Prix above all, caused more discussion, debate and argument than any other single topic; the races to be included, the distances, the points scoring method, whether the points would be awarded on a handicap basis or for first past the post. At one time the members voted for the races, but when the committee took on the responsibility, they could never seem to find the correct dates or whether the nominated races would actually take place.

Some runners didn't want evening races, others didn't want Saturdays and some didn't like afternoon starts. Many members didn't believe a marathon should be included in the Grand Prix. These were some of the same people who would clamour for a London place but have no intention of running any other marathon. Others believed there should be more than one marathon included while others thought double points should be awarded. There was even a walkout at one of the Annual Meetings about a Grand Prix related issue.

The first year I took part in the Grand Prix, there were fifteen or so runners taking part in the Sheffield Marathon and this generated a great deal of interest. In recent years the numbers have slumped making one wonder if it is worthwhile after all to include a marathon. I would normally run the nominated marathon looking upon it as a good chance to accumulate some points, so I didn't tend to grumble.

Out of all this came a small band of runners known as 'The Marathon Men'. They arrived at club nights earlier than the rest of us and they would finish later. They would regularly run sixteen miles on an evening in all weathers. When a marathon came around, it was simply a case of topping up an already deep reservoir of miles.

Others contemplating a marathon would have to start their training from scratch.

They regularly ran five or six marathons a year, and if there was a shorter half marathon option on the same bill, the people who ran in that would be branded as wimps. They often ran in eighteen or twenty mile build-up races and their long Sunday morning runs would see them home in time for the Antiques Roadshow. They were of a useful standard, running consistently below three and a quarter hours, a good deal quicker than me.

On cold winter nights, we would be sitting in the clubhouse enjoying a well-earned tea or beer, when in would come 'The Marathon Men', shrouded in a cloud of steam. One of the long winter circuits was the 'Pineapple Run' over Heath Common from Normanton towards Wakefield and any outsiders who dropped off the pace here wouldn't return for hours.

Greenhorns who had secured a London Marathon place would see these long Wednesday runs as an ideal opportunity to increase their mileage, but naively discounted 'The Marathon Men' and their unrelenting pace. Parts of the 'Pineapple Run' are unlit and people who have dropped off the pace on the common have sometimes not been seen again for days. One guy who had been given up for lost apparently returned with 'The Marathon Men' the following Wednesday after running around aimlessly on the common for days.

The 'Pineapple Run' was still on the itinerary until recently, when a late night bus driver spotted a large black cat crossing the road on the common. It was snowing at the time and the cat made its way across an adjacent field carrying a smaller animal between its teeth. The bus driver was so intrigued he returned the following day with a camera, to take photographs of the tracks. He traced them across a field until they suddenly came to an abrupt halt. This is probably when he decided to run for dear life. The story was enough to persuade 'The Marathon Men' to change their route at least for the time being.

I would occasionally run with 'The Marathon Men' but never considered myself to be one of them. On long evening runs, one guy would shout 'One lightly done please', as we passed the open door of a suburban Fish and Chip shop, where the welcoming smell wafted out across the pavement. They would battle on through illness and injuries, let alone the occasional head cold.

On one long Sunday run, we had already come a considerable distance and at any time I expected us to hang a right taking us back in the general direction of home. Instead of this, we kept turning left extending the run further on each occasion. One lad who hadn't previously gone further than the half marathon distance was never seen again at the club.

I had to wait until 1995 to become a fully paid-up member of 'The Marathon Men'. Each October, a group would run the Snowdonia Marathon and returned with tales about the severity of the course, the horrendous weather and how they had to dig deep upon their resolve. They sounded me out for this during the summer and seemed hell-bent that I would actually do it. I suspected they planned this as some sort of initiation ceremony to see if I was worthy to step up with the big boys. As the weeks progressed they kept asking me if I had posted my application, had I heard anything back from the race and was I still doing it? They appeared to be doing everything within their power to make sure I didn't chicken out.

The literature from the race organisers arrived in good time along with a map of the course and an elevation profile. This usually tends to be in a block diagram with the miles along the bottom and the feet up the side. A continuous line plots the peaks and troughs just like a hospital cardiograph, and these are designed to give you nightmares in the run-up to the race. I couldn't help but notice after a flat half mile we would climb steeply to four miles before enjoying some welcome downhill towards halfway. I prepared for this first section by running the four miles from home to Middleton Water Tower, the highest point in the area, and I did this a couple of times each week. I figured if I could complete this first section in good shape, the rest would be plain sailing.

As I waited in the early morning darkness to be picked up, there wasn't a sound until all of a sudden I could hear footsteps. They began to get louder but I couldn't see where they were coming from. My heart started pounding but almost as suddenly as they had started, they stopped. Was it a ghost returning home from the night club? I began to wish the car would hurry up as I didn't want to be scaring myself to death first thing on a morning, particularly with the big day ahead.

Day break came along the North Wales coastline and the countryside seemed gentle as we passed close to the resorts of Rhyl and Colwyn Bay. The terrain didn't appear particularly severe and I couldn't see what all the fuss was about. Andy was concentrating on the driving, leaving 'The Marathon Men', Kevin, Mick and Les free from any undue exertions or distractions before the big race.

On approaching Llanberis, the rolling countryside took on more of a rugged outlook and the slate sided mountains rose vertically above the village. A road in the distance wound its way up the steep valley like a thread of cotton and this was apparently where we would run.

As usual, we were in plenty of time but ended up having to rush around. Registration took place at the Royal Victoria Hotel where the race would finish. We visited Pete's Eats, a unique mountaineers and ramblers café where the tea was served in bottomless pots. We strolled past the Mountain Railway Station and with a tariff of £14 for the return trip, we had probably made the correct choice in running the marathon.

After changing, we were left with a mile walk to the start at Nont Peris, where among the 1,000 strong field were members of the 'Marathon 100 Club' and the '100 Kilometre Society'. Wally Oakes of Sports Tours was attempting a Snowdonia-Dublin double on successive days, planning to dash to Holyhead after the race for the trip across the Irish Sea. Others were fresh from the exertions of the Seven Sisters Marathon the previous day. Last but not least was Kathy Drake of Spenborough going for her fifth win in this event.

This was to be the fifteenth running of The National Trust Snowdonia Marathon sponsored by the National Grid. It had been dubbed 'The Run on the Wild side' and '26 Miles 385 Yards of agony and ecstasy', and I was about to find out why.

The early stages were through the Llanberis Pass, climbing to 1,100 feet in four miles. The race plan was for me and Andy to run together in the early stages, but he was caught up in the euphoria and soon forged ahead. I ended up running with Les who had come up with the innovative idea of wearing a cap with a huge brim so as not to see the severity of the climbs ahead.

Even though I had run every hill in the area to prepare for this section, I found it particularly difficult on the day as parked cars and runners of different speeds broke my rhythm. Still we climbed as the runners became really strung out between dry stone walls and around the hairpin bends. In the distance, the tiny buildings at the head of the pass looked like Lego models.

Slowly but surely those buildings became clearer. With calves as tight as drums, I completed the final pull just as my lungs were about to explode. A welcome downhill section beckoned with the bright autumn morning providing panoramic views over the Snowdonia National Park. By now 'The Marathon Men' were probably well ahead and there seemed little chance of Mick waiting for me after our disastrous partnership in the Leeds Country Way Relay some weeks earlier. I made a friend for life in Ivor of Hull Springhead Harriers, a man with a heart like a lion. Not only did he run marathons but he supported Hull Kingston Rovers. The next few miles passed quickly as we discussed the fortunes of our local Rugby League clubs and the advent of the Super League. The Springhead club had their own cheerleaders in the shape of two nubile young women who turned up at strategic places to spur on Ivor.

The course flattened passing the sparkling Llyn Gwynant to the right and Llyn Dinas on the left hand side, before we reached the picture postcard village of Beddgelert with its stream, bridges and quaint shops.

Folklore says the name of the village is derived from Beth Gellert or 'Grove of the Greyhound'. The dog had prevented a wolf from harming a baby who had sought refuge under a cot. A fierce battle had taken place between the wolf and the dog and when the owner returned, he saw the dog dripping with blood and felt sure it was from the child. He drew his sword plunging it into the side of the greyhound, before finding the child unharmed. He tried to revive the dog but it was too late. He buried the greyhound within the shadow of Snowdon so passers-by might see his grave.

Back to the race and a testing two mile climb out of the village took us beyond halfway but with the toughest section still ahead. A level section provided opportunities for views of Snowdon, but I gained little comfort from knowing I would have to run part of the way up there. At Waunfur, the action really started with a short climb through a housing estate followed by an arduous drag to 1,200 feet. The narrow road was flanked by high dry stone walls and in some places, walking was compulsory. On glancing back to see how many were behind, I discovered breathtaking views of the North Wales coastline and the Isle of Anglesey.

There wasn't time to admire the views so I pressed on, hands on knees in typical fell running style. The road eventually petered out into a bumpy track and through a disused slate quarry. Six more pulls after the familiar cry of all downhill from here, the track fell away steeply to a narrow road, and now the spectacular views were of Llanberis. I could see the Royal Victoria Hotel where we would finish and could almost touch it, but the stark reality was there were still two miles to go.

The others would have probably finished by now but at least I could take comfort from the fact that I would be up with them next year when I started to take it more seriously. The downhill at this stage was very welcome but a little too steep for aching limbs and cramping muscles. As always in these races there was a sting in the tail as we turned away from the village for a loop on the back roads. Eventually I reached Llanberis running under the railway bridge and towards the finish in slightly under four hours.

'The Marathon Men' were already changed as they applauded me in. I was presented with a well-deserved coaster made from local slate. Andy suggested to an official that perhaps a tee shirt would have been a welcome addition in future, but he was torn off a strip and informed that race profits are directed to projects in the National Park such as maintaining hedgerows, dry stone walls and remote farm buildings.

I joined the others for a drink and a sandwich after I had what a colleague described as 'The mother of all blisters' attended to by St Johns Ambulance Volunteers, which was well worth the couple of quid donation. I remember pleading with the nurse to use castor oil rather than surgical spirit.

I had no need to worry about being near the back of the field as I finished comfortably midway. For the record, John Parker of Tipton was race winner with Kathy Drake once again successful in the ladies' race.

We drove back over the Llanberis pass which seemed far gentler in the car. Les asked if I had a pen so he could start filling in the application form for next year. I was invited with open arms to the Wednesday six o'clock runs and unanimously became one of 'The Marathon Men'.

Even though I haven't run Snowdonia since, I keep threatening to return one day. I gather the start and finish arrangements have changed in recent years but that shouldn't detract from the enjoyment of this excellent event. I would advocate that every marathoner should run this race at least once in their life.

We returned to that part of the world the following spring to run the Anglesey 30 Kilometre Race, a little publicised run but well worth the journey. The out and back course starts at Menai Bridge with sections along the Menai Straits, and considering the location, was pretty flat. This time the rolls were reversed as panoramic views of Snowdonia could be seen with the snow still clinging to some of the tops. That day I ran a shocker and was the last of six or seven runners from my club to finish.

Another race I had looked forward to with anticipation was the New Forest Marathon which we ran around the same time. Four of us travelled by car on Saturday and stayed the night with a cousin of Kevin and his family in Bournemouth. We took him and his wife out for a meal on Saturday evening. Returning home to watch the boxing, I paid our hosts the ultimate compliment by falling asleep on the sofa.

On our way to the race the next morning the heavens opened and the rain was unrelenting for the entire day. The race which I had relished for so long looked like being ruined at the last minute. The headquarters and race start and finish were at New Milton on the edge of the forest, and for some inexplicable reason, best known to the organisers, the start was delayed. Almost the entire field sought refuge under the canopy of a petrol station as we awaited further developments. The half marathon had started some time ago, and the way things were turning out, I would have been better going with them.

Buster Merryfield of 'Only Fools and Horses' fame, started the race from the front of an open top bus, the driving rain doing no favours to his beard. Buster, a resident of the forest, has since sadly passed away.

We set off forlornly leaving the suburbs behind and heading first onto heathland and then into the forest. Running with Kevin and an ultra distance man who claimed to be out for a gentle training run, we pressed on relentlessly past chocolate box houses and through damp woodlands. The ponies and occasional shire horses grazing on the common land looked soaked and dejected, but not as dejected as I felt. If I moved into the centre of the road, the rain was hitting me like knitting needles. If I moved into the sides under cover of the trees, I was treading standing water. There was a short off-road section resembling a bog, which was more the pity as the course had the potential to be beautiful on a fine day.

We passed close to Brockenhurst, Burley and the quaintly named Sway, but what surprised me was the fact that the forest appeared to be criss-crossed with railway lines. There was little surprise when I suffered from blisters and chaffing towards the end of the race, and Mick rubbed salt into already open wounds by jogging back down the course and running in with me. Football fanatic John finished some way behind the three of us and his first words on crossing the line were, 'Did you see Bashley Town's ground?'

Olympian and former London Marathon winner Huw Jones won the race but seemed disappointed not to have lowered the course record. Anybody who finished that day in those conditions had done well whether it be Huw or myself. The journey home was a torrid affair through constant driving rain and spray and we arrived back in Yorkshire, miserable and stiff as crutches late on Sunday evening. Fortunately I had seen sense and booked the Monday off work as a day's holiday.

Another race regularly patronised by 'The Marathon Men' is the Potteries Marathon run in and around the 'Five Towns' area each June. The race is taken to the people and run almost exclusively through towns, suburbs and estates.

The hospitality of the terrific crowds and the carnival atmosphere generated have gone some way towards this race being portrayed as the 'Friendly Marathon'. Although far from easy and usually blessed with red-hot conditions, people return to the Potteries year on year. The supportive crowds and the superb Trentham Gardens finish make this race a must in many runners' diaries.

Like many other races, I have only competed here once but I can remember the long straight drag to the viaduct around the fifteen mile mark and the tea stop beyond twenty. I can recollect the long downhill finish and the annoying humpback bridge leading to the finishing straight within the gardens.

In recent years 'The Potteries', in line with many races, has struggled to keep afloat and seems to have constant dialogue with the police over the route and road closures. Widely regarded as the most popular marathon behind London, 'The Potteries' deserves to prosper, particularly for the sterling work of the organisers and the support of the local people.

The Sheffield Marathon is another favourite that usually brings out the best in the weather. Despite a change from the traditional summer date, the weather still tends to hold fine, the problems now being clashes with other races.

I feel the event has suffered something of an identity crisis in recent years with the route being continually changed due to alterations around the Meadowhall area, the demise of the steel works and the advent of the super tram. My four outings in the marathon here have all been on different courses, the first starting at Hillsborough Park in the early eighties. The supporting half marathon has also suffered changes which have seen it run through most parts of the city. The most recent route has been an out and back course through suburbs, with only a short stretch through Longley Park breaking up the urban sprawl.

The 2003 edition would see further changes, with the route including the Winter Gardens, parts of the Rotherham district and a stretch close to Sheffield Airport. The one positive thing the Sheffield Marathon has in its favour is the start and finish in the Don Valley Stadium. This single factor alone should keep the numbers up and ensure the future of the race.

With the exception of my home town race in Leeds, my favourite of the regional marathons is 'The Robin Hood', not surprisingly staged in and around Nottingham. This is regularly chosen by my club for inclusion within the Grand Prix, but even when I was unattached, I regularly supported this race.

I believe 'The Robin Hood' shows Nottingham at its best and is one of the city's biggest events and charity fund raisers. The course runs through some of the city's squares and precincts in the early stages before running alongside the castle walls on a favourable downhill. You might catch a glimpse of deer in the stages through Woollatton Park. There are long sections on the Trent Embankment, a circuit of the lake in Colwick Park and a stretch alongside the race course. These sections are enhanced by pleasant suburbs with lots of greenery.

A big plus here is the get-out clause of finishing at the half marathon stage should you be struggling or don't relish running a further thirteen miles. Finishers in both races receive a unique framed panel of Nottingham Lace with a different design each year. The tented village on The Meadows provides refreshments and entertainment for your loved ones while you are out there pounding the highways and byways.

Over the years, the race has given me the opportunity to meet a contact from work who tends to run here regularly, while more recently we have been able to meet up with our friends from Luton. My only gripe about the race would be the length of time taken to get through the surrounding side streets onto the carpark and similarly away again after the race.

Several years ago while travelling to the race, I was held up on the M1 due to an accident, and looked to be a doubtful starter. I more or less abandoned my car when I got to within striking distance of The Meadows in what appeared to be a sheltered housing complex. I hurriedly changed, secured my car keys inside my shorts with safety pins and jogged in the general direction of the start. With about a minute to spare, I joined the race towards the front feeling thoroughly warmed up and ready to go. I recorded one of my best times, shading three and a half hours.

The problem now would be to find my car, even though I had made a mental note of the street name where I had parked. To my relief, I found it first time but as I was changing, a young couple walked by with a push-chair. I got talking to them about the race and why I had parked there. 'You're asking for it,' he said. 'They either get pinched or smashed up if you leave them here.' I didn't know whether to consider myself fortunate or stupid.

Last year when I ran the Robin Hood, I was always going to struggle to break four hours, and the way I was running and the way I felt, I considered dropping out at the half marathon stage. A purple patch at around eleven miles persuaded me to carry on but ten minutes after passing the cut-off point, I started to regret the decision. I passed the 23 mile marker on the embankment adjacent to Nottingham Forest Football ground, and a glance at my watch told me I had 33 minutes left in which to meet my target. I plodded on to the best of my ability checking my time at 24 and again at 25 miles. I had 12 minutes remaining to complete the one mile and 385 yards. I dug deep and tried to lift the tempo a little but it was a case of putting one foot down after the other. I turned onto the grass with a hundred yards to go and could see the clock on the finish gantry ticking past 3–59 with the seconds whizzing around. After running 26 miles I now needed to pull a sprint finish out of the locker. On the Wednesday after the race, club chairman Cyril informed me I had run 3 hours 59 minutes and 52 seconds. How's that for pacing myself?

Many of the marathons that followed the running boom of the early eighties are now sadly gone but not forgotten. After several successful years, the popular Bolton Marathon was an early casualty. I ran there once in horrendous conditions but the race stands out for two reasons. A runner around me kept asking members of the crowd for a cigarette and I can recall seeing him at the finish enjoying a swallow as he changed on the grass. The other incident occurred when a woman shouted out, 'Don't let a girl beat you,' as I struggled up the arduous Plodder Lane.

The Selby Marathon which comprised two laps of rural flatlands and the Humber Bridge Marathon have both gone although a Humber Bridge Half is a welcome addition to the calendar. The year I ran here, the usual westerly wind was replaced by a head wind blowing off the North Sea and I struggled all the way to Grimsby.

Meanwhile 'The Marathon Men' were dipping their toes in the world of ultra distance running. I can't recollect whether I was bribed, threatened or how it came about but somehow I was roped into doing the Grantham Canal Run. This comprised thirty-three miles on towpaths, grass and tracks from Nottingham Forest Football Ground to Grantham.

Apparently nothing would prevent us from taking the team prize, that is apart from the unfamiliar terrain, the unrelenting canal banks, the opposition and the big red ball in the sky. I ran along the tow paths of the Aire and Calder Navigation for hours in preparation for the race, but this proved to be fruitless as the terrain on the Grantham canal comprised mainly of short grass and well trodden paths. I would have been better suited running around a school field for hours on end.

The course passed close by Cotgrave Colliery and Belvoir Castle as it meandered through the gently rolling countryside. We passed few houses, hardly any villages, and one pub. Here a sign read 'Photos Taken ahead' giving you the opportunity to smile, polish up your action and not look too tired.

There were many stiles and kissing gates to negotiate and several roads to cross. One bridge required you to really duck down, crouch, limbo or crawl on your hands and knees for twenty to thirty yards. I chose the last option which takes some doing after fifteen miles on the hoof. Some runners wore knee pads specifically for this section but I tended to think that was going a little over the top. Another runner behind me screamed out, apparently cramping up as he knelt down.

As I slowed towards the end, runners who I wouldn't have given a hope for just glided past effortlessly. This sort of race seemed to attract a particular breed of runner who could just plod around all day long. They were lean, mean and without an ounce of fat and many regularly entered the 24 hour races which entailed circling a track over and over again.

Having given my all, and thrown in several walks for good measure, there was still a mile to go as we left the canal and ran under the A1. A more familiar road section brought about a mini revival and I comfortably picked up a couple of places on the way to the finish. The marshal on the final bend into the Blue Bell Yard must have left his position and I ended up in the cattle market and had to be called back.

A generous barbecue was provided followed by a delicious ice cream which I would have killed for at around the twenty mile mark. A man in the pub was drunk with the landlady refusing to serve him anymore. He said he needed to catch a train to get to the Notting Hill Carnival. When the presentations were made, lo and behold, the selfsame man had finished second in the race. Needless to say, we didn't win the team prize or any individual prizes come to that.

I returned some years later but due to repairs on certain sections of the canal banks, the race consisted of an out and back from Grantham Squash Club, and had been reduced in distance to thirty-one miles plus. Once again the weather was unbearably hot and I struggled badly, vowing never to be back. On the way back I could hear the noise of a generator close to the finish which nearly drove me mad. It was a pump draining a waterlogged section of the bank and while it became louder with each stride, it didn't appear to get any closer.

The decision not to run again was taken out of my hands when the race folded with the lack of a sponsor being one of the reasons. A fond memory here is the sight of a runner out on his feet shortly after finishing. He wasn't even given chance to regain his breath and composure before a trombone was thrust into his sweaty palms. He was then hauled up onto the back of a trailer to join fellow bandsmen for a rousing rendition of The Floral Dance, which brought about the biggest cheer of the day.

'The Marathon Men' still meet on a Wednesday evening at a far more sociable time and they don't run as far or as fast these days. Some of the routes tend to be themed such as a run through a district that had recently suffered flooding or a run taking in a street where several houses compete with each other for the loudest Christmas decorations.

We ran through the Freeport Shopping Mall shortly after it opened but the security guards prevented us from gaining entry next time. Another run took us to an address where one of the lads had seen a classic car advertised. There's never a dull run with 'The Marathon Men'.

CHAPTER 19

Letters from America

I HAVEN'T QUITE lived up to my promise that one day I would live in the United States, but I have been fortunate enough to return every few years and have now notched up seven Stateside marathons.

My next trip was to the Boston Marathon in 1991. The oldest marathon in the world requires strict qualifying criteria which I was unable to meet, but by travelling with Sports Tours, I was classed as an invited runner and was welcomed with open arms. Invited runners included people like myself with travel companies, charity runners and United States race organisers. I did feel a little guilty at taking the place of an American 'Middle of the Packer' who would be unable to secure a place, but at least I would finish well inside the 4 hours 15 minutes time limit.

The party was a nice mixture of youth and experience, elite and jogger. There were runners from all parts of Britain, some who I still see from time to time at races. One guy had never run a race before although he had always run. His wife suggested he do the race while they were visiting relatives on an extended break. He had no idea what time to expect, and what he was letting himself in for.

We stayed at the 'Park Plaza' close to Boston Common where the Swan Boats operate. Unlike New York, Boston is pretty compact, far more manageable and by no means as overpowering. A good walking city, it is possible to see most of the attractions over a long weekend.

The Park Plaza was a deluxe hotel with all the facilities imaginable including airline and theatre ticket shops, a health club and indoor pool. There were large public rooms with chandeliers, high pillars and ceilings. The reception concourse area had bags of comfortable seating, ideal for people watching. It was while I was waiting here for other members of the party that I witnessed one of the most peculiar situations imaginable. A man of Eastern extraction, probably an Indian, was standing against a pillar. He was smoking a strong smelling cigarette, perhaps a Gitanes or Camel. He held the cigarette in his mouth allowing the ash to accumulate and then fall onto the floor. He would then take another cigarette from the packet and light it from the butt of the one he had just smoked. He repeated the process over and over again and we sat there waiting for him to do it just one more time. He must have had lungs like bellows and probably felt like I did at the finish of one of the cross-country fixtures.

The race is on Patriot's Day, a Bank Holiday Monday in April. The historic course starts in Main Street, Hopkinton, a rural New England town. White clapboard houses are set among a grassy, tree-lined setting.

The first part of the course is rolling but picturesque and passes through the small towns of Ashland, Natick and Framingham. At around halfway, the girls of Wellesley School form a narrow corridor, with hands held out for appreciative slaps. Their excited cheers make a wall of sound which can be heard from far away.

At sixteen miles, the course plummets to Newton Lower Falls and crosses Charles River. A right turn into Commonwealth Avenue, brings the first in a series of climbs known as the Newton Hills. The last of these at twenty miles is Heartbreak Hill where the race is said to have been won or lost on many occasions.

The course bears right at the reservoir on Chestnut Hill Avenue to Cleveland Circle and then left onto Beacon Street. The last few miles are gradual downhill past Fenway Park, home to the Boston Red Sox.

In the days after the race, we took time out to explore the city, the best way to do so probably being the Beantown Trolley. This is a ninety minute tour on a small coach, should you stay on for the duration. Alternatively you can alight and rejoin at any of the points of interest along the route. The driver provided a humorous and informative commentary and continually rang the bell at each joke. In our case, lady driver Meredith made constant references to any marathon runners onboard.

Boston is a city of contrasts with areas of water and grassland breaking up the mass of buildings, and like other American cities, the streets are set out in a grid system. In the financial district, skyscrapers sit side by side with historical buildings and dwellings.

The waterfront area houses expensive apartments, shopping arcades, restaurants and museums. The New England aquarium is the best of its kind I've seen, with a huge circular tank as the centre piece with a spiral ramp providing a viewing platform. Several hours can be spent comfortably here and at the dolphin show in the auditorium next door. A mock Boston Tea Party ship is moored on the waterfront and for a small fee, you can throw a chest of tea overboard.

The Midtown District is the place to see the shows, the opera or ballet while Downtown Crossing houses Filene's and Jordan Marsh departmental stores. Pretzels, hot dogs, flowers and newspapers can be bought from the many street vendors in the district. Chinatown is small but densely populated and is the third largest of its kind in the States. Luxurious fabrics, porcelain and exotic foods are available here as well as late night dining.

Boston is ideal for a stroll and what better way to see the city than to follow the Freedom Trail, a red line painted on the pavement linking the city's most important and historic landmarks. A list can be collected from one of the visitor centres and you just follow the line and let your feet do the work. Among the landmarks is Paul Revere's house, a former silversmith who rode at midnight to warn of the pending British arrival. Bunker Hill, a 200 foot monument, is a memorial to those killed in the first battle of the American Revolution. The US Constitution named *Old Ironsides* is a heavy frigate undefeated in forty-four encounters, and is the oldest commissioned warship afloat.

The Charles River esplanade is a pleasant place for walking and jogging and Boston Common is the oldest public park in the country. On one side of the common is Beacon Hill, an area of red bricked sidewalks and cobblestone streets with gas lamps. The townhouses and mansions with wrought iron gates and railings portray a feeling of Old England. The Bull and Finch pub, home to TV series 'Cheers' is situated in this area, and it is possible to visit for a beer, a meal or a souvenir.

Faneuil Hall Marketplace, a site for many famous meetings, has been a market for the past 240 years. A lively area in three restored buildings houses gift and clothing shops along with restaurants. Next door is Quincy Market where the stalls range from international delicacies to fast food.

Across the Charles River is Cambridge, home to Harvard University. Harvard Square reached from Downtown Crossing on the T Line is filled with restaurants, historical sites and unique shops. Every corner provides curiosities that mix American flavour with European culture. There are over twenty specialist bookstores, over a hundred eating establishments along with performing arts theatres, cinemas and museums. Many neighbourhood bars have given local jazz artists a step up the ladder to stardom.

Further afield are historical towns of the American Revolution, Concord and Lexington, while Salem, known for legends of witchcraft, is easily reached.

Cape Cod is the areas vacation resort and millionaires' holiday playground. There are miles of beaches and sand dunes with large areas for water sports. The Islands of Nantucket and Martha's Vineyard are offshore and can be reached by ferry from Hyannis or whaling town, New Bedford. These islands provide tranquillity along with sailing, biking, golf and other recreational activities.

I returned to Boston in 1996 for the hundredth running of the marathon. This was the most talked about and reported race I can recollect and a field of 37,000 was swelled by a dozen or so from Ackworth. In the week leading up to the race, fifteen inches of snow had fallen at Hopkinton where the race would start. The snow had then turned to rain with the runners' assembly area resembling a swamp. Duck-boards had been placed in strategic places but even then it seemed impossible not to tread in thick mud or get a shoe full of water. The winter had been the snowiest on record and in the centre of Boston, mounds of snow stood on the sidewalks like statues.

We arrived on Friday afternoon and quickly found our bearings, having our first beer at Samuel Adams Brewhouse on Boylston Street. We returned there for our evening meal, were seated in a dark attic room and had to hold the menu up to the light. Heaven only knows what they served us up. Micro Breweries appeared all over town and we had a nightcap at the Back Bay Brewing Company.

The week was one long list of events relating to the marathon. A centennial monument showing a map of the course along with previous winners was unveiled in Copley Square close to the finish. A pasta party was held at the World Trades Centre and a dinner held for past champions.

The Exhibition and Registration was huge and like no other I had seen. There were trade stalls and stands selling 100th anniversary memorabilia. There were postcards, centennial photographs, jackets, sweatshirts and so much more. There was even a commemorative postage stamp. One of our group Barry, bought a jacket in blue and gold with the Boston Marathon logo on the back. He hardly took it off, probably went to bed in it, and threatened to wear it around Pontefract centre on our return. There was a stand advertising the Cancun Marathon and we walked past here five or six times, pausing to look at the gorgeous Mexican girl handing out the leaflets. I returned to the hotel with a fistful of application forms and a load of information about the race.

On Saturday afternoon we visited Fenway Park, home to the famous Boston Red Sox. We were fortunate to purchase seats behind the diamond and an American man on the row in front was kind enough to explain the finer details of the game to us. This was a real family afternoon out with vendors continually replenishing our appetite with popcorn, hot chocolate and ice cream.

Boston, who were in a bad run of form, were soundly beaten and the crowds started to leave in the seventh of nine innings. I didn't realise the baseball season was so crowded. Over the weekend we were there, they had played three games against Kansas and were starting a further three against the superbly named Baltimore Oriels. Four games a week was normal and over a season they played in excess of 120 games. Imagine having to fund watching your favourite baseball team.

On Saturday evening we saw raunchy rocker Joan Osbourne in concert at the Orpheum Theatre with an equally impressive warm-up band. It had been a hectic day and we were to continue the hectic schedule on Sunday.

In the morning we were among 6,000 International Runners in the Friendship Run. In freezing cold conditions, we jogged from the City Hall to the Charles River Esplanade where we were served with tea, coffee, bagels and rolls. The tour of the course showed us little we didn't know already. We were unable to see much out of the coach windows for the torrential rain.

There had been a new influx of runners at the hotel, among them 'Captain Beany', a prolific fund raiser for children's charities. Beany, from Port Talbot regularly sat in bath tubs of baked beans for long periods of time, with people continually topping up the level, usually by pouring them over his head. He dressed in a selection of space capes, coloured himself in a baked bean shade and then hit the roads. Throughout the weekend he became something of a celebrity, dressing up at the Pasta and Post Race parties and having a photo shoot at The Hard Rock Café. Another new arrival was Colin Fletcher of St Theresa's, a regular on the West Yorkshire Race circuit. When we ventured out on an evening, we had built up quite a gang.

Race day was organised to military precision. We assembled on Boston Common and were marshalled onto one of a fleet of yellow school buses, each with an individual school name on the side. Unlike the previous day or for that matter, the previous week, the weather had saved itself for the occasion and was going to be glorious.

My allocated place was well back from the start line and around a corner from the main street. The announcements and rendition of 'The Star Spangled Banner' could be heard over the loudspeakers but it was twenty minutes before we even edged forward. This wouldn't make any difference as my starting time would be recorded from the championship chip fastened to my shoe lace. As with so many big races, the early stages would be painfully slow until the field spread out.

The race was a couple of weeks after the London Dockland bombings and in a Sunday Newspaper article, a Boston barman had said that Londoners had got what they deserved. He went on to say that he was pleased that this had happened and was just what Britain needed. He added that this was his proudest moment as he never wanted the peace proposed by John Major's government. Like so many other Irish descendents living in the States, he had probably never visited Ireland, or Britain for that matter.

With these words ringing in my ears, I wore my Union Flag vest with pride and in doing so received tremendous encouragement and support from crowds all along the course.

Many greats of the past and present were running today including Ingrid Kristiansen, Alberto Salazar, Bill Rodgers and our own Ron Hill who won in 1970. John A. Kelley who won ten years apart in 1935 and 1945 was running, as was his namesake, John J. Kelley, the 1957 winner. The former had run over sixty Bostons, an unbelievable record, and he was still going strong into his eighties.

No one has come close to that record and anyone wishing to eclipse it would first need to achieve a qualifying standard, perhaps in their late teens. They would have to stay motivated, stay fit and healthy, always be available, avoid injury, not give birth and so on.

After the initial slow start, I responded with some good running. I enjoyed the crowd support even on the remote parts of the course, and the camaraderie of my fellow runners. The noon start meant conditions were initially warm, but they would become cooler in the later stages of the race. With the Newton Hills carefully negotiated, I looked forward to the long descent alongside the railway track eventually leading to the decorated finish area on Boylston Street.

Progress was slow through the finishing chutes, and even though I passed the hotel in the later stages, it took fully an hour to make my way back there. I was handed Gatorade, cheese biscuits, pretzels, a peck on the cheek, you name it. I somehow managed to bend down to remove my championship chip, and then walked slowly towards the baggage buses. Even though I wore a space blanket, conditions, particularly in the shadow of the tall buildings, were extremely cold. I just wanted to reclaim my baggage and return to the hotel for a hot bath.

This was easier said than done however, as my baggage had been deposited on Coach 28 which seemed to have gone missing. I walked past Coach 27, and then Coach 29, but there was no Coach 28. Other people were in the same predicament as me, but after criss-crossing the common and speaking to various officials, Coach 28 was at last tracked down, parked some way from the others along with a couple of other stragglers. Apparently it had broken down on the way back from Hopkinton and had only just arrived. Typical of my luck.

Moses Tanui led home four other Kenyans in the first five places with many more of their countrymen in the first fifty, while Uta Pippig won the ladies' race for Germany. Jean Driscoll won the ladies' wheelchair event for a seventh consecutive time.

In the days after the race, I stiffened like never before, with stepping on and off the kerb feeling like climbing a mountain. I put the blame firmly down to the composition of the roads in the States with many comprising only concrete blocks, with little or no tarmac surface to cushion the impact.

We visited many of the attractions I had seen back in 1991, but which were still enjoyable. We drank wisely and well, sometimes late into the night and we risked visiting the Black Rose Irish Pub, where 'Sunday's Well' played the night away. All over Boston we bumped into fellow Marathoners who told us about some of the great American races, the Grandma's, Twin Cities, Crescent City Classic and many more.

Some weeks after returning home, I received a comprehensive pictorial 150 page results brochure which I can look at in years ahead, to remind me that I was there on the big day. Can I possibly keep going until I am fifty, and make the 3 hours 30 minutes qualifying time? Who knows?

'LA's fine, the sun shines most of the time, the feeling is laid back', is the introduction to a well-known Neil Diamond number. However when I visited, I found that this couldn't have been further from the truth. Contrary to what people had told me both before and after my holiday, I didn't take to Los Angeles and have no desire to return.

Los Angeles is a sprawling metropolis with dozens of adjoining suburbs and diverse neighbourhoods. The car rules, with freeways at virtually every street end and it seemed to take an age to get around through the hold-ups and endless traffic lights.

With forty miles of beaches and the Pacific Ocean to the west and a mountain backdrop to the north and east, this seemed like paradise but don't you believe it. In my time there, the days were scorching hot, but I never saw the blue sky or sun which were continually blocked by a haze. This marathon was going to be warm, sticky and unbearable.

Downtown seemed almost a no-go area at night with shops and restaurants all boarded up and closed by 10 o'clock. On every street corner I was confronted by beggars asking for money, and even though no pressure was brought to bear, I felt particularly uncomfortable. One woman, obviously down at heel, rushed across the road as if attracted to me like a magnet. She hadn't eaten for days and said there was a chuck wagon just around the corner. This America seemed far removed from the one fervently portrayed by Bush, Clinton and other men in office. I did find one cosy bar where they asked for turns from the floor. A guy in a Stetson remarkably called the California Kid got up and sang, 'All my Ex'es live in Texas' and 'The Man who shot Liberty Vallance'.

Marina Del Rey was more like it with waterfront restaurants, bars and shops. I hired a bike to explore the area but had to make a fast retreat when the smog came down rather suddenly. The adjoining district, Venice Beach, is the home of artists and bohemian types, where jugglers, clowns and entertainers strut their stuff as much for themselves as the passing crowd.

At one time the area was a replica of its Italian cousin with canals and gondolas, but now only four canals remain.

I spent a pleasant half day at Long Beach and looked around the *Queen Mary* permanently moored here and flying boat *Spruce Goose* developed as a troop carrier in World War Two.

The goody bag presented at registration contained fifty articles, many of them groceries and this filled out my suitcase nicely for the return journey home. I lost my race number and got into a bit of a flap, but on telephoning race registration, somebody had handed it in. I breathed a sigh of relief and was able to run after all.

I stayed at Inglewood which was handy for the start and finish area at Exposition Park, but I had been ill-advised. Inglewood was a suburb with fast food restaurants, garages and a drive-in cinema and had a distinctly uneasy feel at night.

Conditions on race day were warm at start time and would become unbearable, the worst I had encountered since I began running. The start and finish were adjacent to the Los Angeles Coliseum, home of the 1984 Olympic games where Coe and Cram ran a one-two in the 1500 metres and where Joan Benoit won a popular victory in ladies' marathon for the host nation. I was a little disappointed as I thought we might finish on the track inside the Coliseum.

The early stages were through the high-rise buildings and skyscrapers of Downtown but we quickly reached Sunset Boulevard known as the Strip. Here we have sleazy night clubs and cheap motels rubbing shoulders with elegant restaurants and five star hotels.

Miles ten to thirteen were on Hollywood Boulevard and I tried to make the most of the shade provided by the frontages of run-down shops, pizza parlours and neighbourhood bars. While not as dense as the spectator support at London or New York, the crowds came out along this stretch to provide the runners with every bit of encouragement in the unbearable heat. All the way along here, we ran towards the huge white HOLLYWOOD block letters prominently placed on the hillside. Back onto Sunset and into Vine, dominated by the Capitol Tower Building shaped like a stack of gramophone records.

I was tiring but still had my tourist head on, trying to take in as much as possible, read the many street signs and remember what I could. The course ran along Wilshire Boulevard with elegant department stores and past exclusive leather and jewellery shops on Rodeo Drive.

The Beverley Hills area was spotless and a pleasure to run through. The streets were clean, gardens immaculate and the desirable housing in every shade of pastel imaginable. But I was given a drink of water here that definitely disagreed with me. It reminded me of my football days when we were given water at half-time, poured from a container that at one time had stored petrol. I would put in a four star performance in the second half but for the last ten minutes be running on empty.

I was running on empty too at the end of this race, perhaps a combination of the high temperature and too much walking in the days ahead of the race. The final miles were on agonisingly straight roads back to Exposition Park. Like so many marathons I have completed since, I managed to salvage a little pride by squeezing inside four hours.

I travelled by train the ninety miles south to San Diego, a journey of three hours or so, putting British Rail's performances into perspective. The line was single track for most of the way and the train continually stopped in passing places to let one through from the opposite direction. However the journey along the rugged Pacific coastline was spectacular and easily held my attention for the three hours. As much as I disliked Los Angeles, I adored San Diego. The sky was blue, the sun was visible, there was sea, sand, parks and wide open spaces.

San Diego was founded by Portuguese captain, Juan Rodriguez Cabrillo in 1542 and served as a stop-off point for Spanish Galleons on their way to the South Pacific. To this day it has upheld a seafaring tradition and is home to a US naval base. Throughout the city there are references to Cabrillo with a monument at Point Loma.

There is much to do and see in San Diego over a weekend or longer period and Tijuana over the Mexican border is only ten minutes away. San Diego Zoo, reputably the finest in the world, is set in natural surroundings in Balboa Park, giving the animals as much space as possible. There are lakes, canyons and forests provided for the wonderful assortment of animals and birds. A tramway runs overhead and there is also a guided bus tour available.

Sea World is at Mission Bay Park, but the entrance fee is a little on the steep side. Again there is a sky tram and a sky tower to view the wide range of penguins, sharks, otters and dolphins.

Old Town is situated between Mission Bay and Downtown and is a collection of old buildings steeped in history. The Old Town Historic Park covers thirteen acres, but many of the buildings are now souvenir shops and restaurants.

The Old Town Trolleys, similar to their counterparts in Boston, operate here with the driver laughing and joking his way around most of the cities main attractions. The trolleys even cross the spectacular bridge to the well-to-do districts of Coronado and Silver Strand. I didn't particularly relish the drive across the bridge as the rim was low and there was no safety rail to prevent vehicles from going over the side. I certainly wouldn't have fancied crossing in the trolley on a windy day.

Seaport Village has a prime waterfront location spanning several acres, with cobblestone paths and a wooden boardwalk. There are plenty of tourist shops, a selection of places to eat and plenty to keep the children occupied.

At night time, the place to head to is the Gaslamp Quarter, a dozen or so blocks of restored buildings in contrasting styles from Victorian to Spanish Renaissance. I visited this district some years later and it had been completely transformed with lots of new bars, restaurants and theatres. Ponies and traps, push-bikes and traps and rickshaws plied their trade with business seemingly brisk.

At Buffalo Joe's, there was live music, big screen sports and a wide variety of beers on tap. Dick's Last Resort was an oddball place where diners were provided with paper to throw at each other and the waiters and waitresses deliberately carried out their rude routines. Everyone seemed to enjoy themselves but it wasn't particularly my cup of tea.

I ended the evening in Moose McGillicuddies, which while pretty lively, was not too packed and everyone was kicked out at the not too unsociable hour of 1.30 a.m.

At weekends, queues developed outside the most popular venues as security rigorously checked the identification of individuals by way of a driving licence or passport. Pockets of people huddled together outside buildings, having a quick swallow as California has a no-smoking law in all public places. The celebrations were warming up particularly in the Irish Bars for St Patrick's Day the next week.

My reason for being here was to run the St Patrick's 10K race a week after the Los Angeles Marathon. The race, held exclusively in Mission Bay Park, started at 7.00 a.m. to beat the heat and before the hoards of weekend visitors began to arrive at the park. This is where locals come to jog, bathe, sail, skate-board, relax or simply hang out, and a day can easily be spent in the area.

The course was flat with the exception of ramps leading to bridges and the route followed pleasant paths flanked with palm trees. There were fun runs and children's races with families making a day out. At the finish, refreshments were provided along with beer and I was even approached by a young lady with a clipboard asking me if I was interested in becoming a member of a dating agency. It was my last night or I might have taken up her offer.

Some years later I visited San Diego again, this time to run the January marathon. I couldn't help thinking that this was just a distraction from the main part of the holiday which would be in Las Vegas. Several colleagues had visited Las Vegas some years earlier to run in the marathon, and they had been so impressed they had returned each year, picking out a different Californian race as the purpose for their visit.

The marathon, although in San Diego County, was based some distance north at Carlsbad. We registered on Saturday in order to have a reconnoitre and could have taken part in a 5K fun run had we known. We drove back along the Pacific Ocean Highway, where we were to run the next day. I had the opportunity to drive a left-hand drive car on the right-hand side of the road, which I carried out with trepidation.

The half marathon started at 7 o'clock with my race half an hour later. The Plaza Camino Real Shopping complex provided the race headquarters, adequate car parking and the start and finish areas. We parked close to the exit so as not to get caught up in the queues. A minute or so after the National Anthem and various announcements, we were off, running a mile within the complex before a niggling little climb to Carlsbad and the Pacific Ocean.

Two weeks earlier, I had completed my last long training run, doing an out and back on an unopened stretch of motorway and it had almost killed me. I was hoping I would fare and feel much better today. The route comprised several out and back sections around the Carlsbad Flower Fields and Palomar Airport Road. There were many sections where you could see runners both ahead and behind on the adjacent carriageway as roads appeared to be totally closed for the event.

There were long rolling sections along the Pacific Ocean Highway where bronzed Californians retreated from parked cars and disappeared over the giant sand dunes with surf boards under their arms. That must have been a damned sight easier than what I was doing.

I wouldn't particularly recommend the event. The parts of the course alongside the ocean were beautiful but most of the route was monotonous across dry and sandy terrain. As the miles passed by, the temperatures rose making for difficult conditions in the later stages. I was impeded by the pain from both my knees which were problematical at the time but I knew I would be alright just as long as I kept going. I met with some success in managing to do this and not having to resort to walking. For my efforts, I was once again able to scrape inside four hours.

A paragraph in Fielding's *San Diego* describes joggers as running on bike paths and on streets, paying no attention to oncoming traffic as they continually monitor their pulses. They are sick people.

Well, sick people or not, San Diego caters for them providing two other races. The Rock and Roll Marathon held in June is based in and around the city and sold out on its debut several years ago. It provides a fun to run atmosphere with rock bands playing at each mile post. More established is America's Finest City Half Marathon held every August on a course from Point Loma to Balboa Park. If I should return one day, this is the race I would be looking to run.

Alan decided to join Kevin, John and myself at the last minute for the trip to New York in the autumn of 1993. Sports Tours were fully booked but agreed to put an extra bed into the room if we were in agreement. We stayed at the Travel Inn close to Times Square and with four in the room, could barely swing a cat around. The staff had put the television set in a corner close to the door, in an attempt to create some much needed space. On seeing this Alan decided to give it pride of place, lifting it from the floor and placing it bang in the middle of the dressing table. The idea of doing this was a little misplaced as this set was to a television what a ghetto blaster is to a transistor radio.

After barely a day, clothes were strewn on the floor and on every surface imaginable. When I stressed the importance of keeping the room tidy they just started to 'take the mick' and continued to do so throughout the week.

The weather was cold and clung to you like a vest in the days leading up to the race. We took the Circle Line Cruise but had to stay inside the cabin, and visited the Statue of Liberty, climbing up the narrow stairway to reach the head, not particularly recommended.

There was no record of Alan entering the race when we arrived to register and we had to return the next day and constantly badger the couriers to try to sort it out. Alan wasn't having a great deal of luck.

I managed to lose the other three at the race start in Fort Wadworth. They must have been trying to make a point following my constant moaning about the state of the room.

Seven years had passed since I first ran here but the experience was just as memorable; the crossing of the Verrazzano and the other bridges on the course, the enthusiastic crowds and spectacular Central Park finish. The torrential rain had given way to a warm and sunny day and after starting in tee shirt and singlet, I had to jettison my tee shirt to an appreciative youngster in Brooklyn.

Leading into the race, I had been in a rich seam of form, or as rich as a 'Middle of the Packer' like myself is capable of. The previous week I had dipped under seventy minutes at the Guy Fawkes Ten in Knaresborough, no mean feat for a man of my calibre, and I was really looking forward to the marathon. On the day I started to struggle very early into the proceedings and finished in a disappointing 3 hours and 52 minutes. My time was slower than in 1986 when I ran round with my camera, stopping to take photos. Probably too many rib eye steaks in the days leading up to the race.

The downside to the event is the length of time you have to wait in the holding area before the race gets underway. All competitors need to be on Staten Island before the road closures are put into place, but even then the wait seems excessive.

In the days after the race, I fulfilled one ambition by visiting the Stock Exchange on Wall Street. Asking the security guard if they were trading, he took time off chewing his gum to flick his head, signalling us to enter. Unfortunately we hit the lunchtime lull with little trading taking place. The young men and women in brightly coloured blazers, signifying their positions were stood around talking in small pockets, ankle deep in sales vouchers and tickertape. The exhibits and memorabilia portraying the history of the Stock Exchange made the visit worthwhile.

We wandered into Central Park, the lungs of the city, caught the ferry from Battery Park to Ellis Island, a holding area for immigrants to the States between 1892 and 1954. The process took about four hours with those unsuccessful being sent back on the same ship. There is a record here of all immigrants through Ellis Island and you can check the progress of your ancestors through one of several easy to operate screens.

On the tip of Manhattan, close to the financial district is South Street Seaport, renovated docklands now transformed into galleries, shops, craft centres and a museum. We sat on the veranda with a coffee overlooking the East River and the Brooklyn Bridge. Taking in a spot of shopping, the three of them once again managed to lose me in Maceys.

The Great American breakfast is something I could have become accustomed to; pancakes with maple syrup, prime sirloin steak, eggs served any way imaginable and Danish pastries. We put a fair amount of money behind the counter of a local café and on the last morning there were hugs and handshakes all round when we made it known to the staff we were going home.

Sinatra described New York as the city that never sleeps and he certainly hit the nail on the head. The bar is an institution ranging from the cheap and cheerful all across town to the upmarket in the Wall Street area. The themed café bars such as The Hard Rock Café and Planet Hollywood tend to be in the blocks south of Central Park.

On weekdays bars fill up at lunchtime with shop workers and office staff and again they fill quickly after work for a more leisurely hour. Many bars stay open until the early hours and serve while ever anybody is paying.

We tended to make a couple of bars our locals. One was Dwyers, an Irish style bar frequented by the Sports Tours clientele and the couriers. The other was Coyote Kate's close to Times Square, where they took singers from the floor and where locals played pool in a cloud of smoke. We got to know some of the regulars over several days promising to return on our last evening. Alan got cold feet after becoming somewhat paranoid that we would be hustled big time at pool.

As with the London Marathon it is difficult to secure a place at New York unless you travel with a tour company. But even then you may be required to take an inclusive package of flight, accommodation and entry. Anyone applying direct to the race will go into a lottery just like the residents of the States. Successful candidates are not informed until August, when most flights and accommodation will probably be sold out.

Anyone wishing to run in New York shouldn't become too preoccupied with the marathon. The New York Road Runners Club is a full-time organisation arranging high quality races most weekends across the five boroughs. The Manhattan Half Marathon is particularly high profile and takes place in August, entirely within the confines of Central Park. A shorter race would leave you free to enjoy your stay and not leave you feeling as if you needed another holiday like I did on arriving home.

CHAPTER 20

A Bridge Too Far

WHEN THE ITINERARY was arranged for the 'JOGLE', it seemed as if 'Team D', of which I was part, would make the three major bridge crossings; and with a fair bit of luck and some gentle persuasion, I could be running across all three. On a miserable May Bank Holiday Monday morning, I made the first of the three crossings along the pedestrian walkway adjacent to the Severn Road Bridge, and I looked forward with anticipation to running the other two.

The JOGLE was a continuous relay, undertaken by members of Ackworth Road Runners, from Land's End to John o' Groats. We split into four teams with four or five runners in each, and had three mini coaches, each with a dedicated driver to cover the four teams. Each runner would take turns for around half an hour and then retire to the coach to be replaced by the next person who would be suitably refreshed and raring to go. This continued for eight hours, when the next team would then take over.

The retiring team would drive to overnight accommodation which hopefully wouldn't be too far away. The traditional 6-2, 2-10 and 10-6 shift patterns were used, so each team would move back a shift the next day. The entire run would take between five and six days, and it was reckoned that each team would run twice in England and twice in Scotland.

However the best laid plans were thrown into turmoil when a mystery runner turned up unannounced and ran fifteen miles in quick time. Bob ran out of his skin for 'Team B', so much so that his team mates had to keep dragging him from the road and back into the van so they could take a turn.

A culmination of these events put the JOGLE well ahead of schedule, so following a number of emergency meetings in remote car parks, and several phone calls later, the overnight accommodation was rescheduled to put the event back on track. So instead of running over the Forth Bridge, I ended up in a guest house in a rain-drenched Blair Atholl, with an elderly couple and their smelly dog, watching the 'All Blacks' hammer Wales. We never even got to see Blair Castle and the Duke of Atholl's private army.

The Edinburgh Marathon turned out to be the first and last at least for the time being. The race had apparently proved too costly to stage, running well over budget, so I was pleased to have run the race when I did.

Kevin and I walked ourselves to a standstill the day before the race, climbing the many steps to the castle esplanade where the military tattoo takes place each August. The panoramic views were stifled by the mist, although clearly visible was the Firth of Forth, along with the road and rail bridges where we would run the next day.

Arguably my favourite British city and an excellent short break destination, I would never tire of wandering the steep alleyways, cobbled streets and atmospheric Royal Mile.

In the afternoon, we watched my adopted team, Ross County beat Partick Thistle 2-0. After being held up in traffic and moved on by a steward from a vice president's car parking space into one hardly wide enough for a push bike, we missed the opening goal. In an uneventful game, we had to wait until the penultimate minute to see County clinch the spoils. The biggest cheer of the day came when the pies arrived.

Conditions on race day were cold and misty as runners were ferried in a convoy of double-decker buses to the race start at Pittencreiff Park in Dunfermline. There were many familiar faces among a field of 5,000 including our Luton friends and Sports Tours courier and one hundred marathon man, Wally Oakes. Bernard of Askern, the man who finishes races with a trademark somersault, was also in the starting frame.

The early pace was slow with narrow roads and many roundabouts. After five miles, a long incline brought us onto the walkway alongside the Forth Road Bridge. The views of small vessels in the water below, the spectacular railway bridge to the left and the white Lego-like buildings of South Queensferry were worth the entry fee alone. That is providing you had a head for heights.

I had the privilege of running with three South African young men across the bridge, who were combining an overseas race with watching the 'Rainbow Nation' compete in the Rugby World Cup. Just as I have worn my Union Flag singlet with pride when competing overseas, they ran each with a national flag draped over their shoulders.

From here the course passed through the grounds of the appropriately named Forth Bridges Hotel, before undulating through Dalmeny Country Estate. I seemed to get away from Kevin on the climbs but he tended to come tearing past me on the downhills. The long inclines and steep descents did my knees no favours, but a long flat stretch along the Cramond Esplanade beside the Firth of Forth went some way towards redressing the balance. A series of cycleways in disused railway cuttings brought us into the heart of the city, with the crowd along Princes Street sporadic but supportive.

By now the early morning conditions had changed to hot and humid, making for a difficult last couple of miles. A steep incline led to the Royal Mile where at last there was some downhill to enjoy albeit for the cobbles. The final section passed through the grounds of Holyrood Palace, skirted the foot of Arthur's Seat, and finished on the running track inside Meadowbank Stadium. Once again I just edged inside four hours.

With many road closures in place, our exercise for the day hadn't finished. We walked two miles to Waverley Station and queued for a taxi to return to our hotel in the West End. Organisers quickly announced a race date for the following year and promised improvements to course and organisation. A further announcement some months later stated that plans for a race in the year 2000 had been scrapped, a great pity.

Over the years, my running exploits have taken me over many great bridges from the Verrazano to the Vasterbron and from Tyne Bridge to Tower Bridge. I've run the Forth Bridge, the April 25th Bridge and the 59th Street Bridge.

Running over a bridge gives me a sense of satisfaction, achievement and wellbeing, whether it is a world famous suspension bridge, a pack-horse bridge in the Yorkshire Dales or merely a wooden bridge crossing a stream.

Many of the capital city races tend to have routes that stick close to river banks or the waterfront making for a faster and flatter course, hence the probability that there will be some bridges.

The flagship race for bridges undoubtedly has to be the New York City Marathon, with the Verrazano Bridge start and four other bridges. My favourite is the '59th Street Bridge' or 'Queensboro Bridge', linking Queens to Manhattan across the East River. The views of the New York skyline are awesome and the welcome from spectators packed four or five deep on the pavement, as you run off into First Avenue has to be sampled to be believed.

The Willis Avenue Bridge, a much smaller mechanical lifting structure, links Harlem to the South Bronx close to Yankee Stadium. One year on race day, the hydraulics failed with the bridge not completely closing. This left runners facing a gap of a couple of feet, not particularly recommended for the slightly nervous.

Many races such as the Lisbon Half Marathon have a spectacular bridge start which tends to capture the imagination, but not always the case for the faint-hearted. The 'April 25th Bridge' has huge metal plates as a surface with the River Tagus clearly visible below.

The Bosphorus Bridge at the start of the Eurasia Marathon in Istanbul links Asia to Europe across the Bosphorus Straits. When I ran here in 1996, the early morning mist was so dense, you could hardly see the stanchions and parapets, let alone the water and shoreline below. On the start line, '100

Marathon Club' runner Glynn Parry presented me with me with his business card with a view to running an overseas marathon the following year. I often wondered how many of these he had tucked away in various pockets. The Istanbul course included two other long bridges, the Galata Bridge where dozens of locals dropped their lines into the murky waters below hoping for a catch, and the Ataturk Bridge spanning the misleadingly named Golden Horn.

The Deutzer Brucke at the start of the Cologne Marathon spans the mighty Rhine and provides breathtaking views of the domes and spires of the German city and the unmistakable outline of St Ursula's Cathedral.

The Budapest races use the banks of the not so blue Danube to good effect, crossing the Margaret, Chain and Elizabeth Bridges. The Charles Bridge is one of the main tourist attractions within Prague's old town but all comes to a standstill as runners negotiate the tricky cobbles at the start of the city's races.

The Gothenburg Half Marathon includes two long bridges on its journey through Sweden's second city. The Älvsborgs bron is a large suspension bridge at the harbour mouth while the Götaälvbron brings runners back into the city.

The layout of Amsterdam means there are many bridges to cross over the canals in the running of the city's marathon. For the best part of the race, these were novel, great fun and provided an opportunity to see the best of the city's waterfront houses. As the race progressed and fatigue set in, they became no more than great humps in the road and provided nothing but nuisance value. The gentle ramps leading to the bridges had suddenly taken on the feel of mountainsides.

In the year 2000, I ran the Bridge Race to end all Bridge Races. Some years earlier, a magazine I picked up at the London Marathon exhibition had an advertisement for 'The Bridge Race'. This would take place sometime in the year 2000, but as yet, the date was unknown. This was the race for me so I promptly replied and put my name down.

The Bridge Race would be approximately half marathon distance crossing a proposed new bridge linking Denmark with Sweden. As the months progressed, I received updates and literature with a provisional race date. A Bank Holiday Monday in June had been settled upon so I set about arranging a flight and accommodation. With each update, the number of competitors had grown and 30,000 runners had already signed up a year before the planned date.

Denmark comprises a series of islands, linked by ferries and bridges, with the only border being between Jutland and Northern Germany. Capital city Copenhagen is on the island of Zealand with Sweden a few miles to the east across a stretch of water known as the Øresund. The bridge to be known as the Øresund Fixed Link would take both road and rail from close to Copenhagen Airport at Kastrup, to Malmö on the Southern tip of Sweden. There were apparently people both in favour and against the link, but for Swedes, easy access would be created to Copenhagen Airport with direct and connecting flights world wide.

Few would dispute that Copenhagen is the liveliest of the Scandinavian cities. It is also a walking city with many streets free of traffic including the main pedestrianised Stroget. The Rådhuspladsen or Town Hall Square is the heart of Copenhagen. The Town Hall itself is built to medieval design from red brick. The façade and interior comprise details of Nordic history and mythology. The square is one of the main traffic junctions in the city, and all distances in Denmark are measured from this point.

The Central Station is nearby and opposite are the world renowned Tivoli Gardens. A landscaped amusement park, Tivoli has an open air stage, a concert hall, lakes and gardens. A great place to unwind with coffee, cake or a meal, there are more than twenty restaurants in the gardens ranging from stylish to snack bar. Several nights a week throughout the summer, the gardens close at midnight with a sensational firework display.

Stroget cuts through the medieval heart of the city, a one mile pedestrian precinct with shops ranging from top to tacky. The street changes name several times and crosses many squares where there are street vendors, buskers and musicians.

At one end of Strøget is Nyhavn, a water inlet and famous Copenhagen landmark with old wooden schooners lining the quayside. In years gone by, the north side was a den of iniquity for homecoming sailors with dingy taverns, whore houses and tattoo parlours. Although some of the quaint inns still remain, a combination of restaurants and bars see revellers spill out onto tables and chairs during the long summer evenings. I called at the appropriately named 'Skippers' on Saturday lunchtime for a nice cool beer.

It was at Nyhavn where Denmark's favourite son, the famed fairytale poet and author, Hans Christian Andersen is said to have arrived following his sea voyage from home town Odense. He lived at a couple of addresses along the quayside during his time in Copenhagen.

With Copenhagen Card purchased to cover transport, admission fees and so on, over the several days, I set out to register for The Bridge Race. A couple of train journeys and a bus ride later, (I caught the wrong train at first) a reasonable walk brought me to a huge sports complex on the outskirts of the city, and registration took place in a large hall.

For the entry fee of approximately £40, I received a back pack, rain cape and a drinking belt containing four water bottles. This would come in nicely on those long Sunday runs. There was also a tee shirt sporting the name 'Brølobet' which roughly translated means Bridge Race. Among the literature I picked up was a Danish fixture list with a section on International races. Among the British races shown was the good old Leeds Marathon. Can we now expect a Viking invasion in forthcoming years?

The temperature was scorching hot as I stopped to watch a football match on a local parks pitch. With the exception of the two goalkeepers, the twenty outfield players seemed to be attracted to the ball like bees to a honey pot. Surely I had played in a better standard than this?

The Bridge Race or Brølobet received widespread media coverage throughout the weekend. On Saturday there had been a mass cycle ride across the bridge. Why didn't I know about this? While not a prolific cyclist, I could have still managed this, particularly with bikes for hire all over the city. On Sunday there was a sponsored walk across the bridge. Why didn't I know about this? And on Sunday evening, a sponsored roller skate across the bridge.

On Monday morning I left the hotel with my route planned to the start. I was immediately offered a lift by a German man who was packing bags into the trunk of his car. Introducing himself as Dieter, he explained that he needed to shoot off immediately after the race in order to meet a ferry crossing to his home town of Lubeck. His English was fortunately good as I still hadn't taken those German lessons.

When we reached an out-of-town exhibition centre, he parked up and we boarded one of a convoy of double-decker buses, which quickly filled and set off to the start. After we had been going for a while, the driver pulled in to the side of the road and appeared to make a phone call. He then got off the bus as if to stretch his legs, got back on and made another call. He then climbed out of the cab, came down the aisle and made an announcement which I didn't understand. He then climbed the stairs presumably making the same announcement to the passengers on the upper deck. Apparently the bus was too high to pass under a new flyover, so he turned us around and returned to the exhibition centre. We promptly boarded another bus, this time meeting with more success, and soon arrived at a large sports field.

Here a jazz band provided entertainment, as we waited in a queue eventually passing below a ballooned gantry where our championship chips were programmed. We then followed a human crocodile through residential streets that eventually lead to a newly constructed road. Piles of rocks and pebbles formed a wall on each side of the road and beyond, the sand and the sea. In the distance could be seen the pillars and ramp leading to the magnificent suspension bridge where we would run. After years and months of waiting, I had eventually made it to the start line.

Changing and last minute preparations took place at the side of the road or on one of the many rocks that made up the sea wall. Dieter asked that I take a photograph to mark the occasion. I then vaselined, secured my number, and together we handed in our baggage for safe transportation to the other end. We made our way to the start and waited in a large pen. The whole procedure had started at 7.30 a.m. with the elite runners and would continue until late afternoon. Overseas runners like myself could turn up and run between 10.00 a.m. and midday, while Swedes, Danes and certain age groups were allocated different times. Twelve hundred runners would go every five minutes, from a starting list that had reputedly swelled to 70,000.

The wait wasn't long and after wishing each other the best of luck, Dieter moved comfortably ahead eventually disappearing out of sight. The first part of the race was four kilometres through a tunnel followed by a further four kilometres across the man-made island of Peberholm. The section across the bridge would be eight kilometres with the final section on the Swedish mainland close to Malmo.

The road through the tunnel ran downhill to begin with. The feeling was claustrophobic, and with so many runners, the atmosphere was humid and the sweat poured from me like a tap. Even though I was moving nicely, I felt far from comfortable. Subconsciously I was a little worried about my knees and feared I might struggle.

The tunnel levelled out probably on the seabed and a testing incline brought us into daylight once again. The island lay ahead with the bridge now appearing larger than ever. To the right was the high speed railway line, and on the far carriageway, a persistent convoy of buses transporting runners to Denmark. Some would have already finished their race and were heading back home, while others would be Swedish runners on their way to the start. Several people in each coach would wave across enthusiastically. The occasional TNT vehicle flashed by in the opposite direction transporting baggage to the finishing area.

The red-hot weather of the previous days had given way to a cooler brisker day once we were out of the tunnel, perhaps not a bad thing. The ramp onto the bridge comprised a series of pillars with the railway line now running on a lower deck below the road. The higher we climbed, the stiffer the breeze became, blowing across from the right. With the main span now looming large, a slight left turn brought us below the near tower and onto the platform of the bridge.

Apparently since the bridge was first put out to tender in the early nineties, the specification and design had constantly changed to ensure two of the largest vessels could safely pass side by side between the centre spans.

Volunteers handed out cups of water from a large transporter tanker parked on the hard shoulder. At least I could save my water bottles for later in the run. I caught a glimpse of my German friend Dieter who was one of many paying a call of nature over the side of the bridge.

Running below the second tower, mainland Sweden was now clearly visible and it would be all downhill from here to the far bank. As anticipated, my knees started screaming for mercy on this section, but the relentless walking in the previous days and the sampling of Denmark's fine lagers had done me no favours either. In very much a field of mixed abilities, some runners slipped past comfortably while others huffed and puffed. The only people I seemed to overtake were those who had resorted to walking. What the heck were the cyclists doing here, their race had been on Saturday?

As I came off the bridge, the tented village with hot air balloons and helicopters hovering was clearly visible, but still five kilometres and half an hour away. My stride had shortened and my predicted 100 minutes finishing time looked like being closer to 110. The course cut through an amusement park where overhead sprinklers were available to cool down the runners. I gave these a miss as the only time I have used them, the water trickled down my back chaffing the insides of my legs. Each time they rubbed together it was sheer agony and I ended up running with my legs shaped like a couple of boomerangs.

Eventually I finished in 1 hour and 47 minutes and looked forward to changing into dry clothes. It was my intention to spend an hour or so in the tented village. I would have a drink, a bite to eat and catch the return bus to Denmark hopefully by early afternoon.

However my plans were thrown into turmoil when I was unable to locate my back pack. The bags had been laid out in hundreds of neat rows, each channel marked off with tape and a board indicating the estimated start time and block of numbers. I looked where my back pack should have been but it wasn't there. The bags weren't laid out in strict numerical order and with each one identical to the next, except for the number, I needed to inspect every one. I went to the same numerical blocks but with different starting times and still couldn't find my bag.

The bags were being transported from start to finish by TNT and trucks were continually pulling up and depositing piles of bags onto the grass. Bag handlers were then deployed to take them to their respective rows on the huge playing fields. Many people were in the same position as me, and each time a new consignment of bags arrived, they took it upon themselves to wade in to try find their own. This was pointless – akin to looking for a needle in a hay stack and the situation was turning into a free-for-all.

One Brit who was evidently as frustrated as I was took his anger out on a hapless steward, asking for his name and threatening action. He said that he had TNT contacts back home and had put a fair bit of business their way. I kept revisiting areas where my bag probably could have been but without any luck. The channels for the earlier starters were almost empty with the later ones rapidly filling up.

When I was all but giving up hope, feeling cold and miserable and with panic setting in, I somehow stumbled across my bag by accident. I couldn't open it quickly enough to make sure the contents inside were mine. Thankfully they were but the whole experience had taken me over two hours to resolve, longer than it had taken me to complete the race. I had started to imagine myself returning to Denmark, still in running kit and having to come back the next day to see if my luggage had arrived. Where I would have reported to and how I would have got there is anybody's guess.

Needless to say I neither had the time or the inclination to explore the tented village and the considerable entertainment that had been provided for the weekend's events. I joined what was now a considerable bus queue, but thankfully the turnaround was far better organised than the baggage.

I enjoyed the ride back over the bridge as runners still streamed across on the far carriageway. The occasional TNT truck would flash by no doubt causing more chaos and turmoil on arrival. The Dane who sat with me suggested I caught the train from inside the airport terminal back to the city. He walked with me to the platform, showed me the ropes and again sat next to me. He had run the race as part of a corporate team and seemed to know a fair few people on the train. He stayed on for Helsingor so I thanked him and bade him farewell.

As I walked through the city centre back to the hotel, large crowds were gathering around huge screens placed strategically in the main squares. Denmark as underdogs were taking on Holland and I had planned to find a bar later on to watch England's opener with Portugal. England lost and Denmark in keeping with the other Scandinavian countries suffered an early exit from the Euro 2000 football tournament.

When the race results, photograph and literature arrived several weeks later, an enclosed letter apologised for the trouble caused by the mishandling of baggage. The race organisers had obviously underestimated the task in hand and deflected all the blame away from TNT.

I had believed this race would be a one-off and would probably never be repeated. Road closures affecting major links reputedly disrupt businesses and affect the economy, but I have since seen The Bridge Race advertised for 2002. So who knows in years to come? Copenhagen also stages a popular marathon in May and a well subscribed half marathon in September.

In the days after the race, I had the opportunity for more sightseeing, giving my legs little chance to recover. I walked for what appeared to be several miles to visit the little mermaid but was not overly impressed. I had expected an altogether larger statue further out in the harbour.

I visited the Viking town of Roskilde, a short train journey towards South West Zealand. Dominated by the imposing Domkirke, the cathedral had been started in AD 1000, reaching completion in 1410. This had been the burial place to generations of Danish monarchs. I could have gladly spent longer there but moved on to the Viking Ship Museum where five longboats recovered from the bed of the Roskildefjord in 1962 had been restored. One of these is a warship similar to the one depicted on the Bayeux Tapestry and could seat upwards of forty men.

Having never heard of Roskilde before my visit to Denmark, it made the world headlines shortly after my return home when several lost their lives following a tragic accident at a pop festival.

Helsingor, the main ferry crossing to Sweden, is a historic town with well-preserved brightly coloured buildings. Kronberg Castle, Hamlet's Castle of Elsinore looks out across the strait from a bluff of land. I watched as people carried case upon case of beer onto the ferry, obviously cheaper to buy in Denmark than in Sweden. I wondered how the ferries would be affected by the advent of the bridge.

I caught the hydrofoil to Malmö hoping for a glimpse of the bridge and perhaps travel below the centre span. The crossing took a slightly different direction, with the bridge barely visible in the distance.

As soon as I stepped onto the harbour in Malmö, I saw the friendly faces of Mary and Ken Thompson from Harrogate. While visiting friends in Sweden, Ken had used the opportunity to take part in the race. They were on their way home so after comparing notes, we went our separate ways. The day was perhaps spoiled by the particularly strong wind, with advertising boards and litter being thrust into the air in Malmö's compact streets.

On my final morning, I wandered over pleasant bridges and alongside waterways to Christiania, an area taken over by hippies in the early seventies and known as the Free State. An abandoned barracks within a fortress and much in need of repair, the estimated one thousand inhabitants included motor cycle gangs, down-and-outs and thugs. While regularly patrolled by police, it remains a haven for criminals and drug pushers. I advanced far enough to satisfy my curiosity, thought to myself, 'What the hell am I doing here?' and bid a hasty retreat back to the city.

Back on home soil, my favourite 'Bridge Run' has got to be the Ripon Midsummer Evening Run, held in June each year. The course centres around Studley Royal Park and Fountains Abbey to the west of Ripon and cuts through the appropriately named Valley of the Seven Bridges. The River Skell meanders through the steep sided valley, crossed by a variety of metal, wooden and stone arched bridges. The same course is usually transformed into a mud bath for the festive Jolly Holly Jog, with the gently flowing River Skell now a raging torrent.

My favourite bridge is neither arched, cantilever or suspension. It's a small basic post and rail affair, spanning the entrance to the marina where the narrow boats moor close to Lemonroyd Lock. I regularly pound the tow paths of the Aire and Calder canal close to home and usually plan a stop on the bridge. I may have a time check, a drink from my water bottle, or I may simply gaze out across the water. It's moments like these that make it all seem worthwhile.

CHAPTER 21

Barking Mad

WHILE CROSSING the colliery landfill on an early morning run, a dog had been for a dip in one of the man-made lakes. It caught me up, bringing me to an abrupt halt and vigorously shook its coat, drenching me from head to toe. Apart from this I was barked at, obstructed and chased on three separate occasions. One of the owners apologised for the inconvenience but the other two suitably ignored me, instead attending to the welfare of their respective pooches, and making sure they had come to no harm.

Every runner will have suffered similar experiences on numerous occasions and those who haven't are either extremely fortunate or they are telling lies. The situation today was of my own making as I should have gone out earlier while owners were safely tucked up in bed and before their dogs had made a bolt for the door.

In the early days of the running boom, a celebrity type of dog emerged running at their owner's heel for mile upon mile. They panted like Rolf Harris with tongue hanging out of steaming mouth. Sometimes they would be awarded their own personal number and given a finishing time and position. One ultra distance runner I came across would take his dog for the long haul and I can recollect it jumping into the water to cool down during a hot Grantham Canal Run. But unfortunately that's about as good as it gets.

My love-hate relationship with dogs, or rather their owners, started long before I took up running as a pursuit, in the days when I was starting out in the big wide world.

I tended to park my car, a 1967 Austin 1100 on a spare piece of land adjacent to home. Each morning a man would arrive regular as clockwork and stand with his dog. The man was probably in his late fifties and the dog a spaniel type breed. Sometimes it would be wearing a cone over its head, but that didn't prevent it from regularly depositing next to my car. If I was looking out of the window or in the garden, the owner would stand and stare as if to taunt me.

One day while getting into the car, I suffered a cake on the sole of my shoe. It took me the best part of the day, on and off, to remove it and I never did manage to get rid of the lingering smell. Enough was enough and I decided there and then to declare war on the owner.

Several mornings later he appeared large as life but this time I was ready for him. I asked him not to let his dog deposit near my car, but to my amazement he replied, 'Too late, come and have a look'. I couldn't believe the impudence of the man and it was to get even better. He informed me he could take his dog anywhere to deposit and would do as he pleased. He hadn't liked my attitude and asked me to accompany him to the police station.

This seemed a strange thing to do as he clearly didn't have a leg to stand on. Not wishing to have any police visits to the house after I had left for work, I reluctantly decided to follow him, eventually overtaking him when the spaniel required another pit stop. To cut a long story short, they more or less kicked us out of the police station. When my Dad telephoned later in the day to clarify our position, they had no record of the incident and gave him very little encouragement.

The action seemed to have the desired effect as his visits became less frequent, although occasionally he would drop by just to remind us he hadn't gone away altogether. I would see him from time to time with the spaniel in the passenger seat of the car and his wife sat in the back. One day he and the spaniel stepped off the kerb causing a car to brake and the driver to sound his horn. Immediately he turned and stuck two fingers up at the driver, and I found myself shouting 'Typical'.

When I started running, I would meet him and the spaniel along narrow paths through the fields. Nowhere was there a more polite and courteous runner than myself but there was no way I would give way for this man. He wasn't prepared to give an inch either so I sometimes found myself crashing into his shoulder. I probably felt good at the time, but on recollection, I gained little satisfaction from these acts.

Never having owned a dog, I hadn't particularly taken an interest in the canine species and couldn't tell two breeds apart. In the years that followed I was to learn quickly. I soon got to know the pit bull from the poodle and the pug from the Pekinese. My early running days coincided with new roads and industrial units being built in the area. In turn, this generated spare land, ideal for travellers to park their caravans and set up home.

No sooner were they evicted from one site, than they would move to the next, usually leaving a devastation of rubbish and debris in their wake. They would bring with them bandy-legged horses, a selection of poultry and mean looking dogs that were allowed to roam about freely.

On a night out, I had taken a short cut along a footpath between farmers' fields to catch a bus on the main road. Even though I was a fair distance from the caravans, I was confronted by two mean looking dogs that blocked my path. One managed to stop me in my tracks, and when I tried to move away, tugged at the back of my trouser leg. When I raised my voice and became angry, the dogs fled amidst muffled growling. Only when I returned home did I realise my skin had been severed and there was a trickle of blood down the back of my leg.

The next incident happened in the first Rothwell Half Marathon when the course passed by the same caravans. On a hot day and with only a small field, the runners were well strung out by this time with huge gaps appearing. This was one of my early races and at that time I was more of a 'Back of the Packer' having not progressed to my rightful place as 'Middle of the Packer'.

A dog that looked like a cross between a big greyhound and a bloody big greyhound made itself known, running alongside before turning in an ungainly fashion and almost knocking me over. It did this several times until I became wise to its tactics. As soon as it turned I would accelerate ensuring it couldn't get sufficiently close to bite. It was an awkward beast and took a while to turn just like one of those giant oil tankers. This enabled me to get a fair way in front before it came bounding past me again. A mile further on and half a dozen turns later, the greyhound must have lost interest and decided to leave me alone.

Another incident I encountered with travellers' dogs was when I was completely surrounded by four of the meanest looking ones imaginable, bringing me to a halt. Each time I flinched they edged closer threatening to take a chunk out of my kneecaps. A traveller tinkering with the engine of a van called the dogs to heel, but no dialogue was exchanged between us and no apology forthcoming. I bet they had a good laugh at my expense while telling the tale that night around the camp fire.

I was always told that you weren't allowed to raise a hand to dogs, as you would be hauled before the RSPCA quicker than you can say Jack Russell. These days you aren't allowed to raise a hand to cheeky youths but I sense a mood of change on that one.

I quickly learned to turn situations to my advantage. If a dog bothered me and the owner called out its name, I would use the name to give it the come on and would soon put half a mile between the dog and the hapless owner.

While I don't condone acts of violence against dogs, a colleague of mine would tend to go over the top and take the law into his own hands. If bothered by a dog, he would regularly stick the boot in. He and a friend were reputed to have picked a dog up and bundled it down a banking, when the owner seemed content to watch as it snapped at their heels. This tended to upset him as on each occasion he was confronted by the beasts, the owners were always nearby yet appeared to exercise no control over their pets. Even worse in his eyes, they showed no sympathy or remorse towards the runner.

On another occasion when these two runners were out together, a dog broke free from its owner and chased them dragging its lead behind. One of the runners spotted this and quickly grabbed the lead, and they took the dog for the run of its life, undoubtedly a personal best. They then tethered the dog to a remote fence leaving it for the owner to recover.

This reminded me of an incident in my boyhood years while out playing football in the street. Some particular neighbours wouldn't return the ball when it went into their garden and wouldn't let us retrieve it either. My uncle played tit for tat by confiscating their cat and leaving it in his attic for a day.

Dogs aren't the only animals to take an interest in runners. I've heard tales of a horse chewing a runner's tee shirt and a runner being charged by a bull. However one of my most bizarre experiences was rescuing a sheep from the canal, this being initially sparked off by a dog.

The dog had been chasing a flock of sheep in a field as I ran along the canal tow path, and the owner was nowhere to be seen. The sheep hurried through a hole in the fence onto the tow path, with the dog in pursuit and made towards a narrow gap between the fence and the canal. Too many sheep went for the gap at the same time and the two on the end were edged into the water.

Both swam towards the far bank with one managing to clamber out. The second one was unable to follow suit and after initially reaching the far side, drifted out again towards the middle. I ran back across the lock gates, almost being ploughed down by the first sheep on its way back to the pen.

The second sheep, still in the canal seemed to be treading water, just to stay afloat and seemed to have no definite escape plan in mind. I leaned out to try reach the sheep but was unable to do so, but I did manage to get a clothes prop from outside the lock keeper's cottage. I tried to deflect the sheep back towards the bank but it just drifted further out.

By now it was looking bedraggled, feeling sorry for itself and had started bleating. I could imagine its little legs working overtime below the surface merely to keep afloat. Eventually, I managed to pull the sheep towards the side but was unable to lift it onto the bank. I could lift it part of the way, but the fleece had become too heavy for me to make the final pull. I managed to keep its head above water but each time I tried to lift it, it turned over onto its back.

In the nick of time a cyclist came by and I summoned him to help. At first he ignored me but came when I ordered him to give me a hand. Together we managed to pull the sheep out of the water and onto the grass. It lay on its side gasping for breath, looking up at me through tired eyes, hopefully no worse for the ordeal. I may have prolonged its fate but couldn't help thinking it would end up as somebody's Sunday roast in the weeks ahead.

Another group of people who frequent the canal banks but won't give runners the time of day are fishermen. It's a relief to know that it just isn't the runners these people detest. It's cyclists, horse riders, dog walkers, pleasure boats or generally anyone who disturbs the fish.

They sit silent and motionless, sometimes in damp or freezing weather without a word for any passers-by. They arrive early morning on the rivers, canals and lakes either for pleasure or in a match environment. In the latter, they sit spaced out at their respective pegs, moving only for a call of nature or when time is called for the weigh-in.

They welcome no distractions and won't suffer fools gladly. Many a time I have run the tow paths and hurdled over their poles with barely a glance. Occasionally I have noticed a flick of the head as I run past, to the guy further along the bank as if to say, 'Look at that stupid git'.

A similar thing happened to me while running along the river bank through the centre of Leeds, near the Royal Armouries. A fisherman on seeing me approach indicated to the man along the bank who turned his head to look at me. Reading the situation like a book, I shouted to the first man at the top of my voice, 'Coming through'. Not only would I have disturbed the fish in the immediate vicinity but probably the fish and fishermen up to a mile downstream. That would teach the miserable sods to take the piss out of me.

While I have no axe to grind with fishermen, I couldn't imagine sitting there for hours on end, in all weathers without the hint of a bite. Equally they perhaps couldn't comprehend anyone pounding the highways and byways for hours on end for no apparent end result. I get a slightly different outlook as I press on and keep my body in something like reasonable shape.

Abandoned and burnt-out cars are something else the runner has to contend with, usually on some of the more isolated country routes. There is nothing worse than a tangle of burnt-out metal and upholstery blocking the path and my heart goes out to those people who find themselves minus a car. Dumped lorry-loads of tyres are another eyesore and this is another one that can usually be blamed on travellers.

On two occasions I have reported cars that appeared to have been stolen and then abandoned. In the first instance, I was able to remember the registration number as I repeated it over and over to myself as I ran home. The police thanked me for taking the trouble to report the car and seemed to know exactly where to look for it. The second time I came across a car in a ditch, while out on a long Sunday run. The local police station was closed so I was put through to a central switchboard and generally passed from pillar to post. The officer I spoke to didn't know the area and seemed more intent on logging my details rather than those of the car.

One day while out for a run, I was stopped by children and asked to put out a fire on an embankment. Whether or not they had started it, I don't know but it seemed to be getting out of control. I did the best I could to quash the flames with a convenient piece of carpet and provided the finishing touches with the soles of my running shoes, scorching them in the bargain. It may have been my imagination but when I started running again, I seemed to be on fire.

Many a motorist has stopped me over the years to ask directions, usually to the local motor auctions. One of the strangest requests I have had while out running was to give my name and address as witness to an accident. A lorry clipped a car while cutting in too quickly and failed to stop. I had seen the incident, heard the scraping of metal and was only too glad to help. Who says that running is boring?

CHAPTER 22

Take the High Road

UNABLE TO STAND the smelly dog for a moment longer, we left the guest house in Blair Atholl in search of a suitable establishment to have a meal. We had time to kill as our shift didn't start until ten o'clock that night, but with the rain unrelenting, we didn't venture too far. The Tilt Bridge Hotel would be open for meals at six, so we would be there dead on the dot and first in with our orders.

We returned briefly to the guest house, turning up at the wrong one to begin with. It had certainly looked like our guest house. I don't know who was the more embarrassed, us or the landlady.

Venison was on offer along with other traditional Scottish fayre, but with a stint of running to do in a few hours' time, I kept to the tried and trusted home-made steak pie, chips and two veg.

The minibus arrived with the rain sodden members of Team 'C' looking decidedly worse for a day dodging the showers. As they dejectedly trooped into the guest house, we bade them farewell and promised to see them in a couple of days' time. We loaded our baggage into the minibus for what lay ahead on the night shift.

Dave came into view and in no time at all handed over the horse brass which served as a baton to Roger, and once again we were on the road.

Having completed our day stint between Bridgewater and Hereford and our afternoon leg from Milnthorpe to Carlisle via the notorious Shap Fell, it was our turn for the night shift. We were all looking forward to the experience and up for the challenge.

Throughout May and June providing the weather was good, there would be a murky light until almost midnight in these parts. We would encounter three or four hours of darkness before daybreak, which wouldn't suit the long unlit stretches of the A9 dual carriageway.

I had been to the North of Scotland only once before when I stayed in a chalet at Aultbea on the West Coast with my parents. We visited the remote port of Ullapool where you could breathe the clear air and take in the spectacular scenery. There were wide open areas of isolation and solitude, wide glens and tranquil lochs. This was all well and good on a fine day but if the weather turned, a feeling of loneliness and isolation presided.

Roger finished his stint and handed on to Alberta, just as we reached the A9. Although only a plodder, Alberta, a tireless charity fund raiser, had run some of the great races of the world with a liking for the Médoc Marathon. Yesterday she had run the mile up the steepest section of Shap and wouldn't let us down now.

The JOGLE team relay from Lands End to John o' Groats was well ahead of schedule. This was frustrating from the point of view that I had missed out on running the bridges and our team wouldn't have a further stint in Scotland after tonight.

I took over from Alberta in total darkness with only the rear lights of the minibus visible ahead. Periodically, a heavy vehicle would belt past with the drivers perhaps wondering what we were up to at such an unearthly hour. The going appeared to be tough and I established that most of my stint must have been uphill. The southbound lane of the dual carriageway would occasionally meander away reappearing high above us.

It was mostly quiet apart from the occasional sound of a gushing stream or far-off osprey or buzzard. I would hear an animal dash for cover as I approached or glimpse the floating light of a distant farmhouse or homestead. Fortunately the rain had eased but as I climbed back into the minibus after my stint, I had worked up a real sweat and was glad to towel down and change into some dry clothing.

A determined-looking John took over from me, followed by Roger and Alberta again. We had climbed out of Glen Garry, over the Pass of Drumochter and would hopefully run into some useful downhill stretches. Dalwhinnie was skirted but we saw no further towns or villages until daybreak. When this happened the scenery was breathtaking with the snow-capped peaks of the highlands on the left and the Cairngorms to the right. We spread the workload running half an hour each but it was an undeniable pleasure to run in such surroundings. We passed through peat moors, hillsides covered with purple heather and pine forests, edging our way north towards Spey Bridge and Newtonmore.

Police paid a fleeting interest, slowing down in their patrol cars as they passed our runners and after a lull of several hours, the heavy goods convoy started once again. Banter in the minibus was dominated by the talk of breakfast when our shift had ended and this kept the runners on the road focused.

By now the River Garry had given way to the Spey with caravan parks and chalets looking out across the water. We passed hamlets and villages, many with whitewashed houses and we passed small hotels and holiday homes. The dual carriageway skirted Newtonmore and the distillery town Kingussie, as the terrain became rugged once again with the Monadhliath Mountains far away to the left.

My 'Abba Greatest Hits' cassette had long been switched off and Roger and John kept themselves entertained by firing football questions at each other. Trevor, who had gone over on his ankle on the first day had watched it balloon out of all proportion, but he decided it had improved sufficiently to give it another go.

The River Spey meandered to the east while the A9 headed west towards Carrbridge. Team 'A' made contact and duly changed over with us twenty miles south of Inverness. They took over our minibus with drinks, first aid supplies, blankets etc and we proceeded in theirs towards the capital of the Highlands.

The view on approaching Inverness was worth the drive alone. The town spread out before us, beyond the Moray Firth with the impressive Kessock Bridge taking the A9 to the Black Isle and further north.

John drove around the streets of Inverness, but at this unearthly hour there was only the McDonald's open for business. I suggested we press on across the Kessock Bridge where by rights our team should have run. The views from the centre point were of the Moray Firth, and the scenery was equally good as we started to descend towards the Cromarty Firth and Dingwall. We spotted a suitable place for our traditional Scottish breakfast and pulled over.

Having built up an appetite, we were determined not to be disappointed. There was sausage, eggs, hash browns, black pudding, white pudding, mushrooms and tomatoes supplemented with toast and washed down with mugs of sweet tea. John and Roger still fired football questions at each other but I had the opportunity to fire the football question at them that I had been keeping up my sleeve. Which Scottish League side plays at Dingwall? The answer from John was 'Nobody', while the answer from the others was, 'Don't know'. I had dropped enough hints the previous day and was surprised they hadn't known the answer. Roger would be the ideal choice as 'Phone a friend' on 'Who wants to be a millionaire?' He has an excellent knowledge of sport, geography and all kinds of music.

After establishing the answer to be Ross County and having the recent history of the club portrayed to us by the couple at an adjacent table, we left the café and walked along the high street in search of the ground. We found the ground to be Victoria Park, a compact little ground with neat little stands. The most northerly British club has probably the most beautiful location of any ground. After a spot of shopping, we boarded the minibus once again for the still considerable journey to John o' Groats.

The journey was interesting and varied, with the terrain changing from rolling to rugged. We travelled alongside the Cromarty Firth near Invergordon where drilling platforms had been towed ashore for maintenance. We crossed the Dornoch Firth over a recently constructed bridge at Tain, following the A9 to Golspie, home of Dunrobin Castle and home to the Earls and Duke of Sutherland. The railway line runs along the sea front and I imagine this train journey would more than rival some of the more prestigious scenic lines.

We continued past Brora, with the ground of Scottish Cup giant killers, Brora Rangers alongside the main road. Spectators here in recent years had included my Mum and Dad who took in a game while on holiday in the North of Scotland. At Helmsdale the railway turned inland away from the road and across barren moorland. The road became interesting with switchbacks and hairpin bends and my heart went out to the runners who would have to complete this section later that evening.

The last place of note before John o' Groats is Wick, the town on the weather map. We pressed on, reaching our bed and breakfast shortly after lunch, with some of the party taking the opportunity to catch up with some sleep. But there was exploring to be done so I ventured into John o' Groats, a series of houses, hotels and souvenir shops, all clean and white.

A small ferry berthed at the jetty for the island of Stroma, a few miles offshore. In one of the souvenir shops, I picked up a book outlining the history of Stroma which contained old photographs and documents. Even though I previously knew nothing of the island or its inhabitants, it proved to be a particularly fascinating read.

A large sign post with multiple arms stood in a strategic place on the headland with the mileage displayed to places worldwide. Someone was making an honest crust taking photographs and using 'Letraset' to install your own name or place. In a pub attached to the main hotel was an 'End to End Book' where you could record details of your own particular journey along with suitable comments. I would return the next day to add our entry.

'Team A' arrived at tea time and 'Team B' around midnight. It was left for 'Team C' to complete the journey shortly afterwards. We had been in constant telephone contact and were waiting when the lights of the minibus came into view along the narrow road. Everybody who was available ran the final half mile including some who had never run in their lives. Most ran in the clothes they were standing in, while the keener runners changed into their tackle.

We had been warned to keep the noise level down but despite this, we thrashed out several songs on the quayside. The representative from

Macmillan's, our chosen charity, cracked open a couple of bottles of bubbly in celebration.

After the euphoria had died down the next day, some of the party visited Wick, while others ventured into Thurso. The main visitor attractions in the area, Dounreay Nuclear Power Centre and Caithness Crystal, were both closed so we spent half a day in Wick dodging the showers. One minute saw brilliant sunshine and the next, driving rain. No wonder Wick figures regularly on the weather map. We ended up having a fish and chip supper at three o'clock in the afternoon.

I noticed signposts in and around Caithness to places like Scrabster, Ulbster, Lybster and others. Keen to find out more about these place names, I was told in the Tourist Information that they meant harbour or coast. The girl in the archive department at the local library cleared up the matter. She informed me the 'Ster' element of each place was an abbreviation for Bolstader which was the Norse term for homestead.

In the evening, a celebration dinner took place for all participants, drivers and volunteers to mark the completion of the JOGLE. A couple of wives turned up out of the blue to surprise their respective partners. Speeches were made and mementos presented to the organisers before more beer was consumed. An engaged couple who had been at loggerheads all week had appeared to give each other the cold shoulder. Another member became involved and had rather a lot to say and I was caught in the crossfire. This took some of the gloss off an enjoyable evening and a particularly enjoyable week.

Keen to make the trip again, I entered the Inverness Half Marathon in the March of the following year and have now run it twice. With holidays to be taken before the end of March, I made a long weekend with a night in Glasgow, two in Inverness and two in Edinburgh.

When I boarded the Inter City East Coast main line train at Leeds, I thought I had mistakenly turned up at a Vodafone or Cellnet convention. Everybody appeared to have one of the blasted things and I felt I was very much the odd man out. Passengers chatted away with useless banter such as, 'We're just pulling out of Leeds,' 'I'm five minutes away from York' or 'We've just come through a tunnel, I've lost you'. Some walked up and down the aisle while others spoke up above all the other noise. These things should be banned on trains, but I can see the day coming when I will need one. I've been put off them ever since the aerial of one of the early models went up the nostril of Del Boy Trotter, as he was roughed up by the dreaded Driscoll brothers.

The journey to Edinburgh is enjoyable with the view of Durham Castle and Cathedral from high above the city, one of the best to be had from a train. The Angel of the North is the next point of interest followed by the spectacular Tyne Bridge before the train pulls in at Newcastle. I had picked my seat so I would have the best possible view of the Northumbrian and Scottish coastline but to my dismay, the train reversed out of the station leaving me travelling backwards and looking out inland from the window.

Beyond Alnmouth, the railway travels close to the coastline with the sea, sand dunes and wide beaches clearly visible. I saw Dunstanburgh Castle, a landmark on the popular Northumbrian Coastal Run from Beadnell to Alnmouth. I saw Holy Island with the tidal causeway and Bamburgh Castle before crossing the Tweed estuary into Berwick.

The coastline becomes more rugged north of Berwick and the cliffs become sheer. From time to time there are windswept caravan and chalet parks in isolated places. The train makes a wide sweep to the left, alongside the Firth of Forth, with Bass Rock, home to many seabirds just offshore. Arthur's Seat stands out in the distance and before long, the train pulls to a halt inside Waverley Station. A quick dash across the platform follows, and onto the high speed train for Glasgow. The journey takes less than an hour and I stepped onto the platform at Queen Street shortly before half past eleven.

My room at the historic Central Station Hotel wasn't ready, so I left my baggage and spent a pleasant hour in the Counting House on George Square with a pie in a pot and a couple of pints. I pottered about for the rest of the day and evening, catching the train for Inverness the next morning, changing at Perth. The scenic rail journey parallel to the A9 where we had run didn't disappoint. The line cuts through a steep wooded gorge near Pitlochry and follows Glen Garry and the Spey Valley to Inverness.

My room at Inverness wasn't ready either so just for a change, I called for a pint and then caught the bus to Dingwall where I saw Ross County thrash Cowdenbeath 4-0. The view from my seat across the Cromarty Firth to the snow-capped mountains beyond was worth the admission fee alone.

Inverness is one of those places where you breathe in clean air. I walked the banks of the Ness which appeared to be high and fast flowing. Guest houses, hotels and upmarket accommodation line much of the embankment. In the other direction towards the Moray Firth, the outlook is bleak with drab buildings and shabby docks.

I saw the locks where the Caledonian Canal meets the Moray Firth. The canal runs sixty-two miles through the Great Glen towards Fort William. Only twenty-two miles is made up of canal with the rest of the distance across Lochs. The canal is fifty feet wide and there are twenty-eight locks.

Race day was bright but with a bitterly cold wind. The afternoon start meant I had time to digest a Traditional Scottish, before setting out to find Bught Leisure Centre, the race headquarters. I found it to be a mile from the centre along Ness Islands Road and reached by crossing the river on a footbridge that bounced with every stride.

This is the first major race in the Scottish Calendar with entries from far and wide which is why they perhaps opted for an afternoon start. The seven hundred or so runners completed a small loop within the confines of the leisure centre grounds before heading along the Ness Bank Road towards the town. We were being nicely pushed along by a stiff breeze, but on crossing the river and doubling back along the opposite bank, we felt the full force of the wind.

The course was flat for four miles but then turned sharp left and began a long climb through woodlands and rural areas. More climbing took the course beyond the halfway point and through housing estates and residential suburbs. Occasionally, encouragement would be given from families watching from gardens and spotty-faced urchins shouting, 'Get those knees up'. Several twists and turns and changes of direction brought the course above the castle, leaving a steep downhill to the waterfront. Sections along each side of the river brought the race to a finish on the athletics track at Bught Park. The run was enjoyable with the course and scenery varied and I felt sure I would be back.

I changed into warm clothes, woolly hat and gloves to protect me against the cold and on returning to the hotel, I soaked to my heart's content in a hot bath. I set out for more exploring but in the fading light, ended up having a pub meal and a couple of pints. I ended up in the illustrious company of a local man who said he had been banned from six pubs, but with over a hundred drinking establishments in Inverness, he was nay bothered.

At breakfast the next morning, the waiter asked if I was going home today, to which I replied, 'Yes'. 'And to where would that be, sir?' he asked. Well, I suppose if you want to know something, you should ask, but in a virtually deserted restaurant, he was only making small talk. There were several people in railway uniform having breakfast, who all appeared familiar to the staff. I was safe in the knowledge that while they were here, the train wouldn't leave without me.

The journey to Edinburgh takes about three hours. I visited the usual tourist places, Edinburgh Castle, Holyrood Palace and Calton Hill for panoramic views across the city. I spent some time in Waterstones on Princes Street which spelled the death-knell, for once I visit bookshops, I tend not to reappear for quite some time. I invariably buy a book or two, usually on travel.

The next day I fulfilled a mini ambition by running round Arthur's Seat, an extinct volcano just outside Edinburgh. There were no spectacular views of Mid Lothian and Fife for me, only low cloud and mist which was really disappointing after the testing pull to the summit. I visited Leith and the redeveloped waterfront, but the mist had really enveloped the city and I could barely see fifty yards out to sea.

On the journey home the following day, passengers were packed onto the train like sardines. Where do they all come from, where are they going and what do they do? At the last minute a West Indian, who I later realised to be a man of the cloth, made his way down the carriage and sat across the aisle from me. Almost immediately he pulled the guard asking if he was on the right train for Preston. She promised to come back and sort him out once the train was underway and the passengers had settled down.

When the guard failed to return, I could detect the man becoming restless until all of a sudden he shouted, 'I'm on the wrong train man'. I suggested he change at York and Manchester, but when the guard eventually returned, she suggested he should change at Newcastle.

As the train rounded the sweep on the coast near North Berwick, the West Indian exclaimed, 'Vat's dat sea?' and I told him it was the North Sea. He managed to settle down, at least that is, until Morpeth when everybody became restless. The train embarked upon a go-slow and eventually an announcement informed us a Virgin Train had broken down upfront and was blocking the track. They eventually moved the train into a siding and we were able to get past, but on reaching Newcastle, passengers were packed onto the platform four or five deep.

There wasn't a seat to be had apart from one where a moron insisted on sitting next to the aisle and parking his luggage on the window seat. Couldn't the guy see that passengers were standing in the aisles, between compartments and into any other gap where they could squeeze? But this didn't deter many from using their mobile phones, the only bonus being that they were unable to walk up and down the corridor with them. The downside of course was that the tea trolley couldn't get through. The carriage resembled an underground train rather than an Inter City Express.

At Durham the platform was solid but the passengers seemed resigned to the fact they wouldn't find room on the train, so there was little movement. At York there was a mad scramble as people pushed both to board and to leave the train with the problem aggravated by cases stacked against the doors.

In the years I have travelled by train, this was the worst disruption I can recollect, but even I couldn't imagine how steeply the railways would plummet in subsequent years. The railways are at the hub of our infrastructure and desperately need an overhaul.

A chance invitation to a function at my firm's Glasgow depot on a Friday evening, prompted me to sift through the fixture list to see if I could extend it into a long running weekend. The only race listed was the Isle of Mull Half Marathon, and I duly sent off for an application form and details. I received a ferry timetable with the literature and figured it would be possible to do the race from Glasgow and back in the day.

For July, the weekend weather had been horrific with wall-to-wall rain, but on race day, the rain had stopped and the prospects looked brighter. I left Glasgow early morning driving over the Erskine Bridge and alongside Loch Lomond. The scenic drive across moors, through passes and alongside Lochs was reason enough to enter the race. The West Highland railway line follows the road to Tyndrum, clinging to hillsides and passing through tunnels. The main line continues across Rannoch Moor to Fort William with the branch line heading to Oban.

The town of Oban is the ferry port to the islands, the largest of which is Mull. There are links to the remote island of Iona, where St Columba and his followers established Christianity and to Staffa, famous for Fingal's Cave, immortalised by Mendelssohn's overture. I arrived before the ticket office opened and strolled along the quiet harbour side, calling in a café for a sausage sandwich and a tea. As quiet as the town was today, I would imagine it to be busy on a week day with the arrivals and departures of trains and ferries.

Expecting to board a small boat, I was quite taken aback when the ferry turned out to be the roll on, roll off MV Isle of Mull. Operated by Caledonian MacBrayne, the ferry had room for a thousand passengers as well as cars, coaches and lorries. There were well-upholstered lounges, a buffet and a bar. The journey from Oban to Craignure took forty-five minutes, providing panoramic views of the Firth of Lorne and the Mull coastline. Looking back to Oban, the amphitheatre, McCain's Folly sits proudly on a hillside above the town.

There were quite a few runners on board and I spoke to a young lad who was apparently a flier and an older two-hour man. This would be their third half marathon in as many weeks and when they told me of their travels, it made me feel distinctly like a home bird.

The approach to Craignure is dramatic with a backdrop of mountains dominating the bay, coastline and village. Two girls wearing marshals' bibs met runners off the ferry and a series of arrows directed us to the village hall. Craignure is a quiet village with shop, pub and holiday homes. One of the tourist attractions is a miniature steam railway which runs the short distance to Torosay Castle, one of several on the island.

The village hall provided for registration and changing with kit then being transported to Salen where the race would finish. Looking at the map, the course only accounted for a small section of the island. I had envisaged the race would take in most of the island and was disappointed not to see the colourful waterfront buildings of principal town Tobermory. I had obviously underestimated the size of Mull.

We walked out of Craignure for half a mile or so to the start, but then turned around to face the way we had come. A photograph was taken of the entire field which numbered no more than seventy. When the race started, we ran back along Craignure's main street with houses on the right hand side and shoreline on the left. Before long the leaders returned in the opposite direction, and I counted thirty-one before reaching the turnaround point myself.

Back through the village and past the start, the route stayed close to the coastline providing views across the Sound of Mull to Morvern. The road undulated but there was nothing too severe and I was pressing along nicely hitting the mile posts at seven minutes apiece. I could have stopped to help a couple of golfers look for their ball on the roadside but instead decided to press on. Each runner appeared to have found their own pace, the field had spread out and there was very little movement. Slowly but surely, I honed in on a group of four runners, duly overtaking them and in turn moving considerably up the field.

The dreadful weather of the last few days had given way to blue skies and sunshine and I felt lucky to be running in such stunning surroundings. The main road passed a junction with a signpost to Fishnish, another small port with ferries to Lochaline.

A runner crept up on me unnoticed and drifted by without a word, disappearing effortlessly into the distance. He was the last runner to pass me and after ninety-two minutes, I breached the finishing tape outside the Salen Hotel. Every runner was allowed to break the tape which was a nice touch.

Refreshments were available in the hotel where the presentations were made to the winners. To my surprise, the runner who had slipped by me late on, won an award for the first Mull resident. Several rugby players had completed the run to raise funds for a new clubhouse for the island's local team. Apparently a match against an invitation fifteen had marked the opening of the club house. A guy who I spoke to had apparently scrummaged against former Scotland captain David Sole, not the one of Starsky and Hutch fame. To say this guy looked as if he had never seen an angry man, the things he reckoned to have done to Sole in the scrums was nobody's business.

The organisers had promised a coach would be provided at four o'clock to take us to the ferry. They were true to their word except the coach was the island's service bus, pretty full by the time it arrived at Salen. We had to stand in the aisle for the journey back to Craignure, not a fitting reward for running thirteen miles.

When the ferry arrived, I counted twenty-nine vehicles drive off, plus a push bike, a phenomenal number for an island of this size. When the ferry reached Oban, I said cheerio to the lad who had secured a top ten finish, and his colleague, before starting the two hour journey back to Glasgow. The roads were much busier in the late afternoon but the journey was still enjoyable.

Many Scottish events are held in conjunction with highland gatherings including the Isle of Bute 10K which I ran several years ago. On a red-hot day, I caught the train from Glasgow to Wemyss Bay and the ferry to Rothesay.

The first ferry was full, but extra ferries had been laid on to cope with the influx of people attending the highland gathering. They had called a halt to any more passengers boarding but continued to let cars drive on. A man ahead of me in the queue with a family became hot under the collar, saying he had been victimised for not having a car and he demanded to see the captain. I didn't see what all the fuss was about as another ferry was already waiting to berth.

The ferry, while not as large as the boat to Mull, made the journey in a little over an hour. I followed the flow at Rothesay to the showground, a short walk out of town. The grounds had a small grandstand and there was additional seating around a grass track, where field sports were already taking place in the arena. There were food and drink marquees on an embankment and in an adjacent field, pipe bands were warming up for competition later in the afternoon.

I signed up for the race, but on a warm day and with the Great Scottish Run the day after, I questioned my own wisdom. A few years earlier, I had completed two races in two different countries on the same day. Kevin and I ran the Great Scottish Run on the Sunday morning and on the way home, called at Thorp Arch near Wetherby to run in the British Library Seven. After the stiffness of the car journey wore off, I ran pretty well, but to contemplate something like that today would be unthinkable. When I said that we had called in on our way down from Scotland, our club mates thought we had been joking until I proudly showed them my shiny gong.

A field of no more than fifty people assembled for the start of the Bute 10K of varying ages and abilities. We started with three laps of the grass track before leaving the showground for the island's roads. One girl was lapped by every runner before we even left the showground, but to her credit, she battled on to finish. The day was a scorcher, ideal for spectating but perhaps not participating. An extra two laps of the track were thrown in for good measure on our return to the showground.

I spent an enjoyable hour, staying to watch some of the other events before heading off to explore the town. I ended up eating a fish and chip supper on a seafront bench, fending off a flock of hungry seagulls.

I haven't done justice to the extensive Scottish running calendar but would like to put that right in the years ahead, God being willing. The Lochaber and Moray Marathons whet the appetite, along with the advent of the Loch Ness Marathon. There are attractive races at some of the small Perthshire and Fife towns and having already visited John o' Groats, how about the Caithness Half Marathon? With my penchant for bridge races, the Skye Bridge Run seems a distinct possibility. The list is endless.

The jewel in the crown however must be the Hebridean Challenge, a series of half marathons in remote surroundings on the islands of Benbecula, Skye, Harris and Lewis. Who knows, maybe one day in the not too distant future?

CHAPTER 23

Leeds Leads the Way

In April of each year, an exodus of runners from all corners of the British Isles descends upon the capital for the most recent version of the London Marathon. Those unfortunate not to have secured a place can make the trip and observe the proceedings on the capital's streets, hoping for a glimpse of their friends, club mates or anybody they know. Alternatively, you can watch the events unfold on national television, or get away as far as you can. In 1998 when I didn't make it to the start line at Greenwich Park, I chose to watch my adopted team Ross County take on Queens Park at Dingwall in the Scottish Highlands.

I can never understand why every year, people bend over backwards to either beg, borrow, or steal a London Marathon entry, yet the nucleus of those same people are not prepared to support their regional marathons. Several years ago, my club had a representation of thirty-eight runners across all abilities at London, yet we could only muster eight at Nottingham and six at Leeds. Let's have a look at the respective merits of the London Marathon compared to those of my local favourite at Leeds.

For starters, at London you may have to book your place on the coach and your accommodation in advance of knowing whether or not your application has been successful. At Leeds, once you have applied, you will be welcomed with open arms. For London, applications close before the end of October for the April race. At Leeds, your application has to be in three weeks before the May deadline for a guaranteed entry. For London, the bulk of your training will take place on cold and dark winter nights. Leeds falls a month or so later enabling you to fit some runs into warmer lighter evenings.

Your London number and race literature must be collected from a crowded exhibition hall or marquee, usually some distance from the city centre. Your dignity is challenged by having to answer ridiculous questions to prove you are who you claim to be. At Leeds your number and correspondence is mailed to your home address.

In London, you are required to pay through the nose prices for a hotel room. You are compelled to stay for at least one night as there is no registration on race day. At Leeds, you can sleep in your own bed the night before the race, or if from out of town, competitive hotel rates are available through the race and reasonable weekend breaks on offer.

There is no hustle and bustle on a crowded train to reach the Leeds start two hours early, just arrive in the city centre and make use of the free Sunday parking. There is no laying your kit out on damp grass, under a tree or on a park bench as ample changing accommodation is available at the International Pool. Likewise there is no long queue for the urinal or to hand in your baggage.

There is no arriving in position half an hour before race start to ensure a clear run, no three minute wait after the gun, before breaking out into a shuffle and no bumping and boring as faster runners try to push their way through the field.

So the London route takes in splendid sites such as Tower Bridge, Canary Wharf and The Mall. Leeds has Crown Point Bridge, Sparrows Wharf and The Calls. London has the Greenwich Observatory, Leeds has the Observatory Café Bar. London has Piccadilly Circus, Leeds has King Lane Circus.

At Leeds there are testing climbs on Stonegate Road and the Outer Ring Road while all that London can offer to open the lungs are the incline onto Tower Bridge and the underpass on the Embankment.

At the London finish, you have to locate your respective baggage truck, fight your way to the rail and either catch the eye of the steward or shout up louder than the next man. At Leeds, once the finishing funnels are cleared and medal and goody bag safely in your grasp, keen officials will have spotted your race number and will have your baggage waiting.

Hot and cold drinks are provided before you change back into warm clothing. You can then stroll, hobble or impersonate a poor man's John Wayne walk, back onto the Headrow to see the late order runners coming through the finish.

After reading this, I am sure you will agree that Leeds is by far the better option. There is a shorter half marathon alternative, a children's race and a corporate relay, so I look forward to the numbers being bolstered in future events.

Over the years there have been significant course changes, but with numbers falling in the marathon to around four hundred in recent years, a more manageable two lap course has been used with city centre start and finish. There has also been a change of date from October, then to July and settling at May.

In 1992, overnight snow resulted in the cancellation of the marathon, even though the half which tended to stick to lower ground still went ahead. The decision to postpone on safety grounds brought widespread criticism from people who had stayed overnight or travelled some distance on race morning. I felt most of this to be selfish and unjustified.

Determined this wouldn't happen again, the organisers decided to bring the events forward to the warmer days of July where they stayed for three years. I ran in each of those three marathons, two of them falling on uncomfortably hot days. A double change was brought about bringing the race further forward into May and using two laps of the half marathon course, proving for easier marshalling and policing. This now appears to be the settled date, my only criticism being a clash with several local races, and too soon after the Sheffield Marathon.

The course is a mixture of city, urban and rural, not particularly spectacular but nevertheless, my favourite race. It was my first marathon, it marked my fiftieth and I have run eleven times in all with the half marathon on a further eight or nine occasions.

Dubbed 'The Tough One' in the early days, it has become 'The Friendly One' in recent years with the same runners returning time after time. Many started in those far off days of the running boom and have travelled an almost identical path as myself. I meet many old friends and acquaintances each year, with stories and banter being exchanged usually about running and races.

As I usually go the full distance, I am able to start carefully, chat to friends and notice more around the course. From the Town Hall, a short incline leads onto the city's main thoroughfare, The Headrow. A left turn past the Victorian Grand Theatre leads to the first downhill on North Street.

On the right-hand side beyond the one mile marker is The New Roscoe public house. The original Roscoe was lost to road improvements and each year on the same day, a group of regulars assemble on the very spot in the middle of a roundabout. They drink from barrels of beer and commemorate its passing. The Roscoe was where Irish immigrants came in years gone by, looking for a start. The tenth anniversary was commemorated by The Dubliners and The Pogues appearing in concert at The New Roscoe.

Not too far from here is where the drinks station was stolen some years ago on race day. This is where the policemen walk around in pairs, and that's inside the police station. A flat stretch along the valley bottom on Meanwood Road passes factories, terrace houses and Woodhouse Cricket Ground. They were reputed to have paid there players here, long before the days when each local club carried an overseas professional.

A steady incline leads to a sharp bend at Meanwood and a longer steeper hill on Stonegate Road. This stretch, in excess of a mile, is where the race begins to take shape and separates the men from the boys.

At King Lane Circus, the course drops sharply and turns left onto the

Outer Ring Road. The outlook becomes pleasanter with the road flanked by trees and green fields. On a long downhill, we cross the Meanwood Valley Trail, the setting for another local race.

A second stiff climb passes another cricket ground, this time the impressive New Rover headquarters, before West Park roundabout is reached. Every couple of miles, there are large pockets of runners standing at the road side. But no need to worry, these are corporate relay runners waiting at their changeover points. Start to worry when all the runners have gone.

The next section is around quiet residential streets off Spen Lane, where people support the race with banners and hand out drinks. They have been known to turn an occasional hose pipe the way of runners on a hot day. The worst is now over for the one-lappers with a welcome downhill past the eight and twenty-one mile markers. On this section several years ago, a couple of horses broke their tether and tried to join the race. From Horsforth, a further pleasant downhill on Hawksworth Road approaches the junction at the old Kirkstall Forge.

The last three miles are slightly downhill or flat, past the Vesper Gate Pub where I took a tumble a few years ago. I was running the marathon, on the second circuit and fell flat on my face. My stride had shortened so much that I had probably tripped over a molecule of dust. Half a dozen runners who I had worked hard to catch all came by me, a couple of them pausing to enquire about the state of my health. As I got up and dusted myself down, I looked around expecting to see a window full of faces laughing at me, but I had no need to worry, they hadn't opened yet. I set off in pursuit of those half-dozen runners feeling as if I had been turned upside down and shaken about.

The course passes Kirkstall Abbey on the right opposite the Abbey House Museum. The final stages pass streets of terrace houses on the left and factories and industrial units on the right hand side. The prominent railway viaduct dominates the skyline ahead but seems to take a lifetime to reach. The Yorkshire Television Studios and Napoleon Casino signify the last mile but watch out for fire engines in a hurry.

A niggling little climb leads to the finishing straight in front of the Town Hall steps but keep to the right if you are going around again. You haven't quite finished as a sting in the tail over the last couple of years has seen the finish moved around the corner into Millennium Square.

Leeds fails to attract a top class field, I suspect due to the difficulty of the course, but down the years some well-known names have performed here. Ieuan Ellis and Ian Thompson have been previous winners while Graham Hill, son of Olympian Ron, won the marathon recently. Prolific ultra runner, Eleanor Robinson of Border Harriers has won the ladies' marathon on several occasions, while former London Marathon winner and Olympian Veronique Marot has been a half marathon winner. Locally based Valley Striders have probably been the most successful club in the history of the race.

The other important Leeds race is The Abbey Dash 10K which is a major event in the winter calendar. The course uses the last three miles of the marathon forming an out and back with a loop around Kirkstall Abbey grounds providing the turnaround point. This race attracts a top class field with the winning time regularly below the thirty minute mark, and once again the finish is beneath the steps of the impressive Town Hall.

The nine-thirty start means we are ready to go as the night time revellers are just about to call it a draw. The December date provides pot luck with the weather which tends to be bitterly cold, with the first section run into the teeth of a predominant Northwester. This is one race where I seem to do well irrespective of what form or shape I am in. I try to reach the Kirkstall traffic lights before the leaders return in the opposite direction. This is the benchmark for how I am doing and I usually make it each year.

The return journey can be run into a low sun and one has to look down to avoid the glare. Again the race provides the opportunity to meet old friends and make some new ones. The early start offers the opportunity for a breakfast at the end or at least a tea and a cake before the journey home.

Another event I rate highly is the Leeds Country Way Relay held in the area in late August or early September of each year. Organised meticulously by Kippax Harriers, the race starts early morning at Garforth to the east of Leeds, and follows The Country Way on footpaths, tracks and to the edge of fields. There are sections on disused railway lines, river flood banks and small stretches of road, not to mention the numerous gates, stiles and fences.

The total length is close to sixty miles and the race is split into six similar legs each run in pairs. It makes sense for the pairs to be of similar ability and in the early years it was useful to reconnoitre your leg at least a couple of times. This proved difficult for out of town teams, even though the route is marked with discs on posts and fences. It paid dividends for these runners to attach themselves to pairs in front and stick to them like glue. While this ploy can work well particularly on the first leg, it is useless in the later stages when you sometimes don't come across any other couples.

At the changeover points on legs five and six, a cut-off point is implemented where all the teams still waiting to go at a particular time, set off together. This in itself is a race within a race and can be quite competitive. I have waited at the start of leg five, hoping above hope that our fourth leg pairing would arrive giving us a couple of minutes' breathing space ahead of the massed start.

Realistically, only two or three clubs locally have the strength in depth to be in with a chance of winning the main race. From my point of view, the idea is to go out, make the most of a pleasant run in the country and enjoy a change of scenery.

In the weeks ahead of the race, the Kippax organisers would run, walk and inspect the course removing any obstacles and ensuring sufficient signs are in place. They would cut down any unduly long grass and ensure 'Rights of Way' had not been ploughed over. Generally they make sure everything is in order and usually do a first class job with the organisation.

Organising a team for this event can become a nightmare and my sympathies lie with Dave who each year organises two or three teams for my club. Each year he says, 'Never again' but the following year with batteries recharged, he comes up trumps. He was treated pretty shabbily a couple of years ago, when there were several withdrawals in the days leading up to the event. Even on race day a pairing failed to show, resulting in disqualification for the entire team.

It will be of little consolation to Dave, but most clubs suffer in a similar way. The majority of runners prefer to go on a morning to get their leg out of the way while most prefer a leg they have previously run. Naturally people prefer to run with a friend if possible or somebody with whom they get along. Last minute changes usually mean that pairs are asked to do legs they have never previously run and aren't familiar with. Sixty minute men can be sometimes placed with girls who have never run ten miles.

Apart from pairing people together, there are also the transport arrangements to consider. All runners must be able to reach their starting points and equally importantly, be able to get back to their cars. Ideally both runners should be able to drive so a car can be left at both start and finishing points.

Several years ago, the heavens opened and my partner Mick and I were soaked to the skin. He brought me back to where we had started and I looked forward to changing into warm clothing. When we had left a couple of hours earlier, the car park had been solid but now there was only a sprinkling of cars probably all belonging to competitors. Someone had managed to enter my car and had stolen my trousers of all things, along with twenty pounds in the pocket.

Another year, I received a string of phone calls in the days leading to the event, asking me to run the second leg, then the first and finally a more familiar fifth leg. Exclusively to the north of Leeds, this leg starts at Golden Acre Park, skirts Eccup Reservoir and takes in parts of the Harewood Estate.

The route passes through the rural village of Bardsey, through the churchyard and alongside the steepest field in the world. The changeover point is at the top of another steep hill on the outskirts of Thorner. The scenery makes the run worthwhile particularly the views over Wharfedale on an elevated section of the leg.

The first year I took part in the relay, I ran in a team thrown together from a group of five-a-side footballers. I was only asked to make up the numbers but ran with Ken, a friend and runner of similar standing. We were down for the first leg so aided by a map, we ran the section in midweek prior to the event and hopefully would iron out any mistakes on the day.

To my astonishment we were handed a baton which had to be safely delivered around the sixty mile course. Batons were used in shorter track races but surely we weren't expected to carry this over stiles and through undergrowth. I could picture it ending up down a ditch or in the river.

We discussed the need to start carefully but still seemed to get caught up in the euphoria, going off far too quickly. I pleaded with Ken to slow down as a gap was developing between the two of us. This was one of the first stagings of the event, many people were unfamiliar with the route and hadn't come to terms with the concept.

At one point while running through some woods, I got the impression we had company. On glancing round I wasn't wrong as three couples, obviously unfamiliar with the route had backed up behind us. When a long straight stretch provided vision of the teams upfront, these teams were around us in a flash.

I gained some satisfaction after we had finished our leg and were talking over a well-earned drink. We had been waiting for several minutes when suddenly, the same three teams entered the field in a mini convoy. They had obviously gone wrong towards the end of the leg, had stuck together and lost valuable time. 'What kept you?' I said to one runner who I knew by sight, but he seemed none too impressed.

In this event, people have been known to go well off course and be missing for hours. Others inadvertently take short cuts and save time while others deliberately take short cuts to save time. People too numerous to mention have run into difficulty with farmers, ramblers, dogs and cattle.

As I mentioned earlier, all participants receive an exclusive pottery souvenir with a different item each year. The runners who return to Garforth Leisure Centre on Sunday afternoon are provided with a slap-up meal. Long may this continue.

As a city, Leeds has made massive strides in recent years as a great place to live, so it must be a great place to visit. Certain hotels offer discount weekend rates and special rates can be negotiated for both the Leeds Marathon and Abbey Dash.

After work and at weekends, young people flood into the city's, with many pubs, cafés and bars with new venues seemingly opening each week. People from all over the North of England visit the city's much acclaimed night clubs.

If shopping is the order of the day, there is something to suit every taste. The Victorian Quarter is a series of renovated arcades with top fashion shops. Queen Victoria Street contains Europe's largest glass canopy. The Corn Exchange is a carefully restored domed listed building with craft, jewellery and music shops inside among others.

Kirkgate Market is the largest covered market in England with up to eight hundred shops in its heyday. Granary Wharf below the City Station is set in a series of tunnels and vaulted arches and houses hand-crafted goods made in workshops and studios. There are a number of cafés and usually street entertainment on a weekend. The popular high street shops can be found in pedestrianised streets between Briggate and City Square.

There's plenty to do on an evening with nightly shows at The Playhouse, home to National Theatre North, The Grand Theatre, The Civic Theatre and The City Varieties. Or just stroll down the many alleyways and passages off Boar Lane and Call Lane towards the renovated waterfront area. Here cosy pubs sit side by side with trendy restaurants and wine bars.

By day, stroll along the riverside path to the city's flagship attraction, the Royal Armouries, featuring weapons, uniform and militaria throughout the ages. The City Museum features traditional exhibits and information while the Leeds City Gallery houses contemporary works, the Henry Moore Collection and the splendid Pablo's Restaurant.

Out of town is the Cistercian Kirkstall Abbey with the Abbey House Museum and recreated period street just across the road. Temple Newsam House to the east of the city is open to the public and has extensive gardens and a rare breeds farm. To the north of Leeds is Tropical World at Roundhay Park while Harewood House has a superb collection of furniture and paintings. The manicured gardens designed by Capability Brown and the bird garden are well worth a visit. Opera in the park has taken place here in recent summers.

So remember if you are a London Marathon reject, 'Leeds leads the way'.

CHAPTER 24

Eastern Promise

THE DRIVE FROM THE AIRPORT to the hotel was one of the holiday highlights. Four lanes of traffic were all moving at differing speeds, overtaking on both sides, vehicles cutting in front of us and hopping lanes all to the perpetual sounding of horns. Somehow the inevitable accident failed to materialise and we arrived safely at our hotel.

The Hotel Avicenna was comfortable, had a rooftop breakfast lounge, a grill and a smashing little bar. Some of the city's innumerable sights were a mere stroll away.

Istanbul is a city of contrasts and curiosities situated at the confluence of three stretches of water. The Sea of Marmara separates Europe from Asia and flows into the Agean Sea to the west. The Bosphorus Straits flow into The Black Sea while the Golden Horn is a seven mile inlet which divides Stanboul from Beyoglu and Galata.

We were here to run the Eurasia Marathon in October 1996, the race that spans two continents and crosses the majestic Bosphorus Bridge. Running club member Bob had an ambition to run here, regularly visiting Turkey on holiday. His in-laws lived in Turkey and he had friends here. John and I arrived on Thursday while Alan and Ken would arrive on Saturday. Hazel and Jenny would run in the popular mass participation seven kilometre race.

The main thoroughfares of the city are busy but well maintained although some of the back streets are in urgent need of repair and in some cases peter into dirt tracks. The pavements are steep and narrow, with sturdy walking shoes a necessity. The one tramway runs from the city walls near Topkapi to the ferry terminal and railway station at Eminonu.

Most commuters appear to travel on the many ferries from Eminonu to the suburbs along the Bosphorus and along the Asian waterfront, where trains depart for Ankara and Southern Turkey. Three ferries a day journey the wooded Bosphorus shores to the mouth of the Black Sea, and the strategic position of Istanbul close to the Balkans guarantees the shipping lanes are always busy.

The Greeks founded Byzantium in this spot in 660BC and it has served as capital to the Christian and Islamic Empires. In 1500 this was the world's largest city with 1.2 million people, but today the figure stands at 8 million with shanty towns and sprawling suburbs being systematically replaced with tower blocks.

We awoke on Friday morning to the call for prayers. Most of the population are Muslims which entails adhering to 'The Five Pillars of Islam' including praying five times a day. The rooftop breakfast lounge provided fascinating views of the city's domes and towers, mosques and minarets and the Asian coastline beyond the Sea of Marmara.

Because of my running exploits, I had become something of a minor celebrity at work. My colleagues and the company had generously supported me with sponsorship over the years for a number of local and national charities. If people knew I would be on holiday, they would ask 'Where are you running this time?'

Since the advent of e-mail, I tended to send out any last minute instructions along with a cryptic message as a wind-up. For example when I visited Amsterdam, the message I sent out read, 'Happy Bottling while I am running along the canals and over the bridges'. In Norway the message read, 'Happy Bottling while I am running through the forests and along the fjords'. Before I left for Istanbul, I put out a message, 'Happy Bottling while I am running by the mosques and the minarets.' A colleague quickly replied perhaps tongue in cheek and said, 'Andy, what the hell's a minaret?'

Many of the tourist attractions are situated in the Sultanahmet District close to Hippodrome Square, a long narrow park flanked at one side with bars and restaurants. Chariot races and other events had taken place here in the days of the Roman Empire.

Istanbul is a paradise for historians, archaeologists and anyone who is a keen sightseer, with too many places to list or mention. The skyline is dominated by the Blue Mosque, a cascade of leaded domes surrounded by six fluted minarets, built between 1609 and 1616 as the Mosque of Sultan Ahmet. Once inside the turquoise tiles glisten in the light of innumerable windows which give an atmosphere and presence of blue.

The design was obviously influenced by that of Hagia Sofia which stands adjacent. Known as 'The Church of Divine Wisdom' it was completed in AD 537. This was the greatest achievement in Byzantine architecture and for over a thousand years, the greatest church in Christendom.

The Topkapi Palace is only a stone's throw away and as a museum is the most popular tourist attraction in Istanbul. This was originally the government seat of the Ottaman Sultans and forms a small town with libraries, stables, treasuries, barracks and government offices all joined by a series of courtyards. A full day could be spent here but if pushed for time, the Harem, the Treasury and the Pavillion of the Holy Miracle are priorities. The gardens and restaurant provide excellent views across the Sea of Marmara towards the Bosphorus Straits.

The Underground Palace of Yerebatan Sarayi is a forest of pillars reached by a steep stairway, with a maze of walkways two feet above the water. Constant drips echo around the dimly lit chambers in the largest Byzantine cistern which supplied water to the palaces and other buildings on the site of Topkapi.

With so many attractions to see in such a short space of time, we found a map essential. Even though many of the sites are within the Sultanahmet District, there are others worth seeing, within walking distance or a mere tram ride away. The Theodosian Walls stretch from the Sea of Marmara to the Golden Horn and many sections are still walkable today.

The Dolmabahce Palace is set on the banks of the Bosphorus in Besiktas and was built as a monument to extravagance, with the highlights being crystal chandeliers, tapestries and lavish carpets.

The best view of the city and surround can be had from the Galata Tower in Karakoy. Reached by 'the Tünel', a short stretch of underground railway up a steep slope, the tower, built in 1349, houses a restaurant and a night club. The narrow balcony outside provides breathtaking views of the domes and spires of the Old Town across the water, providing you have a head for heights.

Venturing uphill towards the Istiklal Caddesi, the side streets provide for a seedier lifestyle and are probably best avoided if you aren't streetwise. At the top of the hill, the street broadens into Taksim Square, the heart of modern Istanbul with five star hotels, fashion boutiques and stylish bars. Taksim Square hit the headlines recently as the scene of the tragic incident involving Galatasary and Leeds supporters.

The Egyptian or Spice Bazaar near the ferry terminal at Eminonu has eighty shops selling tea, coffee, herbs, spice and fruit while the Grand Bazaar, the world's largest covered market, is a must for the visitor or tourist. With over 4,000 shops along with cafés and banks, this is the ideal place for browsing an hour or two. Your bargaining skills will be put to the test, but frankly, I tired of the banter and started to feel a little intimidated.

We were approached innumerable times on the streets with a view to buying a carpet. John and I were tricked into a situation after being polite to a young Turk, who asked if he could help us. As we found to our cost, looking at your map in a public place can be critical as Turks rushed around to assist like bees around the proverbial honey pot.

We told the young man we were looking at the map to establish our bearings, we were not looking for anywhere in particular and certainly weren't lost. He invited us to his studio for tea, and having read that it would be offensive to refuse, we duly followed him. The studio turned out to be a carpet shop, and we ended up having the hard sell from 'big brother' before we set eyes on any apple tea. I explained that we didn't want a carpet, hadn't budgeted for a carpet and had no means of getting one home. Obviously unimpressed by what I had to say, he brought 'even bigger brother' to persuade us that it made sense.

The situation had changed from being quite funny to distinctly uncomfortable, with panic starting to set in. I could picture myself carrying a carpet over my shoulder just like Rowan Atkinson in the Barclaycard advert. We managed to get out of jail when customers came into the shop, 'even bigger brother' went to deal with them and we made a bolt for the door.

We laughed and joked about the situation afterwards particularly in a restaurant the same evening when three men kept entering, each time carrying carpets to an upstairs room.

Even youngsters selling guide books and items you couldn't possibly want such as yo-yos and kites, were persistent, clinging to your shirt tails for hundreds of yards.

The Galata Bridge at Eminonu is the hub of the transport system where bus, tram, train and boat all interconnect. During the daytime, the bridge is packed with fishermen casting their lines into the murky waters of the Golden Horn. At rush hour, the area becomes chaotic with an influx of people either heading for work or returning home. Claxons can be heard as the ferries compete with each other for vacant berths.

Smaller boats are equipped with a stove and a frying pan to cook mackerel sandwiches for hungry workers and shoppers alike. We had visited the area with the intention of trying one of these but I chickened out at the last minute.

The food was surprisingly good although the portions were modest. For the Friday evening meal I started with 'Wedding Soup' which is a mutton broth thickened with egg and flavoured with lemon juice. I had kebabs on a skewer which seemed a popular main course but I noticed Sea Bass, Red Mullet and Blue Fish figuring on the Sea Fish menu. The desserts were quite appetising with excellent ice cream and to round off the meal, the most popular Turkish drink, tea. For the less ambitious, McDonald's and Burger King were never far away.

The best value for money we came across was the Pudding Shop, a reasonably priced self-service restaurant in Sultanahmet that served up stews, pies and meat balls.

We called in one bar where there was music, were seated on extremely low stools, but a pillar prevented us from seeing the musicians. Moving back towards the hotel, we were asked if we wanted a drink and directed up a shabby flight of stairs. The room beyond opened out into a dance floor and stage. We were seated on stools at a bar and stood out like sore thumbs

We arrived just in time for the cabaret as a singer started on the stage and then walked around the room with one of those magical microphones without a wire. His songs were pretty much the same style, tempo and thickness with the introductions similar to the soundtrack of a Vincent Price or Peter Cushing horror movie.

Next up was an oriental belly dancer strutting her stuff as young men waved their liras, hoping for the chance to place them down her cleavage. I had my notes ready but she could obviously tell we were on a budget and didn't bother us. Attractive young Turkish girls of dusky complexion then took to the dance floor, but the young Turkish men seemed intent on chasing the one blonde girl in the room. We enjoyed ourselves so much, we returned for a second helping on Sunday night.

Bob had arranged to bring our race numbers to the hotel on Saturday lunchtime which saved us the hassle of having to register. As we sat in the hotel lounge, he duly strode across the square flanked by a smaller man he introduced as his father-in-law. The other man, larger and much younger was Bob's friend Akim, who ran a haulage business.

We left the hotel for a bite to eat but an unexpected cloudburst saw us isolated in a restaurant, when as many inches of rain fell in several minutes. The drains on Hippodrome Square were hardly able to cope. This put paid to our trip up the Bosphorus Straits with Mike, an American staying at our hotel, who we had arranged to meet at the quayside.

Mike was something of a modern Indiana Jones, travelling across Turkey and then into Greece looking at ancient buildings and relics. He later told us that the best part of the trip had been spent huddled undercover to avoid the thunder, lightning and rain. We left Bob and his companions arranging to meet them the next morning at Inonu Stadium. From here coaches would take us to the race start on the Asian side of the Bosphorus Bridge.

Having missed the Bosphorus cruise, John and I opted to catch a ferry to Uskudar, one of Istanbul's suburbs on the Asian shoreline. The return trip in early evening captured the silhouettes of the city's mosques and minarets against the brilliant sunset, a memory that will come flooding back whenever I think of Turkey.

Our taxi sped through the early morning mizzle and mist, across the Galata Bridge to Besiktas where the race would finish. We met Bob who had brought Akim and his young son along to watch. Alan, Ken, Hazel and Jenny soon arrived. As they would be here for several days after we had flown home, we filled them in on the sights and places to go and not to go to.

We boarded one of the special buses provided to transport runners to the race start, but a Turkish runner started gesturing to us and trying to make himself understood. The coach squeezed forward several times but was just bridging the gap. Still the Turk persisted with instructions, this time pointing out of the window. I didn't understand what he was trying to say and just thought he was another person who had taken a dislike to me.

Eventually the coach set off and after a short drive we crossed the Bosphorus Bridge shrouded in mist and to the marathon start. We saw runners on the opposite carriageway warming up, but the coach didn't stop and carried on for perhaps a mile. We had been brought to the Fun Run start and this is what the Turk had been trying to tell us. We had basically caught the wrong bus.

With time at a premium, the five of us said cheerio to Hazel and Jenny, and jogged back along the carriageway eventually reaching the start line with five minutes to spare. Not the ideal preparation for a marathon as if twenty-six miles wasn't enough. You are advised to warm up, but this was probably taking things to the extreme.

Expecting thousands of runners, there were only several hundred with the vast majority of participants obviously going for the shorter option. There were a handful of Brits, among them Glynn Parry, a member of the exclusive 'One Hundred Marathon Club'. He had reached the milestone earlier in 1996 at Boston where he ran dressed as a Centurion.

We were quickly underway, John and I running together with the other three not too far behind. A long downhill took us to the Bosphorus Bridge but the experience was tinged with disappointment as the mist prevented us seeing the straits, the water and the mosque at Ortakoy. We climbed out of the mist on a long hill beyond the bridge and with the temperature already on the increase, we would be in for a hard morning's work.

The next section of the course was an out and back on wide dual carriageways. The surface comprised large concrete slabs which would play havoc with the joints in the later stages of the race. The outlook was not pleasant with office blocks, factories and flats making up the early miles with very little greenery. There were flyovers, underpasses and traffic lights but we were waved through, even on red.

The first turnaround at Mecidiyekoy saw Africans in the lead as is so often the case in big city races. John by now was well ahead and he waved across as he returned on the opposite carriageway, and I did likewise to Bob, Alan and Ken. I didn't feel particularly good but with a distinct lack of mile or kilometre posts, it was difficult to gauge my progress. I noticed many Turkish runners were wearing track suit bottoms, respecting the Muslim beliefs of covering their knees.

The route passed Taksim where there were several twists and turns. The long downhill stretch which I had been looking forward to crossed Ataturk Bridge on reaching the foreshore and entered the Old City. Another climb brought us to the Aqueduct of Velens which I tackled quite well and after running through another Istanbul suburb, we reached the Sea of Marmara.

We ran to the impressive City Walls and turned around to tackle the long arduous stretch along the waterfront towards the city. John once again acknowledged me as he passed down the other side, and when Alan, Bob and Ken came by at various intervals, I must have been almost a mile in front.

I passed the same man and woman for a third time as they walked and chatted away to each other. They can't have bothered with the out and back sections and must have known some good short cuts.

The section skirting the Bosphorus is one of the most spectacular I have encountered in marathon running. I only wish I could have done it more justice, neither feeling good or running well. There were panoramic views of the Blue Mosque, Galata Tower and dozens of mosques and minarets either side of a sheet of glistening water. I was made to feel at home, coming in for abuse from a group of yobs outside a bar, but wearing my Union Flag vest, I was perhaps an easy target. If my memory serves me correctly, I swore at one of the youths but nothing too severe.

Having dug deep into my reserves, I had now resorted to the occasional walk. By the time I had reached Eminonu, the runs had starter to become shorter and the walks longer. I could see the many fishermen lining the Galata Bridge, perched on any available parapet or vantage point from where they could drop a line. They paid little regard to the constant stream of athletes drifting across the bridge.

As badly as I was doing, I had said to myself that there was no way that I would walk on the Galata Bridge. This psychological ploy had served me well previously and had come up trumps several times in the past. It had done the trick on a couple of occasions towards the end of the London Marathon when I had said to myself, 'There is no way I will walk down the Mall'. Unfortunately today it wasn't to be.

As I stopped to walk, I turned around to see Alan approaching the ramp on to the bridge. I couldn't believe he had come from so far back to catch me, but if I kept running, I could surely fend him off. There was little chance of that as he had a heart like a lion and obviously had the bit between his teeth.

On leaving the Galata Bridge, the route still followed the Bosphorus through Beyoglu but moved away from the waterfront. Alan soon caught me up, passed me and drifted effortlessly out of sight in a matter of minutes. 'How far do you think now?' I asked, as he came up to my shoulder. 'At least two miles' was the reply. He was probably about right as twenty minutes and several walks later, I saw the grounds of Dolmabahce Palace and knew the job was almost complete.

A large crowd on the stadium steps applauded the finishers and after running around three sides, we entered a long tunnel before finishing on the track where the applause was even better. However, the announcement of finishers' names was being drowned by loud, constant, repetitive disco music.

So little attention was been paid to the marathon finishers once this din had started, that my overall impression was the marathon very much played second fiddle to the fun run. Bob and Ken finished in due course, tired but happy with Ken saying, never again. Now where have I heard that before? Alan seemed to revel in his victory over me, tormenting me for some time afterwards and occasionally reminding me of the outcome.

We all got together on Sunday evening for a celebration meal with Bob's father-in-law and Akim coming along. I had no real desire to return to Istanbul particularly after the much publicised football violence, but writing this chapter has whetted my appetite. We packed a lot into a short space of time but left so much still to do, particularly the journey through the wooded Bosphorus Straits to the Black Sea. If I should return one day, it would be for the shorter race option rather than the marathon.

CHAPTER 25

A River Runs Through It

HAVING LOST MY FATHER in the July of 2000, the last thing I wanted was a weekend break at the start of September. I wasn't up for it one bit, hadn't read up on the destination as I normally would, and I felt it was a distraction I could nicely do without. How wrong could I be? The weather was terrific and I enjoyed every minute. It was probably just the pick-me-up I needed at that time and one of the best short breaks I have had.

Medieval Buda is linked to elegant Pest by eight bridges spanning the mighty River Danube. Buda rises vertically from the waterfront and has cobbled streets, quaint shops and intriguing alleyways. In contrast, Pest has wide avenues and magnificent buildings with charming squares and pavement cafés. The flatlands stretch out from here towards the Great Hungarian Plain.

The weekend had been planned for some time with a group of us expressing interest but as so often is the case, only John and I made it onto the plane. I secured a good deal booking through an Eastern European specialist, but by the time we had driven to Heathrow and paid through the nose for Pink Elephant Parking, we were no better off.

The early morning flight from Heathrow by Hungarian carrier Malev, enabled us to have a long afternoon in Budapest on Friday. This would be followed by three full days and a part day on Tuesday with a late afternoon flight home. The Budapest Half Marathon in which we were running would take place on Sunday morning.

The passport control at Budapest's Ferihegy Airport was pretty slow. We were among several people who rushed across as an extra desk suddenly opened, but my old queue continued to move quicker than my new one, so I actually wasted time. Whether the incoming immigration officer was more meticulous than the others or whether he just hadn't warmed up, I don't know. I always seem to lose out in these situations.

A minibus was laid on to take us to the Hotel Stadion, a huge tower block on the outskirts of the city. While the driver wasn't in the same league as the one in Istanbul, he nevertheless seemed pretty impatient and took his fair share of chances. The hotel was under extensive refurbishment and the rooms were basic but comfortable.

It seemed ideal weather for shorts, so after unpacking and changing, we ventured outside to take whatever the city could throw at us. When it comes to planning I am pretty meticulous and tend to know where I am going and what I want to do. Running pharmacist John is a modern day Ernest Hemingway or Phineas Fogg and tends to take the planning onto a different level. He had read up as usual on the destination and not only had worked out where we were going in the afternoon but had an itinerary planned for the evening.

We were soon able to find our bearings even though we had difficulty with the street pronunciations. We purchased three-day cards entitling us to use the metro, buses and trams as well as discounts to museums and other attractions. Instead of travelling, we chose to walk into the city, underestimating the distance. This took quite some time with a number of subways to negotiate and traffic lights to cross. Fast food counters are based in the subways and metro stations and I purchased a hot dog which was a little too heavy on the mustard for my liking. I would probably get used to handling the Hungarian Forints when it was time to go home.

Hungary is in the transition from communist state to democracy. Years of borrowing from the West came to a head in 1989 with the removal of barriers and links to the east, and Hungary experienced problems moving towards a free market. Much additional western investment has been at hand but Hungary is still burdened with large debts.

A programme of restoration has taken place on both sides of the river, streets have been renamed, communist symbols removed and new traffic systems introduced to avoid the congestion. The restaurants and nightlife are good and a large number of cultural events available. Although many of these are beyond the prices of most Hungarians, they sit comfortably within the tourist's budget.

A brief diversion took us inside the grand Keleti Station where trains depart for Vienna, Warsaw and Bucharest. There were men exchanging currency and women offering accommodation, rogue taxi drivers touting for trade and scantily dressed women touting for business. Imagine arriving on a train to be confronted by this assortment of characters.

Down-and-outs and the homeless slept rough in the subways leading to the Metro station. Many had basic furniture for all the world to see while others lay fast asleep on mattresses and blankets. Whether this happened in the communist era or more recently, it was a crying shame so many people had to live this way.

We walked the banks of the Danube, not so blue here, and passed many of the pleasure craft moored along the water's edge. Some of these were now floating restaurants with well-heeled people standing at the head of gangplanks offering menus and trying to drum up business.

We crossed the Chain Bridge, one of Budapest's best known landmarks, constructed by Scotsman Adam Clark and completed in 1848. The six hundred yard span seemed a favourite spot for beggars, many disabled and some particularly disfigured. We took one of the steep uphill paths to the Castle District where narrow streets and cobbled squares portrayed a feeling of being taken back in time. A sneak preview enabled us to gain our bearings and plan for the days ahead. We sampled the night life ending up in a bar where a group belted out seventies and eighties British pop songs.

The first job on Saturday morning would be to register for the Budapest Half Marathon at Szechenyi Thermal Bath in the City Woodland Park. We discovered as overseas runners that we were entitled to our own individual changing cubicles within the baths. The bag presented to us had final race details, number, championship chip and a tee shirt. The start lists were displayed and I looked at the British Runners to see if any of our top athletes were here or if there was anybody who I knew.

On our way out of the park, we passed Vojdahunyad Castle, a replica of the original in Romania. Children and adults alike were enjoying themselves in the outdoor pool which doubles as an ice skating rink in winter. The zoo, circus and amusement park are all in and around the park.

The main entrance to the park leads into Heroes Square dominated by the Millennium Monument and the statues to King Arpad and the leaders of the seven Magyar tribes. The Magyars were descendants of Finno – Ugric people originally from the foothills of the Urals, and still the dominant people in Hungary today.

The three underground lines are colour-coded, cover both sides of the Danube and are fast and efficient. Above the ground there are over thirty tram routes and numerous bus and trolley bus services to all parts of the city. Keen on fare dodgers, civilians would suddenly double up as inspectors by pulling on an arm band and a clip on badge in order to surprise hapless commuters. With the threat of an on-the-spot fine hovering, I dug deep into my pockets to produce my card in the nick of time.

We caught the train from Heroes Square to the Castle District, exploring the charming streets which have been carefully restored. A massive rebuilding programme took place after 1945 and occupied the next thirty years. Germans and Russians fought house to house here for months on end and there were more casualties to civilians than combatants. The district is closed to through traffic unless you are staying at the Hilton which has somehow found its way into this UNESCO protected area.

Horse and carts for hire with coachmen in traditional uniform meander the streets while Japanese tour groups follow their guide, usually unmistakable holding an umbrella aloft. We enjoyed a coffee at the Fisherman's Bastion, a Romanesque stronghold with seven turrets again representing the Magyar tribes. The terrace provides panoramic views over the Danube, Pest and the surrounding area.

Matthias Church is close by, in front of which is the Plague Monument commemorating lives lost in an epidemic in 1691. Within the Royal Castle are three museums and we visited one of these, the National Gallery exhibiting works by Hungarian artists. We left Castle Hill by the Siklo Funicular railway eliminating the criss-cross walk down to the waterfront.

In the evening, England were playing France in a football friendly international and we found a bar where it was been shown on a large screen. With one eye on the race the following morning, I told John I didn't want any more than three pints. He suggested one in the first half, one at half time and one in the second half which seemed fine by me.

The bar was full of French people who were noisy and boisterous whenever France were leading, but when England equalised, John and I plus one other person applauded. He then came to stand with us providing safety in numbers and owned up to being a Newcastle United supporter. When we were ready to leave and opened the door, it was raining bucketfuls. There was no taxi in the rank so we returned inside. We ended up breaking our three pint pledge and finished up watching most of the Holland and Ireland game which was next on the bill.

With not the ideal preparation for the race, we awoke as reluctant starters perhaps thankful that it was only a half marathon. 'Only thirteen miles,' said John which proved little consolation as I dragged myself from under the covers. The walk to City Woodland Park was a mile or so from the hotel. On showing our race numbers, we were directed as promised to our own private changing cubicle by white-coated female attendants. Why weren't we treated like this in races at home?

The race started on one of the main roads through the City Park and we waited in our places to the incessant sound of rap music and bongo drums. It was impossible to hear each other talk so I was glad to get started. We crossed the bridge near the outdoor pool, cut through Heroes Square and ran slightly downhill along the wide Andrassay Boulevard towards the Danube. Last night's rain had given way to sunshine and the possibility of a scorcher, while all around the course we were treading water.

The race hadn't quite captured the public imagination as pedestrians were crossing Andrassay Boulevard in front of runners. One elderly lady almost caused a pile-up as she crossed pulling her shopping trolley behind. Small pockets of spectators gathered close to the bridges but crowds were generally pretty sparse.

John and I ran the first three miles together but I could see he was chomping at the bit for some action. Eventually he could hold back no longer and gradually eased away eventually disappearing out of sight. The course was flat except for the ramps onto bridges and there was plenty to hold the attention of a plodder like me. We crossed the Chain and Elizabeth Bridges and ran past the magnificent Parliament Building, and below the Royal Castle, Fisherman's Bastion and Gellert Hill.

There were long stretches along the quays and on one of these I took a tumble. I felt quite humble at the amount of sympathy shown and the number of people who stopped to help me, despite not understanding any of the dialogue. I had been pressing along quite nicely but now felt all shook up with a mouth full of gravel for my trouble. The soaring temperatures didn't help my cause and I began to regret the Amstels consumed last night.

A small motor boat with Nike Logo travelled the Danube following the race leaders and providing a commentary. We had seen the very same boat the day before and it resembled a larger scale model of one of those boats made by folding newspaper.

With five thousand runners from thirty different countries, the course was busy but manageable. In overseas races, I tend to take an interest in the colours worn by the competitors around me and a guy running in a Star of David design wished me luck on seeing my Union Flag vest. We seemed to interchange and finished in around the same time.

The stretch on Margaret Island was the most enjoyable on the course once we had passed some more of the dreaded bongos. Margaret Island sits in the Danube within the heart of the city and provides a recreational area with baths, gardens, parkland and hotels. A stiff climb took us onto our fourth bridge, the Arpad, and a dual carriageway and a couple of doglegs brought us within sight of Heroes Square. I was now within earshot of the loud speakers in the park and John was waiting at the finish area with a well-earned drink.

After changing we bidded the ladies in white coats farewell, promising to see them next year should we return. Our fortunes took an upturn when we met two friendly young ladies in Mel and Tina who struck up a conversation after recognising my Great North Run tee shirt. They invited us for a drink and we spent a happy hour in a beer garden comparing notes and discussing running with members of the Chapel Striders Club from North Leeds.

John has a knack of finding out what is happening in these places and he came up trumps once again when he found out Hungary were playing

Italy at football in a World Cup Qualifier. I can remember England visiting the Nep Stadium in the Keegan-Brooking era when the tickets could have been sold several times over. The stadium was an intimidating place to visit and England were given little chance.

Whether the change to a democracy had pushed the ticket price range out of the grasp of many supporters or whether interest had waned, I don't know. There were spare tickets up to the day before the game and we bought a couple at one of the booths around the perimeter of the ground and were even able to pick our seats.

Italy had just returned from a successful Euro 2000 tournament while in contrast Hungary had suffered some resounding defeats at the hands of mediocre opposition. The stadium seated 70,000 with little covered accommodation. I could imagine how the atmosphere would be tense for the opposition as a full house of Hungarians waved flags and banners. The atmosphere was moving particularly during the rendition of the national anthems.

The game was end to end with Hungary's performance above all expectations. With the scores level at 2-2, the home side were going for the winner when time ran out. This was an unexpected extra which I thoroughly enjoyed and since returning home I have kept a close eye out for the Hungary results.

Bill Bryson said in his bestseller *Neither Here Nor There,* that without exception, Bulgarian girls were the most beautiful in the world. I can't argue with that as I haven't visited Bulgaria, but what I can say is that there were some stunning Hungarian girls. One in particular was Eva, a dark mysterious Magyar girl who served food and drink in one of the expat Irish Pubs. We talked, laughed and joked with her grasp of English being so good, she was able to torment and tease. If only I had been ten, fifteen or even twenty years younger. I haven't been as smitten since I rushed home from school all those years ago to see Stacey Dorning in 'Follifoot'. We returned here time and time again, got to know Eva's shift pattern and kept turning up like bad pennies. John tended to get a little annoyed because he fancied a change of venue.

On Monday we continued sightseeing and climbed the dozens of steps and the steep cliff pathways to Gellert Hill at 750 ft above the Danube. There are magnificent views of the city and surrounding area with the Danube disappearing into the distance. Industrial smokestacks are visible on the outskirts while prefabricated tower block housing encircles the city.

The hill took its name from Bishop Gellert who came here to preach Christianity. He became a martyr in 1046 when he was bundled into a barrel spiked with nails and rolled down the steep cliff-face. There is also a citadel here built after a conflict in 1848. We took the more sedate route down past tacky souvenir shops and refreshment stalls. Cars and buses used this route to bring townspeople and visitors alike to the observation platform for spectacular views.

On our way to St Stephens Basilica, we stopped for a nice meal at the Columbus, one of the restaurant boats. I had deep fried schnitzel which was about the size of a diver's flipper. The waiters here resembled the hunky dancers who support the likes of Geri Halliwell and Jennifer Lopez in their routines, but even the Dale Carnegie techniques of 'How to win friends and influence people' wouldn't bring a smile from the sultry barmaid.

St Stephens was completed in 1906 after it had previously collapsed but the extensive renovation taking place made it difficult to appreciate the masonry, statues and treasures within. The showpiece is a glass casket in which is said to be the severed hand of St Stephen. The hand had been involved in something of a tug of war across Eastern Europe before coming home to Budapest. Each year it would be paraded through the city streets on August 20th to mark the anniversary of St Stephen's canonisation.

We climbed the stairs to the dome and ventured out onto the narrow balcony, for more views of the city skyline. I wasn't altogether comfortable with the arrangement and had to edge my way around staying close to the wall of the dome. The woman behind me looked how I felt and wouldn't move out of the doorway.

The trams rattled past late into the evening as we looked into shop windows for a bargain and watched elderly men patiently playing chess in the many picturesque squares. We went for a few beers, but John insisted we call at a couple of bars before calling to see Eva for one last time.

Our flight on Tuesday afternoon missed its slot and was late taking off. This meant that we consequently lost our slot at Heathrow, but on landing, the plane had to sit on the apron as there was no available stand. To rub salt into wounds, they failed to send out any coaches to transfer passengers to the terminal.

When the first coach arrived it quickly filled and passengers were left on the tarmac or still on the plane awaiting follow up coaches. One businessman remarked, 'This would never happen on Swissair'. Due to the various delays, the luggage had beaten us to the carousel within baggage reclaim, and it had backed up to the funnel causing some of the cases to be squashed and mutilated. When we eventually cleared passport control and customs, we were presented with a hefty bill by Pink Elephant Parking.

Despite the sting in the tail, I look forward to revisiting Budapest, the sooner the better.

CHAPTER 26

Irish Eyes

THE FIRST TIME I visited Dublin, the weather was so cold that we kept sliding into the expensive woollen and leather shops on Nassau Street to have a warm against the large hearth fires. On my next visit, the rain fell like knitting needles confining us mainly to indoors. This time the rain was like stair rods so the best laid plans were thrown into turmoil.

I was to be made redundant from my job so I was fitting in my outstanding holidays. It was the last break that I was likely to have for some time so I was determined to enjoy myself. I was in Dublin for two nights before moving on to Cork for a further three and I would take part in the highly recommended Ballycotton Ten.

Leaving my house at 8.00 a.m. the journey couldn't have been easier. An hour flight from Leeds and Bradford and I was settled into my hotel and unpacked by eleven. The heavy rain put a damper on my plans but I always had work colleague Frank Connor's pub crawl of the Temple Bar area up my sleeve. This pub crawl was designed for those with hollow legs who didn't easily fall over.

Dodging the raindrops, I ventured into the concourse of the prestigious Trinity College and saw the Book of Kells in the famous Long Room. I returned to the Temple Bar area and had a spot of lunch in the busy Buskers Bar. I moved on to St Patrick's Cathedral and then Christchurch, both founded during the Viking occupancy of Dublin in the eleventh and twelfth centuries. The crypt of Christchurch is the oldest standing building in the city today.

Friday was all planned but ended up a washout. I was to visit Howth, a pretty waterfront town with steep winding streets. I had previously run through Phoenix Park in the Dublin Marathon and fancied revisiting in not so testing circumstances. The park, the largest in any European city, has the Wellington Monument and the Papal Cross, put up in 1979 when a million people gathered to see the Pope. I wanted to walk the quays and see the Waterways Visitor Centre, a history of Ireland's canals.

I did none of these things; instead dodging in and out of shop doorways and spending time in St Stephens Centre and Dublin Castle. The upside of the day was that I had a Bewleys breakfast and Dublin's finest fish and chips.

On Saturday morning I left Dublin by train and travelled to Cork. The rain was unrelenting, falling on already saturated fields. The girl next to me worked in Dublin but was returning home to Tralee for the weekend. Further down the carriage were members of a rugby team travelling to a match all resplendent in matching sweaters with club crest. Four of them started to play cards and the others gathered around. They stood in the aisle, leaned over the back of seats and perched anywhere to have a glimpse of the game and to put forward their advice. What a way to while away a journey. It almost beats watching a marathon.

I changed trains at Mallow sprinting along the platform to avoid the prolific rain. I can remember singing 'The Fling at Mallow' in my younger schooldays and wondered if this was the one and same place.

Half an hour later we approached steep hillsides, entered a long tunnel and emerged at the other end in Cork. The rain had eased a little but it was a little breezy as my taxi sped around the one-way system and along the waterfront to my hotel, The Jurys at Anderson's Quay.

For so long overshadowed by Dublin, Ireland's second city is experiencing something of a boom and has much to offer as a short break destination.

Built upon an island in the River Lee, a network of bridges connects the city with the steeper outlying streets. Cork was founded by a seventh century monk, St Finbarr and today, a nineteenth century Gothic cathedral stands on the very spot. The surrounding area was flooded, hence the name 'Corchai' which means marshy place.

The city is best discovered on foot, be it a pleasant walk along the river banks or a stroll through the bustling streets. St Patrick's Street and Grand Parade are the main thoroughfares on which modern departmental stores rub shoulders with other establishments. Narrow alleys lead to fascinating little shops, pubs and restaurants, Carey's Lane and French Church Street being typical examples. The streets are thronged with pavement artists and buskers, along with traders selling their goods out of suitcases. The Grand Parade has a covered market and the Merchants Quay Centre, housing Dunne's departmental store, can provide a welcome diversion should the weather be inclement.

My first stop would be the bus station to check the times for Ballycotton the next day. To my dismay there was no Sunday service. Out of panic, I checked in the office and the inspector said, 'There's no Sunday service if that's what it says'. I suppose it was a silly question anyway. I could go as far as Middleton, probably halfway, but then I would need to find some other mode of transport to Ballycotton.

I walked the quays leaning into the stiff breeze and watched a ship approaching up the River Lee. The name of the vessel was *The Seahorse Serpent* and I was left wondering the ship's port of origin and the nature of its cargo. I stood on one of the bridges to the south of the island where the River Lee flows through a narrow channel and fairly cascades over the weir. I explored the English Market with a wide range of traditional stalls and stopped for a tea.

On returning to the hotel, I could hear an enthusiastic crowd watching rugby in the bar. Ireland were playing in Paris where they hadn't won for many years and were quoted at 50-1 to win. There seemed to be a good feeling about this game. Several experienced players had been recalled and the press were fairly upbeat about Ireland's chances. When I saw Ireland were leading going into the final stages, I began to rue not having a flutter, but France broke their hearts snatching the spoils late in the game.

The Sunday afternoon start meant I had time on my hands, so after a light breakfast, I took to the deserted streets. The early morning showed Cork at its best, particularly as the shocking weather of the past days had been replaced by sunshine and blue skies. Perhaps the race wouldn't be too bad after all.

The bus trundled around the city's one-way system, along the quays and followed the Lee Estuary. Turning inland through pleasant countryside, the bus reached Middleton, home of the Jameson Distillery and visitors' centre. I briefly walked the main street but soon realised the only way to travel the half dozen or so miles to Ballycotton would be by taxi.

The driver was a German who had settled here after marrying an Irish girl. His home town was Lubeck, a place I had visited, so we chatted away with something in common. He had recently returned to driving after a traumatic accident involving people he described as tinkers. I took these people to be travellers, but whoever they were, the man had been unable to claim damages through their insurance and the police had been unsuccessful in pressing charges.

I noticed the grass verges, hedgerows and undergrowth were coated in black from mud sprayed up by vehicles in the wet spell. As we approached Ballycotton, people with sports bags were walking towards the village, obviously, like me, unable to catch a bus. I caught a glimpse of the sea to the left on the final climb to the village. A banner at the side of the road welcomed the President and all runners to the village, but at that stage I gave no credence to the mention of the president.

The taxi pulled over when it could progress no further for parked cars and a line of traffic. I alighted, paid the driver and thanked him, but had no idea how I would return to Middleton after the race. I thought about booking the taxi there and then, but with heavy race traffic and the probability of runners still finishing, an agreed pick-up point may have been a problem.

Ballycotton is a small Cork seaside village with picturesque island and lighthouse. I walked the long main street with single houses, terrace houses, businesses and shops, pretty much what you would expect to find in a small village. People were standing in their doorways and at their gates, watching the steady stream of people. Many spoke as I passed, a nice gesture to a complete stranger, and with two hours still to go before race start, they were already tasting the atmosphere.

At the top of the street, I reached the Cliff Hall Palace which was throbbing with energy. Competitors and their families were milling around the refreshments and trade stands with others studying the map of the course and start list. I had a tea, well sweetened, and walked down the slipway towards a small jetty.

A fair crowd had assembled here and an official party with a smart red-haired lady stood out from the rest of the gathering. I walked along the jetty but stood back as the official party approached. The lady acknowledged sections of the crowd and spoke to me as the group passed by. It was then I realised the lady to be Mary McAleese, the Irish President who was visiting Ballycotton to officially launch the new lifeboat. I now realised what the references had meant on the banner. Mary would also start the race in which her husband Martin was running.

The first Ballycotton Ten took place in 1978 with thirty-one runners, thirty running below seventy minutes with Richard Crowley winning in a shade over fifty. Twenty-one years later, the race reached its 1,400 limit with the first 1,000 places going on a first come, first served basis. The remaining places would be drawn from a ballot with the rest of the applications being turned down. Three runners, including prolific race organiser John Walshe, have competed in all twenty-one races and the list of winners reads like a *Who's Who* in distance running. Among past winners have been Gary Staines, Jerry Kiernan, Marion Sutton and Karen MacLeod.

The main race sponsor is Nike and for a modest entry fee, a tee shirt, goody bag and mug are provided to all competitors. The entire village is involved in the race organisation from the ladies in the post office who handle the correspondence and send out the race packets, to the schoolchildren who tidy up the village the day after the race. The event has a big impact on East Cork tourism with many people returning year after year.

Returning to the Cliff Hall Palace to change, the atmosphere was alive with friendly banter, many runners obviously knowing each other and as start time approached, there was a buzz of expectancy. I saw a friendly face in Tony of Wakefield Harriers and together we made our way to the start on the narrow main street between high walls.

'The Ballad of Ballycotton' was sung by Dick O'Brien, a race tradition, and Mary McAleese got the race underway. We were tightly packed but soon spread out running along the main street, out of the village and beyond fields which had doubled as car parks. On the initial downhill, the panoramic coastal landscape was visible and at the bottom, the course flattened towards Shanagarry.

A left turn by a pocket of spectators brought us onto a straight, flat, country lane towards the drinks station at three miles which I completed in a little over seven minutes each. The course followed a loop of flat but contrasting terrain bringing us back to the same spot but this time at seven miles. Once again, drinks were handed out with words of encouragement from the enthusiastic volunteers.

The local clubs, Leevale, St Finbarrs and East Cork were well represented but there were athletes from all over Ireland, and I couldn't help noticing large contingents from Garstang and Cheltenham. Appropriate messages had been painted on the road in strategic places such as the one on the hill at nine miles which read, 'The only way is up'.

Still maintaining a seven minute pace, I reached the main street crowded with spectators. People leaned out of windows to watch while children stood on walls or any vantage point to get a glimpse of the finishers. I was able to pick up pace towards the crest of the hill before starting the short descent below the finishing banner. My seventy-one minutes had secured me a place in the five hundreds, slightly in the top half of the field.

I decided to hang around for a while after the race, wait until most of the traffic had cleared and then try for a taxi to take me back to Middleton. The bus to Cork didn't leave until seven, and it was barely five, so I had time on my hands. I had promised myself a hamburger from a van at the finish, but it somehow didn't have the same appeal to it after the race. A video was being shown later that evening but I would be on my way well before then.

My mind was changed for me when I received the offer of a lift part of the way back to Cork, enabling me to catch a bus. The man had run and brought his wife and young son along to watch. Apparently she had been a fairly useful runner before giving birth and intended to start again as her son grew older. The race had obviously whetted her appetite and captured her imagination. Their car was parked on the fringe of the village and progress was slow to begin with. They eventually dropped me on a main bus route, on their way to catching a ferry across the Lee estuary. They refused payment and wouldn't even let me give the boy any money. I'm not sure where they dropped me but I was soon on a bus heading back towards Cork.

A few days later, I found out that a special coach had run from Cork Railway Station to Ballycotton, returning in the early evening after the race. Never mind, I'll know better next time.

From my experiences over the few days, I realised that a car is recommended for exploring the immediate area, as public transport is limited. However in the city, a network of one-way streets can be problematical particularly for a stranger. In some instances, a detour is required to reach somewhere that is actually quite close as I discovered when I caught a taxi from the station to my hotel. The city can grind to a halt in rush hour and huge expectation surrounds the recent opening of the long awaited Lee Tunnel.

On Monday I took the half hour train journey along the Lee Estuary and waterfront to the pretty hillside village of Cobh dominated by the magnificent St Colman's Cathedral. Formerly known as Queenstown, this was the start of the journey for thousands of Irish emigrants, desperate to find a new life in America. Convicts were also brought here from Cork for the prison ships bound for Australia.

Cobh became the premier port for transatlantic liners, the *Titanic* having berthed here before the fatal voyage and the *Lusitania* sunk off the coast by a torpedo in 1915. The station buildings have been transformed into the 'Queenstown Story', an excellent small museum. Through photographs, models and exhibits, the maritime tradition of the area is documented through the years.

The picture postcard fishing port of Kinsale lies twenty miles south west of Cork and can claim the title of gourmet capital of Ireland. In 1975, twelve restaurants formed the Kinsale Good Food Circle and excellent sea produce is served in all of them. The Cottage Loft on Main Street and the Blue Haven on the site of the old fishmarket are particularly recommended. A Kinsale Gourmet Festival is held annually in October.

The many well-signposted coastal paths make Kinsale an ideal place for walking and there is an abundance of bird life to be seen. The Kinsale Museum contains memorabilia from the sinking of the *Lusitania.*

Cork City Gaol is well worth a visit and is open all year round. Remarkably untouched, the prison gives a genuine insight as to what life must have been like for a nineteenth-century prisoner. Blarney Castle is six miles west of Cork and tourists line up, all intent on kissing the Blarney Stone. The stone itself is a limestone block set high in the battlements. To kiss the stone involves a climb of 120 steps, being dangled by the legs and leaning over backwards. Needless to say, I gave this one a miss. Blarney House with splendid gardens and Blarney Woollen Mill are worth a visit.

Ballycotton came to prominence recently as location for the film 'Waking Ned'.

This area of Ireland is a hotbed for running with many races throughout the year. Apart from the ten mile race, Ballycotton Running Promotions also stage a summer midweek five mile series, around the surrounding area. There is a West Waterford Summer Series and a Cork Business Houses Fixture List. I'm sure to get my teeth into some of these if I'm still moving forward when I retire.

CHAPTER 27

A Tale of Two Cities

WITH MY KNEES crying out for mercy beyond six miles and on any severe downhill, my marathon days were clearly numbered if not behind me. For the first time in my life I visited a physiotherapist who was on a routine visit to my firm, otherwise I wouldn't have bothered.

He was apparently a sportsman so knew his business, but I didn't like what he had to say. By lying on the bed and doing some simple exercises, he was able to diagnose the problem. The quads around my knees were apparently firing in the wrong sequence and he gave me the impression this was either rare or severe when he called our nurse over for a second opinion.

He said I had to reduce my mileage to around ten per week alternating with swimming, cycling and some weight training. He gave me a special exercise to do which involved standing with my back to the wall while holding a brief-case and then squatting down. I had fifteen of these to do three times a day.

On my follow-up visit, the physio asked to see my running shoes so at least something good came out of this, they had a good wash. When I told him I hadn't any great pain from my knees, he recommended I should keep running unless I suffered any reccurrence.

My dodgy knees had limited me to shorter runs so it seemed my sixtieth marathon would be my last. I certainly wouldn't hang around long enough to join the 100 Club. Without the usual three or four long training runs under my belt, a gutsy effort on the day would probably get me around in reasonable shape but there would be no personal best.

If this was to be my last marathon, I would sign off in great style by running a race that had been a long time ambition. Some years ago I subscribed to six issues of the American magazine *Running Times* at a special offer price. They continued to send it well beyond the six issues and when I contacted the magazine for payment, they saw fit to send me a second copy under separate cover indefinitely.

Throughout this period, one race was regularly advertised and stood head and shoulders above all the others. It eventually developed into a must do event. The race was the Twin Cities Marathon held in Minneapolis and St Paul. *The Ultimate Guide to Marathons* written by Dennis Claythorn and Rich Hanna rates the Twin Cities as the second top destination marathon in the States behind Big Sur. It was also rated the third fastest and fourth scenic. It is widely acclaimed as the most beautiful urban marathon in America consisting of winding parkways, stunning foliage, blue lakes and the majestic Mississippi River.

One aspect I like about travelling to these races is that not everyone on the plane, unlike travelling to New York or Boston, is running the marathon. There is no talk of anticipated times, personal bests or injuries and half of the passengers are not in shell suits or lycra. This provides the opportunity to meet some really interesting people such as the man on the flight to Stockholm who was receiving an award. There was the young girl travelling to somewhere in the frozen wastes of Norway to demonstrate a photocopier. My travelling companion on this trip was involved in a long distance courtship with a girlfriend in San Diego. He visited as often as he could; both had failed marriages previously but neither were prepared to move to each other's country.

I knew little of the Twin Cities apart from what I had read. Minneapolis first came to my attention years ago when a very young Cybill Sheperd featured in a film as little more than a schoolgirl on vacation in Miami. A bungling young man fell for her and pursued her back to Minneapolis. Apart from Cybill, the winter scenery really made an impression on me. More recently another film, the black comedy 'Fargo' was based in and around the Twin Cities.

I read that Minnesota is known as the Land of Ten Thousand Lakes, that Minneapolis is very prosperous and that St Paul, the State Capital, has a slightly older and conservative feel.

Chicago is one of the world's busiest airports and where I would transfer to my flight for the Twin Cities. The flight was a little over an hour, crossing the shoreline of Lake Michigan before heading towards the fertile belt of the Midwest.

I had no idea how I would transfer from airport to hotel but my problem was resolved as soon as I passed through the check-in. A Twin Cities Marathon desk sat in a prominent position within the airport concourse and I made my way over. The young lady told me a minibus was provided to ferry the elite runners to the hotels. If I waited outside the terminal there would be one along shortly. I told her I wasn't an elite runner but she had probably realised that anyway. I was nevertheless assured there would be a place for me.

To say I felt out of place on the coach was perhaps an understatement.

There were two African runners weighing probably six stone apiece and they sat silently throughout the journey just staring ahead. Most of the others were lantern-jawed thoroughbreds all looking for under two and a half hours. It was no surprise that the conversation was all pretty high-powered stuff.

At last things started to look up as a young lady boarded and sat next me. She was from Orlando, here for a fifth time and let me have a map of the course which I needed like a hole in the head. I wasn't motivated for the race and with very little training feared the worst. We left the terminal only for the driver to take a call on his mobile asking him to return to pick up a straggler, who looked like another five and a half minute man.

The driver was a confident American of about forty years and wore a broad stetson. He gave an informative commentary on the landmarks we passed such as the world's largest dog food factory and the home of post-it notes. He gave us a rundown of the course, not that my colleagues needed it, the weather forecast for the day and places to visit and where to eat.

On reaching the hotel, the coach was involved in an accident when it reversed into a Daimler. I was impressed with the swift manner in which the respective drivers exchanged details and the amicable way it was conducted.

When I nudged a car on my way to work, the woman driving the other car became hysterical refusing to give me her telephone number and each time I got close to her she backed away. She refused to sit inside my car to exchange details and wouldn't let me sit inside hers either. Instead she chose to write outside on the bonnet with the ink running in the pouring rain. She even turned down my offer of an umbrella. The only noticeable damage to her car was to her mascots which appeared to have been knocked from the dashboard and onto the floor. The fact that she was upset prompted her to turn around and return home rather than attend an interview, but that was her choice.

The woman got back into her car and drove away, but it didn't stop her claiming for whiplash, taxi fares to hospital and lost wages on top of substantial damages to her car. I received a letter from her solicitor informing me measures were being taken to prosecute and I received various phone calls from the police. Finally I received a letter from the police stating that it would be in nobody's best interest to press charges.

What a contrast between similar accidents in different countries. I thanked the coach driver and gave him a five dollar bill. It was the least I could do.

I had secured Twin Cities special rates at the Regal Inn and found myself on a floor with elite athletes. This proved to be a pain as they congregated in groups along the corridor and I could hear muffled voices whenever I was in my room. They limbered up, gently jogged or just sat on the floor against a wall. It was most annoying and an invasion of my privacy. What a way to spend a weekend.

Following a brief reconnoitre on Friday evening, I set out early on Saturday to familiarise myself with Minneapolis. Approximately twelve blocks by twelve, the city is quite manageable and I soon gained my bearings. Many buildings are skyscrapers and high-rise, some are very new with spectacular and no expense spared shopping arcades. The people were well turned out and there appeared to be an ambience of prosperity. The main street, Nicollet Mall is pedestrianised and houses some of the best shops and restaurants.

The weather was gripping with the occasional snow flurry so I decided to move indoors. The skyways are a brilliant innovation comprising passageways and overhead corridors linking most parts of the city without venturing out into the fresh air. I joined the skyway at my hotel, crossed a couple of streets, walked through the convention centre and along the balcony of a bank. The key to the skyways is to follow the signs and markings and I duly passed through the Hilton Hotel and a large department store. A map is essential and a good deal of concentration necessary. I had to backtrack several times and on one occasion came to a dead end at the Lutheran Centre.

The skyway system would be ideal for Britain's northern cities but I couldn't see the business community reaching agreement over rights of way and access. Minneapolis is a city the rest of America looks up to, with very little crime, no poverty of note and little noticeable begging, so these factors make the city ideal.

Thousands of Northern Europeans settled here and there are constant reminders across the city. The American Swedish Institute recounts the Swedish experience in America through exhibits and artefacts.

The shops were very quiet for a Saturday, with many closed within the financial district. I wondered if the presence of the Mall of America, several miles outside the city, may have impacted upon this. With 520 outlets under one roof, this was at one time the biggest out of town mall in the world.

One shop I visited was the Thomas Kinkade Gallery containing art, gift items and collectables by 'The Painter of Light'. The shop was empty apart from the assistant and she was good enough to spend time with me. By lowering and switching on lights, the paintings took on a significantly different appearance which is why Kinkade is known as 'The Painter of Light'.

I love paintings and have often fancied myself as a collector, but I am short on the paintings. I was tempted by a work called 'Dawson', featuring a Canadian lumber town, the waterfront, some log cabins and a backdrop of snow-capped mountains. The price was a couple of hundred dollars and I promised to return on Monday when I had an idea what would be left in the kitty. Needless to say, I never did return.

My priority was to register for the race but I still couldn't generate a great deal of enthusiasm, putting it off until lunchtime. The registration and exhibition was taking place at the Hyatt Regency Hotel. As I approached, I observed runners and their families in brightly coloured sportswear, coming away with their goody bags in Twin Cities Logo. In contrast, I turned up looking much smarter in casual clothes.

I secured my number and championship chip, commonplace in these races today, and then started to look around the stands and exhibits. A promotions girl handed me half a dozen key fobs from the boot of a VW car; these would make ideal souvenirs for the people at work. There were stands advertising races at interesting places such as Nashville and Green Bay. The exhibition was one of the best I have visited and unlike some of the bigger races, I wasn't pushed or jostled and was able to walk around in comfort.

I filled in a form for an exotic holiday at a stand exhibiting electronic gadgets. They then invited me to join a queue, all attempting to throw a rolled-up sock through a trapdoor in a cardboard cut-out, from behind a marked line. A small crowd had gathered and everyone before me failed. I threw underarm and the rolled up sock wiped its feet before dropping through the trapdoor. The stallholder said in a Midwest drawl, 'Say, he's only the second person to do that today and both threw underarm'. The small crowd suitably applauded and he handed me a pocket calculator for my efforts.

On Saturday afternoon I walked the Mississippi mile, consisting of parks, scenic pathways and restored buildings. I gave my legs a rest by taking a paddle boat from the landing on Boom Island, but the cold was so bracing it enveloped me like a coat. On the way back to the hotel, I called at 'The Local', a traditional pub, where I treated myself to a steak and a Guinness. With the big day ahead, I then turned in for the evening.

Race day was again bitterly cold and it would stay that way. Yellow school buses ferried runners from the city's hotels to the start at the Hubert H. Humphrey Metrodome named after the Twin Cities politician and former US Senator. Changing was available around the concourse and within the seating of the Metrodome, a completely covered stadium housing a full size football field, home to Minnesota Vikings among others.

The only similar venue in Britain is at Cardiff where they have a sliding roof and tend to play with it open. Minneapolis is only a provincial city yet still boasts a venue like this.

The ten mile race which perhaps I would have been better suited to, started at half past seven. Just imagine, I would have been finished at nine o'clock in time for a full breakfast, but it wasn't to be. When the ten milers were clear, the marathon runners were requested to stand in their particular time zones which quickly filled up. I had opted for a long sleeve tee shirt underneath my vest, topped with a bin liner. I wore gloves for extra insurance and had a woolly hat tucked down the side of my shorts to call upon.

The guy who lined up next to me was perhaps a similar age and was looking forward to a personal record. I cried wolf making my excuses upfront, and told him that in my condition I would be only too glad to get around. My race tactics would be to set off steady and then ease back. But seriously, it was just a matter of seeing how far I could go before my knees started to hurt and then hanging in there for dear life. I had a couple of recent half marathons to my name but was lacking in those so important eighteen milers.

After a couple of Souza marches and a poignant rendition of 'The Star Spangled Banner' we were underway crossing the mat on the start line to the unmistakable trill of championship chips. My new companion sounded like a steam train with his feet hitting the ground like a couple of sledge hammers. It became clear that his personal record wouldn't match my just grateful to get around. We wished each other luck as I forged ahead.

We passed beneath the cold shadows of the downtown skyscrapers and by the famous Guthrie Theatre and Walker Arts Centre early on. Out of the shadow and into the sun, I at last gained confidence to remove my bin liner, tearing it from around my person and tossing it to the side of the road. Immediately, I started to feel the biting cold once more.

A short hill and residential stretch at three miles brought us onto the parkway system and towards the first of four lakes on the course, 'The Lake of the Isles'. The autumn foliage and the contrasting colours of the trees were brilliant, and I only wish I had felt more comfortable to enjoy this marvellous scenery.

The crowds around the course, particularly around the Lakes were warm and generous in their applause with the race providing them with an opportunity to get out into the pleasant surroundings. At races like this with large crowd support, I often wonder how many had run in races themselves. I know that after many years of running, spectating goes down very badly. Several years ago I watched the London Marathon, choosing to stand at a couple of places on the docklands where I was able to pick out the runners much more easily. I moved on to a place within the square mile but soon retired to the Victoria Station bar for a couple of pots. While I appreciate the encouragement of the crowds, I couldn't revert to being a spectator after spending so much time on the other side of the fence so to speak.

Next stop was Lake Calhoun, home to local running club and then on to Lake Harriet. The bright sun turned the surface into a silver mass and it was hard to believe we were only several miles from the city. The tree-lined boulevard, Minnehaha Parkway, ran alongside a beautiful creek and with ten miles gone, I felt comfortable, if not fluid, with no pain at this stage. A good proportion of the field comprised girls, young ladies and women, a far greater proportion than in races at home. Some moved along effortlessly chatting away to each other and making the most of the day.

The straight Cedar Avenue stretch crossed the corner of Lake Nokomis, our fourth lake. I risked removing my gloves but despite the brilliant sunshine, I quickly put them on again. From fifteen to nineteen miles, the route followed West River Road with the Mississippi down below flowing through a steep wooded gorge.

I was slowing considerably and while not in pain, effort and determination were the only factors keeping me going. After crossing the Mississippi, we followed East River Road to mile twenty-one where a testing climb elevated the course onto Summit Avenue.

Summit Avenue is located one block east of Grand Avenue and boasts five miles of Victorian mansions. The majestic boulevard extends from the banks of the Mississippi to the Cathedral of St Paul, and all the way along this stretch, crowds gathered on manicured verges and lawns to encourage those in particular who had reverted to walking.

I reached the stage around twenty miles when I realised my projected finish time would be around the three hours fifty mark, and I began to enjoy this historic stretch. Among the many mansions were the Governor's Residence and the former home of author F. Scott Fitzgerald. The cathedral of St Paul comes into view but takes a very long time to reach. Modelled on St Peter's Cathedral in Rome, this is one of the largest churches in America with a spectacular 186 foot high dome.

The course takes a left here onto John Ireland Boulevard for a long downhill run to the finish with the State Capital Building providing an equally impressive backdrop. As soon as I finished, I felt freezing cold and stiff as a crutch. My plan to hang around for a while, sample the entertainment and see the presentations took a knock when I decided to gather my belongings and head straight back to Minneapolis. I collected my freebies by way of bread rolls, chocolate biscuits and bananas and put the medal that had been placed around my neck into my shorts pocket. Clutching the foil space cape, I went in search of my bag.

After struggling to pull my track suit bottoms over my feet, I was soon sorted and on one of the shuttle buses speeding along the freeway to Minneapolis. I reflected on the day with some satisfaction at completing one of the best events in which I have taken part.

There were 5,907 finishers from 20 countries and 48 states with a further 2,200 in the ten miler. I finished a creditable 2,161 to maintain my status as 'Middle of the Packer'. The 2,000 females who finished constituted 37 per cent of the field, a far higher proportion than in Britain. American based Russians finished in the first two places in both the men's and ladies' races.

I showered and changed but was still conscious of elite athletes continually prowling and warming down in the corridor. I took to the streets ending up at Zela, a sophisticated eating establishment. The place was quiet with waiters outnumbering the punters but it was only mid-afternoon. I ordered medallions of lamb which arrived in the centre of a huge plate, accompanied by a dollop of mashed potatoes and a selection of vegetables. The mash alone was worth the price being amongst the creamiest I have tasted. As I ate, I couldn't help but notice the valet car parking chauffeurs who huddled on the pavement clapping their hands and flapping their arms to keep warm.

I turned down the chance to go bowling in the evening. In the first instance I couldn't bend down and secondly I hate trading in my shoes for those tatty pairs they allocate at the bowling alley. Instead I visited 'The Local' hostelry described in *Where Twin Cities* magazine as a place for upwardly mobile twenty to forty somethings. Surely I squeezed into this category. After a couple of beers I returned to the hotel and slept like a baby.

Monday was all mapped out, the first stop being Keys Café for the best breakfast in town, and I wasn't to be disappointed. I ordered two eggs, sunny side up, Italian sausage, hash browns and a rack of toast. When my breakfast arrived, I felt bloated just looking at it. The sausage provided a base with hash browns stacked high and two eggs, sunny side up perched on top. This was only from the bottom end of the selection and for just six dollars.

Two heavies came into the café, gave the waitress the spiel and ordered the full works. Their breakfasts duly arrived resembling mini mountains.

Today was Columbus Bank Holiday in the States but some premises were open for business as usual. Office workers formed in small pockets beneath the tall buildings, puffing on cigarettes and no doubt looking forward to the next smoke break. I walked across the Metrodome car park where early arrivals were gathering for the evenings football match between the Vikings and Tampa Bay Buccaneers.

The Vikings' supporters wearing replica maroon and gold, sported the names of their idols, usually Rudd, Culpepper or Moss. Why were these people here so early before the game and how were they going to occupy ten hours?

Feeling rather full with my Keys breakfast laying heavily, I moved sluggishly on to my next point of call, St Anthony's Falls, the only waterfalls on the Mississippi. I crossed the historic Stone Arch Bridge and marvelled at a huge barge being manipulated by a small tug into the chamber of the giant locks.

I followed the Heritage Trail walking cobblestone streets, past historic landmarks and along woodland paths. I moved onto Nicollet Island where squirrels continually crossed my path, moved on to Boom Island and returned along St Anthony Main Street.

I walked off my breakfast in time for lunch which would be at Tuggs River Saloon in the shadow of the giant Pillsbury Flour Mill. I sat overlooking the Mississippi and the Minneapolis skyline on a large deck and tucked into Tuggburger, fries and relish. With enough walking under the belt for one day, I used my bus pass to ride back to the city.

When I left my hotel room on Monday evening, the preliminaries were underway for the big game which was being shown on television and large screen in bars all over town. I visited the Rock Bottom Micro Brewery, a large beer hall with five home brews which was packed to the rafters. Next stop was Kiernans, a laid back Irish Pub with a band playing among others 'Ghost of the Liberties'. I made a mental note to tell Anne, a friend and runner from The Liberties area of Dublin.

The Brits Pub with roof top bowling green and red standard telephone box looked full as I passed so I moved on to a German-type Bier Kellar. There were references to the German roots all across town with appropriately named bars and restaurants such as Black Forest Inn, Bavarian Hunter and Glockenspiel.

Everywhere I went, punters were transfixed to screens, some in replica maroon and gold. The match see-sawed one way and then the other, before the Vikings snatched the spoils at the end to maintain their unbeaten start to the season. Most places served food until late and I could have comfortably slipped into this lifestyle. Businessmen straight from work mixed with locals of all colours and creeds.

On Tuesday morning I left Minneapolis for a couple of days in Chicago. There was so much I hadn't seen. I had only visited St Paul on race day, so had missed the waterfront and the historic buildings. I hadn't seen Little

Stockholm or the villages along the beautiful St Croix valley but there is only a limited amount of time and only so much you can include.

Chicago was enjoying an October heat wave which provided a fitting end to an excellent autumn break. For a real marathon experience in a manageable race and a taste of the real America, I could highly recommend the Twin Cities.

CHAPTER 28

A Day at the Races

A HORRENDOUS WEATHER FORECAST was given out on Saturday evening and the outlook for Sunday was no better. Following a succession of early morning phone calls, we set out but if one had cried off, we all would have followed suit. As we hit a blanket of snow across the Pennines, only one faint heart would have been enough to persuade us to turn around at the next exit.

The snow fell more sedately in Cheshire but as we approached the start, the 'Beware Runners' signs indicated very much that the race would go ahead. 'We're not running in this lot surely?' I said to the marshal as we left the car but he just returned a rueful smile.

The location of The Four Villages Half Marathon is Helsby Sports and Social Club with the rugged peak of the Old Man of Helsby as the backdrop. In the opposite direction, the flatlands spread out towards the industrial landscape of Ellesmere Port and Runcorn with the Manchester Ship Canal beyond.

As always we were far too early but warmed ourselves in the clubhouse drinking coffee from Les's magic flask. Roy completed his last minute preparations eating an obligatory pork pie. The one thing about these sort of races is that nobody knows you, until that is our club chairman Cyril, and Mrs Jones burst onto the scene with fists full of application forms for our own promotion, the Ackworth Half Marathon. If only a small proportion of runners turned out from the forms distributed, the narrow lanes in the area wouldn't be able to cope, with clear road not appearing for several miles.

We reluctantly changed into our usual gear bolstered by woolly hats, gloves and tracksters. I have never worn tracksters or track suit bottoms feeling far more comfortable in shorts, preferring instead to flash my painfully white knee caps. The only reason that Les wore two tee shirts was that he hadn't packed three.

The car park was like a skid pan, so what would the course hold for us? There had been considerable changes since the years we ran here regularly. The circuit around the oil refinery, power station and filter beds had been replaced by flat country lanes, undulating country lanes and bloody hilly country lanes. The fast flat course gesture on the application form was a blatant lie.

The fifteen hundred or so runners headed out through Dunham on the Hill but after that we barely saw a house and passed only the occasional farm building. On the narrow lanes we were treading ice, snow and slush with the combination playing havoc with my calves and aggravating already sore knees. Mouldsworth and Manley made up the four villages and it was here the fun started with a considerable climb to the ten mile clock where a band of marshals and spectators cheered us on.

The Paul Simon number 'Slip Sliding Away' sprang to mind as particular care had to be taken with each stride. A useful downhill section provided the impetus to try and make up for lost time, but the slippery surface and the runners ahead kicking up spray didn't help the cause. At least the snow had held off and the wind had dropped to a comfortable level.

The marshalling both on the course and at the start and finish area was excellent and an attractive boxed medal was presented to all those who survived the course and the elements. Changing rooms and warm showers were available with free hot refreshments provided. Adequate car parking was on hand and a reasonable departure afterwards for such a big field, in our case to the Dunham Arms where we enjoyed a carvery roast washed down with a pint of Banks Bitter.

As we left a pretty sunny Cheshire, everyone had enjoyed the day despite the conditions and another pair of socks for the bin.

In 1993, a new event came onto the calendar, the Stamford St Valentine's 30K. Only a couple of hours down the A1, this would be a good workout and useful stepping stone for would-be London Marathon competitors, and, being in Lincolnshire it was sure to be flat.

But how wrong they were, the thirty kilometre course probably contained as many hills, with long heartbreaking stretches and sections along windswept ridges. Stamford is a historical coaching town on the River Welland with splendid stone buildings. The race headquarters are the impressive Stamford School, set in spacious grounds. The rural course passes through the villages of Ryhall and Great Casterton along with several smaller communities and passes Tolethorpe Hall on the way out and back.

Somebody within the club must have taken a fancy to the race as it was included in the Grand Prix the next year. In the weeks leading up to the race, many runners expressed interest, but as the day of reckoning drew closer, one by one they gave backward. I felt really run-down and under the weather in the days before the race and didn't feel up to eighteen gruelling miles. The fact was, I had promised Ian a lift, he was well trained, raring to go and I didn't feel like letting him down. Instead I opted to take my kit and see how I felt when I arrived at Stamford.

The weather was as bad as it gets, bitterly cold, a biting wind and driving rain. By taking my kit however, I had made a statement of my intent to run and I very nearly regretted it. I started off well enough but after several stretches into the teeth of the wind, I slowed badly and runners started to pass me at will.

At twelve kilometres, a slight rise brings the road parallel to the main London railway line and a left turn up a further incline produced a stretch into the prevailing wind. A first aid station was strategically placed on the grass verge. As I passed I made my intentions clear to the St John's Ambulance volunteers, telling them I wanted to retire from the race, the next time the sweep-up vehicle was in the vicinity.

I plodded on for half a mile, a mile, probably two miles, but there was no sign of the sweep-up vehicle. I have never dropped out of a race before, the nearest being when I pulled out of the Robin Hood Marathon at the half marathon stage. I was most annoyed when the club newsletter had me down as 'Did not finish'. By now the conditions had become pretty unpleasant with hailstones peppering my face and the strong wind pushing me all over the road.

But suddenly out of the blue as if by a small miracle, I began to pick up pace and started to pass many of the runners who had previously overtaken me. My tired legs and aching limbs had suddenly staged a minor recovery.

The stretch from Great Casterton towards Tolethorpe Hall had the stiff breeze blowing at our backs and I was being fairly whipped along. I passed a succession of runners including some of my club mates. Towards the end of the race as if to make up the distance, there are several twists and turns around a housing estate. When you think all is over bar the shouting, there is a demoralising stretch around the perimeter of Stamford School field.

In recent years, *Runners World* pacers have been added to encourage groups of different abilities to make it around in under a particular time. Generous prizes particularly for teams are awarded and in keeping with the St Valentine's theme, a prize is awarded to the couple with joint best times. The downside to the race is usually the inclement February weather and the tough course which would probably be better suited to a summer event.

In contrast to Stamford, a race where I have usually been blessed with better weather on the occasions I have visited is the Dentdale Run. Sitting on the North Yorkshire and Cumbria border close to the South Lakes, Dentdale is a steep fertile valley at the head of Wensleydale. The River Dee meanders or rushes through the valley depending upon the weather and the time of year. The race organisers make provision for this in their mail out by stating that in case of flooding, a further three hundred yards may be added to the course.

Originally intended as a fun run to raise funds for Dent Primary School, the race started out with children running in fancy dress and mothers pushing prams around a much shorter course. Now the race is the unusual distance of fourteen and a half miles, so a personal best is always on the cards.

Dent is a picturesque village with mazy cobbled streets with many of the stone houses formerly hand knitting and weaving cottages. Nowadays, some have been turned into antique and craft shops or cosy cafés. The village boasts two pubs, the Sun Inn and George and Dragon. Both are owned by Dent Brewery and serve the renowned Ramsbottom Ale.

On race day, the population trebles for several hours with the six hundred limit regularly reached. The race starts at one o'clock and winds through the narrow streets before heading out on tight country lanes flanked by neat hedgerows or dry stone walls. Despite the steep valleys, the circuit isn't too severe providing you have some long runs to your name. Sheep perch precariously on vantage points watching the runners tackle the many short sharp pulls.

A pack-horse bridge is crossed at four miles before the return trip down the far side of the valley. Glancing across, it is possible to see the back markers and the flashing light of the rear vehicle. Some useful descents enhance this section to eight miles with a pleasant stretch alongside the River Dee. Family and friends walk the half mile from Dent to cheer on their loved ones, and on one occasion I was able to jettison my tee shirt here on an unusually warm March Saturday. The drinks handed out just hit the spot before the next series of climbs towards Lea Yeat and Dent Head where the railway station is the highest above sea level in England.

Throughout most clubs, runners of similar ability enjoy friendly rivalry. One particular year I slowed for a drink and Ian thundered past me. I caught him on one of several climbs and thought I had shrugged him off. I had to slow as a tractor and Range Rover travelling in opposite directions tried to pass. I glanced round and to my astonishment Ian was so close I could have given him a kiss. A planned steady last couple of miles turned into panic stations and ended with a mad scramble back to the village.

The roads on each side of the valley run parallel so you can see the runners strung out in the distance. The scenery is pleasant on the eye and if running comfortably, you won't fail to enjoy the event. A generous descent in the last half mile provides views of Dent's white buildings and after a slight detour around back lanes, the finish in the school grounds beckons.

The ladies of Dent provide ample refreshments, included in a modest entry fee, and a couple of pints in one of the hostelries usually rounds off a successful day. Not without its problems, the race tends to attract a notorious farmer who makes a point of driving a high-sided trailer through the streets shortly before race start time. This usually necessitates in the start line banner having to be taken down. The twelve mile marker has also made a habit of mysteriously vanishing throughout the years.

Anyone fancying the race should make a point of finding out exactly where Dent is. One year we improvised and found ourselves on a scenic but narrow winding road across the tops. From time to time someone would have to get out of the car to open and close the gates intended to secure the sheep.

A number of farmhouses take paying guests and an overnight stay can provide a pleasant early spring break if the weather stays fine. Friends still enthuse at the home-made steak pie served up at one such establishment.

In contrast to the other years when I have run here, the 2003 event saw torrential rain with a strong wind blowing across the valley. We were treading water for long stretches as the river overflowed in places and water gushed from the already saturated fields. Needless to say, the organisers saw fit to implement the extra 300 yards.

As I removed the application forms that had been secured under my windscreen wipers while I had been pounding the roads, the place name on one of them seemed to ring a bell. It was only when I got my breath back, stopped coughing and collected my thoughts that I realised that in fact I had been to Walkington. In my younger days, I had played cricket there in an afternoon friendly, best remembered for a fist fight involving a player from each side.

The game was organised through a work contact of one of our players and we set off early stopping for a couple of jars on the way through at Holme upon Spalding Moor. The player on our team had a remarkably short fuse and probably fuelled by the beer, he ended up fighting over something and nothing. The same player was on his second circuit of local teams, having been thrown out by most clubs over similar occurrences or falling foul of their committees.

I played football against the same guy with the match ending up as a free-for-all as the referee saw fit to jump ship. The word on the street was that he had put a contract out on one of our players, a young raw-boned lad. The two mysteriously avoided each other for weeks and when they eventually met up, they greeted one another like long lost brothers.

So as a couple of car loads travelled along the M62, I was at least safe in the knowledge there would be no fisticuffs tonight, just a sociable evening run. Walkington Playing Fields, a couple of miles west of Beverley brought the memories flooding back as it was the same venue where the fight had taken place all those years ago.

A friend who had run here previously warned me not to get too far back at the start and I soon realised why. There is a reasonable walk from the field to the start with a bottle-neck caused by everyone having to negotiate a kissing gate. Only when each and every runner is through can the race start.

The runners line up in a column which can be fairly long in a sizeable field. When the start is signalled, a human crocodile disappears into the distance before I have even moved off the spot. The early stages are through a lush meadow where some grass appeared to have been cut down especially for the event. The volume of runners mean that some have to run in the long grass on each side of the path in order to play catch up. Tight laces are essential here, particularly in the early stages.

The path leads through another gate and a marshal directs runners up a steep track which joins Risby Lane. A dip and stiff pull come almost immediately before the road levels out towards Walkington. Spectators walk the short distance from the start and gather on a corner to lend their support as we turn left towards Little Weighton.

The road undulates and a stiff breeze sometimes persists but the scenery more than makes up for any discomfort. This is what running should be all about and is just about as good as it gets.

On high ground the stanchions of the Humber Bridge, several miles away come into view if you know at which point to look. Volunteers hand out drinks in Little Weighton near the village duck pond and after a steep rise, the road levels out running along a ridge towards Skidby. The fields to the left are colourful with lavender and rape, and beyond are the tiny buildings of Walkington where we are heading.

We cross the fields by way of a cart track which switchbacks at least three times. If the next road section looks familiar, then it is with part of the first mile doubling as the last. Again spectators congregate on the corner but this time we turn right along a track and through a leafy glade. The run in to the finish covers three sides of the sports field with many people starting their bid for home, only to ease off again when they realise there is still some distance to go.

The commentator mentions as many names as possible and an unusual souvenir has generally been up for grabs including a pair of gloves and a luminous hat. The fun run starts and finishes before the main race and is a mile and a half long. Competitors range from our next generation of champions to parents going around with toddlers. With usually over two hundred entrants, the runners are coming through solid at peak finishing time.

The races organised by Beverley Athletic Club have taken place on a July Friday in recent years with Royal Nuffield Hospital being the usual sponsor. Refreshments are provided at a local school but if you get a move on, there may still be chance of a carvery or bar meal at the Ferguson & Fawsitt Arms or one of the other local hostelries.

Last year the course was changed in light of the Foot and Mouth epidemic with a different start and the country sections replaced, but this didn't detract from any of the enjoyment. My lasting memory is of the dozens of youngsters coming away, wearing their luminous hats which stood out like beacons in the fading light.

A race that I was well aware of, but didn't run until recently is the Yorkshire Wolds Half Marathon. Fell Runners and Orienteers within our fraternity seemed to love it but the road runners claimed it to be a killer. Run in conjunction with the Bishop Wilton Show at the foot of the Wolds near Pocklington, the race is usually held on the third Saturday in July. When I say at the foot of the Wolds, the land starts to rise steeply just across the road from the showground.

The Bishop Wilton Show is a celebration of country life, arts and crafts. There is show jumping, rare breeds of cattle, sheepdog trials and activities with a farming theme. Marquees house arts and crafts along with refreshments and a beer tent. Several local painters display their excellent works here and I usually go with the intention of buying a painting to start off my prestigious collection. So far I haven't managed to get out of the blocks.

The race starts on the road outside the showground and runs initially in the opposite direction to the winter race held in these parts, the Snake Lane Ten. The first couple of miles are pretty gentle by anyone's standards, but on mile three, you are left staring at a range of hills which draw closer and closer.

Eventually you realise as the song goes, 'The only way is up'. The first climb is steep, and while subsequent climbs are gentler, they soon sort the men from the boys. The road is flanked by rolling fields and woods but after a while, the scenery provides little consolation. Concentration and determination are the key qualities required as the climbing lasts for three miles with no level or downhill to break the monotony.

With heart and lungs on fire, a right turn into a narrow lane signifies the end of the climbing for the time being and the start of the downhills. You feel on top of the world but have neither the time or the inclination to take in the panoramic views. After persevering for almost half an hour to reach this lofty position, you are soon almost back to square one with most of the downhill coming in one exhilarating mile.

From the narrow lane, a right turn leads onto a wide track which starts to plummet through dense woodland. The track twists first one way and then the other as runners move from side to side to secure a firmer surface. The track goes down and down as daylight is replaced by darkness interrupted only by the occasional shaft of light. With the valley bottom certain to be around the next bend, the track still continues to fall away sharply.

At last the track levels as daylight pours in and a well-trodden path beckons through a narrow steep sided dry valley. Drinks are served by a gate at the end of the valley and soon we are back on a road. An undulating section with miniature hairpin bends leads to Millington at ten miles. The second long slog is from the crossroads before the eleven mile marker to Great Givendale beyond twelve. This is the sort of section you don't relish at this stage of the race and many experienced runners resort to walking. A good run up here can make all the difference between a successful race or not.

With half a mile to go, runners have a bird's eye view of the showground as the country lane drops almost vertically crossing the main road and finishing adjacent to the rare breeds. Time can be made up in this final stretch but beware that on the steep hill and around the tight bends it is easy to go out of control.

The second time I ran here, I was in a rich seam of form, at least for a 'Middle of the Packer'. My five or six previous half marathons were all within a hundred minutes, but I was unlikely to figure as well here. For the first and only time, I wrote down my predicted mile splits which ranged from six to eight and a half minute miles. I secured these to a band around my wrist hoping they would help in my quest. A breakneck last mile in under six minutes saw me reach my target with only seconds to spare. The following year on a scorcher of a day, I trudged in ten minutes slower.

Finishers here receive one of the coveted Fangfoss Pottery Mugs for a morning's work well done. There is still time to browse around the many stalls and exhibits, have a bite to eat and a well-earned cuppa and purchase that elusive painting. Well maybe next year.

The massive flooding in the autumn of 2000 resulted in race cancellations, among them the seventeenth running of the Guy Fawkes Ten. Despite several crossings of the River Nidd, the course was still negotiable even though some of the car parking areas were soft. But with police resources severely stretched in more important areas, the organisers reluctantly followed their advice, and on Friday afternoon postponed the race.

They made broadcasts on local radio and phoned around asking people to pass on the word. I received a phonecall from a club mate on Friday evening and passed the message on to a couple of colleagues who had entered the race. By doing this, only thirty runners turned up on the day, a magnificent effort on behalf of the organising club, Nidd Valley Runners. Several weeks later, a jiffy bag duly arrived through the post containing a race tee shirt, a letter of apology and an account of the sequence of events that led to the postponement. There was a concrete date for the 2001 race which unfortunately didn't happen due to the Foot and Mouth outbreak in the area. Instead, a five miler took place exclusively in the confines of the Yorkshire Showground at Harrogate.

The Guy Fawkes Ten has experienced something of a nomadic existence using different venues and courses around the Harrogate and Knaresborough area. The early races took in Harrogate centre, parts of The Stray and a section along the waterfront at Knaresborough. We ran below the famous railway viaduct, a regular photograph on Yorkshire calendars. A later route took in the villages between Knaresborough and Wetherby forming an out and back course with a loop. Hopefully through the courtesy of Sir Thomas Ingilby, a regular venue has been found for the race at Ripley Castle.

The programme notes of several years ago stated that the course remained unchanged and the countryside as beautiful as ever, but Nidderdale remains and hopefully always will be decidedly lumpy. The race commentator also made a point that the course hadn't been ironed flat as promised.

The race headquarters are the historic grounds of Ripley Castle, home to the Ingilby family for seven hundred years. Cromwell is said to have had prisoners shot here after the Battle of Marston Moor and sought refuge overnight against the wishes of Jane Ingilby. Some years ago, the castle and grounds were used as location for the television series 'The Flaxton Boys'.

The race starts is in Ripley Main Street but a loop of the grounds and the need to climb several steps cause a bottleneck culminating in a pretty slow first mile. The early stages are on farm tracks with a steady gradient until almost two miles when a minor road joins the main road at Burnt Yates. We stay on the main road briefly before turning left, and a stiffish climb leads to a long overdue downhill. The River Nidd is crossed for the first time in Birstwith.

We are punished for the welcome interlude when a side road leads to a nasty little hill. Parishioners attending the local service weren't sure whether to pray for us or pity us. I'm a big believer in taking whatever courses tend to throw up and not one to moan, but this hill borders on the unfair. A left turn provides some welcome respite and spurred on by the magnificent marshals, we embark upon one of the few flat sections on the course. But this doesn't last for long as a nice downhill provides fine views of Lower Nidderdale with the runners strung out ahead over the next long climb.

Another long downhill beckons through Hampsthwaite where again we cross the Nidd over a splendid pack-horse bridge. Last time here I caught John Bell in my sights, a useful over-sixties veteran. Closing on him with every stride I eventually drew level which was the worst thing I could have done. Glancing across at me, he effortlessly slipped up a couple of gears and the next time I saw him was at the finish.

A further couple of miles of pleasant winding country lanes, and the final mile is reached on wooded bridleways. After a furious descent over a roaring stream, the final pull leads to the finish in the historic castle courtyard.

You can forget any thoughts of a personal best here but the scenery, the clean air and the organisation more than make up for the testing course. The castle grounds and park are open on race day and Ripley Main Street includes a saddlery, gift shop, delicatessen and art gallery. The Boar's Head, a former coaching inn, has a fine restaurant and serves bar meals.

The race holds a special place for me and I will return as often as I can. It was the last race that my father, a keen follower of my fortunes, attended with me before he passed away in 2000.

On a bright crisp and frosty morning, a coachload of Ackworth runners and supporters travelled over the North Yorkshire Moors to Loftus, a community north of the coastal fishing town of Whitby. The 'Poultry Run' came highly recommended as several of our number had run here in previous years and apparently a large prize list of festive produce would be there for the taking.

The journey across Fylingdales Moors was very pleasant but even with the sun shining brightly, the temperature was still close to zero and the frost hadn't lifted. I didn't know whether the coach driver was about to laugh or cry when he was told tongue in cheek that he would have to follow the race as a sweep-up vehicle.

Any chances of prizes disappeared when a six hundred strong field toed the start line with large contingents from New Marske, Swaledale and Billingham Marsh House. The representation from Newcastle area clubs emphasised the fact that the North East is still the hotbed for running in the UK. There were two delightful young ladies from Hartlepool Burn Road and we duly invited them to run in the next Ackworth Half Marathon.

At the time I didn't realise the significant impact this race would have upon myself and my colleagues. The fixture has become a must in the race calendar and each year the club subsidises a coach for the day. The event is talked about for months in advance, and the day out provides an excuse for a Christmas fuddle. People can be heard to say 'Put me down for Loftus,' and one person reckons his entire year's training is geared to peak on this day. I'm not sure if he means running or drinking though.

In the early years, the race started and finished at Loftus Cricket Club, but more recently the headquarters have moved to the Leisure Centre. I first ran here in 1992 when the conditions underfoot were treacherous. Some parts of the course hadn't been exposed to the sun and were still very icy at midday. In subsequent years, we have encountered a variety of conditions albeit usually bitterly cold. There have been bright and crisp days with a sprinkling of frost while other years have seen snow and a biting wind.

A Brass Band plays Christmas carols, there are festive stalls and runners dress up as fairies or as Santa Claus. All of these things provide a seasonal atmosphere and a feel-good factor when perhaps you aren't up for the rigours that lie ahead. Each year, one of the men dressed as a fairy carries a big rubber hammer and hits people along the way. His efforts are rewarded by raising money for the Life Boat Appeal.

The early stages involve a series of stiff climbs to Hummersea Lane where the views are stunning and the wind and the cold are bracing. Passing the occasional house and farm building, the moorland road continues to climb until a right turn leads to the first of the off road sections. Encouraged by a man and his dog, we embark upon an uneven track towards Easington. This stretch is predominantly downhill and can be firm or over the ankles in mud depending upon the weather conditions.

Generally there is a pocket of spectators outside the Tiger Inn before a niggling little pull by the church leads onto the coast road beyond the three mile post. To the right is Boulby Potash Mine and beyond the rooftops and gables of Staithes nestled in a cleft between steep cliffs, Penny Nab and Cow Bar.

A left turn leads up a steep gorge with a running stream and occasionally along with dozens of other people, I have resorted to a walk. A gap in between fields leads to a farm track which again can be firm or muddy. At the top beyond a farmyard is the highest point on the course at Boulby Bank close to the Cleveland Way. Rock Cliff nearby is the highest point on the east coast of England at 666 ft.

The remaining three miles or so are mostly downhill with some annoying little pulls to keep you interested. Several years ago, the wind on this section was so severe that runners were having their ankles whipped from under them and were battling to remain upright. On one occasion, an additional section was added including the knee-jarring descent to the former fishing village of Skinningrove.

The last two miles are the first two miles in reverse with last year's course providing a generous downhill through residential streets to the Leisure Centre finish. The distance is indeterminable, somewhere between seven and eight miles and all finishers usually receive a long sleeve tee shirt. There are numerous spot prizes on offer in keeping with the time of year.

All competitors can have a free swim in the pool at the leisure centre but our lot are more intent in getting to the pub which in the last few years has been The Mars Inn. After a meal or a sandwich and a few pints, all benefit gained by doing the race is blown away. One or two usually arrive back at the coach decidedly worse for the drink.

An end to a great day is the image of a dozen men standing in a lay-by, paying a call of nature, with the backdrop of Roseberry Topping silhouetted against the moon.

Another favourite race takes place in my home town of Rothwell. The 10K runs through 'God's Country', has an elevation drop from start to finish and is downhill with the wind at your back all the way. This usually takes place in April, perhaps a week or so after the London Marathon.

I have covered the Leeds Marathon, Great North Run, Great Scottish Run and Robin Hood Marathon in previous chapters, and collectively, these make up a dozen of my favourite races. I can't pick one that stands out above the others as each has individual characteristics and qualities. Some races are in town, some are in country, some have large entries, others a few hundred. But one common theme throughout all of these events is the extremely high quality of the organisation.

I was disappointed to hear that the Robin Hood races were in jeopardy due to Nottingham council being unable to fund the race budget. Fortunately the races were saved at least for the time being with Sweatshop coming forward as a main sponsor. These races have meant so much to so many people over the last two decades and their demise would be a sad loss to the racing calendar.

CHAPTER 29

Onwards and Upwards

IT BECAME APPARENT very early in my running career that I wouldn't break any pots. I wasn't prepared to tolerate any more pain than was necessary, so much preferred the long haul to the quick burst. The half marathon seemed a much better proposition for me than those heart pounding and pulse racing 5 mile or 10K events.

Rather than go for broke from the gun and try to hang on for dear life, the half marathon provided the opportunity to settle in, see how I would feel and cut my cloth accordingly. And so my love affair with the 13 mile 192 ½ yard race began. Averaging ten a year, I have managed to maintain my enthusiasm and a certain level of fitness for almost twenty years. My 150th half marathon was at Ackworth in 1996 and my 200th on the same course in 2001. At my current rate of progress I should clock my 250th in 2006, hopefully at Ackworth.

I ran my 50th Marathon in 1997 at Leeds to join three colleagues at the club, Ken Bingley, Les Adams and Kevin Blackshaw all on that milestone. My 600th race was the Flora London Marathon in 2000 where I ran a shocker. I have run on four continents, in twenty different countries and Vienna was my fifteenth capital city race. Regularly averaging thirty miles a week, I should pass the 30,000 mile mark sometime next year.

I have never been a prolific Charity fund raiser but must have contributed £10,000 over the years to local hospices and organisations. My work colleagues and company have always been very supportive but I have been careful not to bite the hand that feeds me, keeping more of a low profile in recent years. Persuading people to sign up for sponsorship is the easy part but collecting the money can be a pain. I have often had to dip into my own pocket to make up the shortfall or close the books with monies still outstanding.

After a recent midweek event, a friend asked, 'Is there anywhere you haven't run Andy?' My reply, rather tongue in cheek, was 'You must be joking, I've hardly scratched the surface'. So after being fortunate to compete in so many places across the world, where could I possibly want to go, and which races are still to be run?

The Two Oceans Marathon in Cape Town is undoubtedly the best event in which I have run and is also my best performance. I would love to return but couldn't come close to recreating the events of Easter Saturday 1995.

A logical progression would have been to run the Comrades Marathon, the daddy of the ultra marathon calendar. The Comrades runs through The Valley of a Thousand Hills from Pietermaritzburg to Durban. This course is known as the down route and each year alternates when the race starts at Durban on the Indian Ocean and runs up country through Zulu Natal.

The distance is eighty-nine kilometres and runners use the Two Oceans as a stepping stone or to gain a qualifying time. A four and a half hour marathon will be good enough to secure a place on the starting line of the Comrades. I firmly believed that at one time, this distance was well within my grasp, as sometimes I felt as if I could plod along all day. However these days, five miles in training feels like running to the other side of the world. But who knows, I may feel differently in a few years' time and relish the challenge.

Another race I rated very highly and enjoyed was the Stockholm Marathon although in 1990 I was moving easily and felt comfortable, but I have provisionally pencilled this one in again for next year. *The Ultimate Guide to International Marathons* rates this race as number one in the world and awards full tens for course beauty and organisation. It describes the Stockholm Marathon as exceptional, gorgeous, well-organised, boisterous and somewhat unusual for its late afternoon hours.

The advent of the internet, web sites, e-mail and the likes has opened up a whole new range of running possibilities and several I have come across seem to be must do events. A recent television documentary portrayed the Von Trapp children of Sound of Music fame reunited in Salzburg where they relived some of the magical moments in the Austrian city where the musical was made. The River Salzach flows through the city overlooked by the giant fortress Hohensalzburg.

Wolfgang Amadeus Mozart was born here in 1756 but only became fêted in the city after his death. He was more or less kicked out of Salzburg, saying he wasn't appreciated. Apparently there was no theatre, no opera and the people didn't like his music. He died impoverished in Vienna and was buried in a massed grave. Today the city thrives on Mozart with streets and a square named after him, a Mozart week and a festival. The city stages a high quality half marathon in October. What better place to run than with mountains, music and Mozart?

Another event I came across which merited a full page spread in *Distance Running Magazine* is the Quebec Marathon and Half Marathon. My father spoke fondly of Quebec which had featured in one of the old cinema 'Pathe

Newsreels' and described as 'City of a Thousand Dreams'. Quebec is one of the few walled cities in North America and stands on the mighty St Lawrence River.

The population is mainly French Canadian and the province predominantly French speaking. Several years ago, a referendum decided that Quebec province would remain part of Canada rather than go it alone as a separate state. But the republican movement won't give up easily and in time are expected to force a similar ballot in which they may hold sway. The race start is reached by ferry and the route runs along the foreshore, crosses a long bridge and finishes in the Old Port of Quebec.

I recently saw the 1983 film 'Flashdance' for about the fifth time. Reports in the Sunday paper described the film as naff and the writer said at the time that he was embarrassed at owning up to seeing the film. The next Monday at work, we were presented with slides and a short film monitoring the company's progress. When these were finished, our manager struggling to come to terms with the projector said there was one more slide to show for the boys. Meeting with little success he said that he had hoped to show a slide of Jennifer Lopez. A man in the audience who had obviously seen Flashdance called out, 'Never mind about Jennifer Lopez, how about Jennifer Beals'. Too right, a man out of my own heart.

Who can forget the wonderful Jennifer cycling from her home in Pittsburgh's warehouse district to her daytime job as a welder, crossing the city's spectacular bridges. At night time she was an exotic dancer who harboured an ambition of becoming a ballerina. I will never tire of seeing Flashdance with that haunting melody 'What a feeling'. Naff!? I won't hear a word of it.

The City of Pittsburgh Marathon is held each May and seems like another must-do event for the calendar. Crossing three of the city's bridges, the race finishes at Point State Park at the Three Rivers Nexus.

So there's still plenty to keep me on the streets and the incentive to keep dragging my weary body out of bed, early on a Sunday morning. Let's face it, if I didn't do this, what would I be doing? Well after getting rid of last night's curry or Chinese to make way for a full English, I would take a stroll across to the park where twenty-two angry young men would be kicking a bladder around a field. They would shout comments like 'Keep going fella' and 'Well played my son,' while all the time hurling abuse at the man in black.

At the stroke of twelve, I would make my way to the pub, or probably to the club in time for the stripper. I would return home after three for a nap on the sofa. Then I would repeat the cycle all over again. I don't think so!!

CHAPTER 30

The Finish Line

THE SETTING was Golden Acre Park to the north of Leeds early on a Sunday afternoon towards the end of August. The Leeds Country Relay was taking place, and regular partner Mick and I were running the fifth leg as far as Thorner.

We had travelled in separate cars, Mick leaving his at Thorner from where we used mine to reach Golden Acre Park. On completion of our leg, Mick would drop me back here to collect my car and we would look forward to an ice cream cornet and flake topped with lashings of strawberry juice.

A year ago today, I woke to the news that the Princess of Wales had been tragically killed in a car accident. Mick and I had followed similar arrangements as those today but when we returned to Golden Acre Park, my car had been entered and my trousers and money taken. There had been a torrential downpour while we had been running and most of the cars had left the park. The ice cream van had gone too but I wouldn't have had the money to pay. Maybe better weather and better luck today.

This would be the fourth or fifth time we had run this leg together. After a traumatic first year, we had formed a useful partnership and I like to think we served our club well. The first year, Mick was on top form and I struggled to stay with him. The fact that I had reconnoitred parts of the course worked in my favour as from time to time, Mick wasn't sure which way to go so had to ease back and wait for me.

Mick reached and opened every gate first. He waited while I had safely passed through before fastening them and catching me up once again. He was first over every stile and carried the dreaded baton for all but half a mile. A very quick first mile had knocked the stuffing out of me and I struggled every bit of the way. As badly as I ran however, we still managed to pass one pairing and weren't headed ourselves.

To my surprise, when the pairings were discussed for the following year, Mick was still keen to run with me on the same leg and didn't wish to be relocated with another partner. It was important that I ran well and didn't let him down again. Fortunately I did run well and we formed a solid partnership for several years.

At Golden Acre Park, the runners would complete the fourth leg along the main Otley Road and as they approached, a marshal would call their numbers to officials below. The runners enter the park through a tunnel under the road where the next pairing is in the holding area ready to go.

A spectator had made a chance remark to us that he had been to the previous changeover point at Thornbury and couldn't recollect seeing our pairing pass through. This immediately started us thinking about the possibility of going in the massed start, when all pairings still waiting would set off together at half past two. The massed start on the final two legs enable the event to finish at a realistic time and prevent runners waiting indefinitely at the changeover points.

As the time moved closer to two-thirty, teams finished and teams set off but there was no sign of our pair. The Ackworth 'A' Team had been long gone with the fourth leg pair probably at home now with their feet up. Mick commented that this was the last time we were waiting here and next year we would ask to run a morning leg. We didn't seem to have much luck as a couple of years previously, one of our fourth leg pairing had twisted an ankle and couldn't finish so our team were disqualified. We still went through the motions completing our leg, but didn't pick up a placing.

Sure enough, all the runners still waiting were called to the massed start and we were soon underway. There were between a dozen and fifteen teams in total, some of them veterans, some comprising a man and woman and others with two girls. One thing for sure was that none of these teams were crackerjacks.

Drawing upon my experience of when I had first run with Mick, I told him to take it easy early on. I could tell he was annoyed at having to wait until the cut-off time, there was fire in his belly and he was up for it. Leaving the park, there were two teams ahead of us, a couple of veterans from Horsforth and two runners representing one of the Abbey teams. Having said that, we were veterans ourselves but were quicker than these two, soon passing them and tucking in behind the Abbey Runners. I kept having a quiet word with Mick telling him to ease back, but he was chomping at the bit and raring to take on these two.

We climbed the steady gradient in the opposite direction to the excellent Eccup Ten Race. The incessant barking could be heard as we approached the boarding kennels where dogs were running rings around their volunteer walkers.

One of the Abbey Runners appeared to be struggling to keep up with his mate, a fact that hadn't gone unnoticed with Mick. He was quickly around the back runner with me hotly in pursuit, my lungs blowing like a pair of bellows.

At the next gate, the first runner had to wait for his partner to catch up, and we were now holding the proud position of leaders of the massed start. We had clear countryside ahead and started to focus on a couple who had set off ahead of the massed start. We passed four such teams on our journey through Harewood Estate, Bardsley and Scarcroft to Thorner.

The cut-off time had elapsed at Thorner so we were unable to personally hand over the baton to our last leg pairing. We were pretty pleased with our efforts, recording our best time for the leg. Mick ran me back to Golden Acre where fortunately my trousers were still intact. We bought and enjoyed the ice cream we had been so looking forward to for the past two hours and then said our goodbyes.

This was the last time I would see Mick as he passed away the following week.

Mick had been ill some time ago but in running terms had got back to somewhere near his best. He was a stalwart of 'The Marathon Men', going the distance nine times in 1995 alone. While others around him appeared to struggle, Mick always looked the part, running upright and effortlessly and appearing as if he could move up a couple of gears at anytime.

His first marathon was at London in 1993 and as the blue and red starts merged after three miles, we found ourselves running side by side. I had the privilege of running the best part of the race with Mick until he proved the stronger of the two and eased away in the final miles.

Mick left a wife, Trish and a grown-up family, and will be sadly missed by all who knew him.

I like to think the passing of Mick persuaded me to look upon running from a slightly different perspective. Rather than be dictated to by personal bests, I have tried to derive more enjoyment and satisfaction from my performances. I have become much more aware of the surroundings than of my stopwatch.

As I move effortlessly back down the field, I am confident that by taking this approach and with a favourable breeze at my back, I will be penning my memoirs again in another twenty years.